GODS AT WAR

UNDERSTANDING THREE MILLENNIA OF RELIGIOUS CONFLICT

OLIVER THOMSON

AMBERLEY

First published 2019

Amberley Publishing
The Hill, Stroud
Gloucestershire, GL5 4EP

www.amberley-books.com

Copyright © Oliver Thomson, 2019

The right of Oliver Thomson to be identified
as the Author of this work has been asserted in
accordance with the Copyrights, Designs and
Patents Act 1988.

ISBN 978 1 4456 9471 9 (hardback)
ISBN 978 1 4456 9472 6 (ebook)

British Library Cataloguing in Publication Data.
A catalogue record for this book is available
from the British Library.

Typesetting by Aura Technology and Software
Services, India. Printed in the UK.

very best wishes

Oliver Thomson

GODS
AT WAR

'Welcome to UN Army, Navy and Airforce, the Crusade of World
Peace and Justice.'
Banner in the streets of Seoul, 1950

'In every country and in every age, the priest has been hostile
to liberty. He is always in alliance with the despot, abetting his
abuses in return for protection to his own.'
Thomas Jefferson

CONTENTS

Contents

PREFACE

What do Vladimir Putin and King Eannatum of Lagash have in common? The answer is that both leaders looked to religion to justify an invasion. Putin did so by getting the blessing of the Russian Orthodox Church to endorse his annexation of the Crimea in 2014. King Eannatum of Lagash, an ancient Sumerian town in what is now Iraq, justified his attack on nearby Umma in around 2450 BC by claiming that his god Ningursu had told him that his enemies would be piled high up to the gates of heaven. The carved record of this incident is on a stone monument now in the Louvre Museum, Paris.

Over the past few decades there has been a revival in the bitter confrontations between rival religions and between rival sects within religions, so it makes sense to look back over the centuries at the role religions have played in starting wars and ask the question, why do religions and sects fall out with each other so often? This book is not intent on blaming religion for any more wars than necessary, there are after all plenty of other culprits, but on achieving a balanced view of the part that religion has played in causing or inspiring wars both civil and international. The proportion of so-called religious wars may at times have been exaggerated, but it has always been significant and perhaps surprisingly has very much increased during the twentieth and twenty-first centuries.

It also seems that whenever an element of religious extremism is added to the spectrum of causes for any war, then the toxic mixture thus created tends to make the subsequent conflicts more rather than less prone to atrocities. This book looks back at the damage this has done over more than four millennia, from the wars of ancient Babylon to twenty-first-century terrorism, from the Spanish Armada to Pearl Harbor, 9/11 and the emergence of ISIS.

The main structure of this book is chronological but when there have been copy-cat wars or a series of wars with very similar features I have covered these in the same chapter. I have however provided cross-references for those who want to follow a particular theme, region or religion.

I apologise for any offence caused by any apparent criticism of a particular faith but remind readers that most religious wars were not the fault of the faith as such, but of the interpretation put on it by human leaders.

So far as the spelling of names is concerned I have generally followed what might be regarded as the most common form rather than the most authentic.

'The French wars of religion (inflicted) evils which cannot be measured by battle losses alone. Town was divided against town, village against village, family against family. Armed affrays and assassinations became ordinary incidents of life.'
H. A. L. Fisher, *History of Europe*

'Around the globe the perceived value of acquiring nuclear weapons has gone up while the repercussions of violating treaties have declined.'
Hans Christensen, *Time*, January 2018

'The infidels of Hungary bowed their heads to the temper of his blade.'
Poem by Baki referring to Sultan Suleiman

INTRODUCTION

I Which wars were truly religious? The spectrum

'Gott mit uns' (God is on our side)
Motto of the kings of Prussia

Before embarking on a survey of religious or semi-religious wars throughout history it is useful to establish a kind of scale by which we can evaluate the importance of faith among the many other complex causes that have led to each war.

There are I suggest nine broad categories of war on which the influence of religion should be considered, though nothing to do with wars is simple and the edges between our categories are often blurred. They should be seen as a spectrum ranging from the unadulterated fanaticism of genuine religious wars at one end of the scale to the cynical exploitation of religion by warlords with absolutely no genuine religious motives at the other. The two things all categories have in common is that their god is always on the same side as all the participants in every war, and all religions without exception promise an excellent afterlife to fallen warriors. All the examples mentioned in this introductory chapter will be dealt with in more detail later in this book, so at this stage we are just establishing a few criteria.

Firstly, come wars waged deliberately to expand the base of a particular faith, to provide it with more territory, more people and perhaps more wealth. This would be true of the Old Testament

Israelites and the jihad of the first Muslims. It could also be true of the conquest of pagan Germany by Charlemagne or the original expansion of the Ottoman Turks and is certainly true of the Aztecs in ancient Mexico or the Taliban in Afghanistan. These were all basically holy wars, but most of them were also waged to bring at least some material benefits or to satisfy the imperial ambitions of the men in charge.

The second type is different in that it focuses on antipathies between opposing religions. Again, the motivations have often been far from purely spiritual, for the original differences of opinion may have been toxified by ethnic or economic factors or years of irrational prejudice. This is true of many of the Christian versus Muslim conflicts including the first Crusades, the wars of the Muslims against Hindus and Sikhs in India or Buddhists in China, and also the extreme level of antipathy against Christians generated after the Jesuit conversions in Japan and against the United States of substantial numbers of Muslims owing to the sponsorship of Israel.

A third somewhat similar category covers sectarian warfare, of which the two most frequent examples in world history have been Catholic versus Protestant Christians and Sunni versus Shiite Muslims, though there have even been wars between rival Buddhist monasteries. This category accounts for the Eighty Years War in Holland, the French and German wars of the Reformation, the Spanish Armada attack on England, the Thirty Years War, the first stages of the English Civil War, or the Cameronian rebellion in Scotland. It is also true of the wars of the Shiite Shah Abbas of Persia against the Sunni Muslims of Samarkand and of several other Sunni/Shiite confrontations, including the most recent in Iraq 2014. Similarly, it is true of the Mogul Emperor Aurangzeb in his wars against the Shiites in India, since he did perhaps genuinely hate all those he regarded as infidels, including Sikhs and Hindus.

A fourth variant are wars caused by power struggles within particular faiths. The most obvious example of this are the frequent conflicts between Holy Roman Emperors and the supporters of various popes, most of them arising from the disputed rights of investiture. These led to frequent invasions of Italy by German or French armies from around 750 to 1527, all of them causing considerable hardship and significant casualties. The Italian wars of the three German emperors, Otto I, iI and III, were typical, as was the war waged by Pope Julius II against France and Venice. Perhaps also in this group should be included the wars between rival Buddhist monasteries in Japan.

Fifthly, there are those numerous wars where religion is simply exploited by an ambitious empire-builder to motivate his armies and justify his aggression, used as a disguise and an excuse, a propaganda tool. This would be true of Charlemagne's revival of the Roman Empire and of most of the later Crusades, particularly the notorious Fourth, which led to the capture of Constantinople, or the Baltic crusades leading to the conquest of East Prussia by the Teutonic Knights. It would also be true of the Muslim conquest of India, the Fatimid conquest of Egypt and many of the later jihads including the Ottoman conquest of the Balkans. It would certainly also embrace the Spanish conquest of South and Central America and many other examples of Christian empire-building where missionaries were not far behind the armies. It also includes the aggressive Sacred War in the Pacific fought by Japan in 1942–45 with the backing of so-called State Shinto, which caused more deaths than any other war in this or perhaps any category. It even includes the First World War, when both sides believed that God was on their side: Field Marshal Douglas Haig believed he had a divine mission to conquer the Germans on the Western Front.

Our sixth category includes those wars where religion almost accidentally provided the flash-point for a war that really had altogether different causes. An example would be the Crimean War of 1856 whose nominal cause was a disagreement between Catholic and Orthodox clergy over control of the Christian holy sites in Jerusalem, which were at that time inside the Ottoman Empire. The real reasons were political, the fears of France and Britain that Russia would become a major threat to European stability if it expanded its territories towards the Mediterranean. Another example would be the Indian Mutiny a year later, where the underlying cause was resentment of British exploitation of India, but the accidental flashpoint was the belief that the new rifles supplied for Sepoy soldiers involved Muslim recruits in having to taste pig fat and Hindu recruits having to taste beef fat when they used their weapons. Perhaps there was an element of this even in the American Civil War where one of the initial flash-points was the raid on Harpers Ferry by the religious fanatic John Brown, underlying which were the moral and commercial differences between southern and northern states. Alternative interpretations of the Bible's views on slavery played a part.

Our seventh and eighth categories are opposite sides of the same coin, with religious groups either supporting or attacking the establishment. It is understandable that establishment churches tend to side with their political masters, to pronounce any war that they undertake as 'a just war'. Thus throughout the centuries archbishops or patriarchs or imams have shared in the responsibility of blessing otherwise non-religious wars. A classic example would be Pope Pius X apparently encouraging the Emperor Franz Josef to attack the Orthodox Serbs in 1914, and contributing at least in a small way to the Armageddon that followed. Establishment churches also tend for their own sakes to contribute to the infrastructure of war, they provide appropriate ceremonial, sing warrior hymns, reassure by praying for victory, console the wounded and the bereaved, perform impressive funerals for the fallen with appropriate reassurance of an afterlife, ring bells, raise cenotaphs, sell poppies, generally add respectability to the warmongers' causes.

A facet of this inter-establishment mutual support has been the fact that so many rulers in the past have been kings or emperors by divine right, blessed by the support of their favourite faith and in turn gaining the right to wage war when they felt like it. This was true of the Chinese emperors as 'Sons of Heaven', the Japanese as descended from the Sun God, the French Capets and virtually every legitimate or semi-legitimate king worldwide whose authority stemmed from a birthright endorsed by an appropriate religious ceremony and enshrined in appropriate mythology. The kingdom of Prussia had 'Gott mit uns' as its motto and in 1848 Bismarck insisted that he wanted Germany to be ruled by a monarch chosen by God, not one elected by a human assembly. Vladimir Putin's favourite Night Wolves similarly had 'God, Russia and Putin' as their motto. The United States had their republican version of the same divine theme, their 'Manifest Destiny' to be a great nation and at one stage almost eliminate the indigenous population of North America.

So close has been the alliance of church and state in times of war that very often the personnel were almost interchangeable.

As well as divine kings and emperors there were church leaders who doubled as generals. Two popes provide good examples, the German Leo IX and the Italian Julius II, known as 'The Warrior Pope', not to mention the belligerent Bishop Odo who joined William the Conqueror in 1066 and helped suppress one of the last rebellions against his rule, or the fighting Bishop of Beauvais during the Hundred Years War. It is an unfortunate verbal coincidence that many of the words most popular in religions such as 'glory' and 'self-sacrifice' are also very frequently used in wars.

Turning to the anti-establishment version of this theme, our eighth category, it was common for new underdog sects to side with underdog political equivalents to attack their opponents currently in power. Classic examples of this would be Wycliffe, John Bull and the Peasants Revolt in England, or the White Lotus Buddhist revolt that brought the Ming dynasty to power in China. It could be argued that the Dutch Reformed Church as an underdog sect in South Africa allied with the Boers who regarded themselves as an oppressed minority. And certainly extreme Muslim sects of the late twentieth century allied themselves with groups of ethnically or economically oppressed peoples to start a whole series of wars.

It is clear that many of the originally underdog groupings that were allied to fairly extreme Islam in the late colonial period after 1918 subsequently became more like category 7 as they in turn became part of the establishment, as for example with the bellicose and devout Muslim Colonel Gaddafi, who first staged his coup as an Islamist underdog figure but over the years as virtual dictator of Libya pursued aggressive strategies as a head of state using his own interpretation of the Koran to justify his domestic policies and his aim to drive Christianity out of Africa.

Finally, we come to what might be termed religion as the last resort, when a nation struggling against the odds to avoid defeat turns to faith. An early instance of this was when ancient Rome faced disaster at the hands of the Carthaginians and to raise morale dumped most of its old religion in favour of a new goddess, the Magna Mater or Great Mother, imported from the East to please the soldiers. Perhaps even the Angel of Mons falls into this category of divine or semi-divine females coming to the rescue.

The classic example of this was France in the last stages of the Hundred Years War, when after numerous defeats at the hands of the English the French establishment very reluctantly accepted the help of the visionary Joan of Arc, turning a non-religious war overnight into a religious struggle with divine blessing and making its objective the sacred crowning of the dauphin in Reims Cathedral. Similarly, when Babur, founder of the Moguls, found himself in a desperate position near Delhi he suddenly turned his war of conquest into a jihad. Tolstoy gives a wonderful description of the Smolensk icon of the Mother Mary being carried among the Russian troops before the bloody battle of Borodino when around 40,000 men were killed on both sides without achieving any useful gain for either. Similarly, when the supposedly atheistic Stalin was faced with defeat by the blitzkrieg in 1942 he suddenly abandoned his principles and turned for help to the Orthodox Church, which he had done so much to destroy. Soon afterwards, the Japanese when faced with defeat revived the concept of 'Divine Wind' or 'Kamikaze' to continue the hopeless struggle, one which had anyway been motivated by obsession with their semi-divine emperor. The fact that a typhoon in 1274 had arrived conveniently to sink most of the Mongol warships invading Japan was seized on retrospectively in 1945 to prove to the Japanese that the gods were on their side and that they had the right gods. There is even the suggestion that religion can provide a last resort not just to cope with defeat, but also with victory, for when Alexander the Great had accomplished a rapid succession of conquests he proclaimed himself a god to help smooth the ruffled feathers of his new subjects, many of whom had previously been ruled by kings or pharaohs who claimed divine status.

Another curious example of retrospective credit for an imagined victory being granted to a religion was during the Mongol/Tartar invasions of Poland, Hungary and Bohemia 1241. None of the European armies had managed to stop the booty-hungry and ruthless Tartars, but a crowd of villagers had sought shelter in a castle at Hostyn (now in the Czech Republic) where they soon ran out of water and prayed to the Virgin Mary for help. The result was a massive lightning storm, which both replenished the water supply and drove off the Tartar besiegers. The survival of the villagers was militarily of no account, but it was of huge importance to the church as it turned Hostyn into a major pilgrimage site. This shows how a religion can be bolstered by participation in a successful military action. It shows that gods and war were often engaged in a two-way trade: the warriors benefited from religious support while the credibility and popularity of the religions could be enhanced when there was a victory. When King Clovis of the Franks won the battle of Tolbiac (496 or 508) against the Alemanni tribes of western Germany, he chose that moment to gain credibility for his own personal conversion from anti-Trinitarian to pro-Trinitarian Christianity, thus creating a platform for the development of the French kingdom as a pillar of Catholicism and sanctifying his career as a champion of orthodoxy against the Arian Goths.

There are also examples of retrospective blame. When the Scottish Covenanter army was defeated by Cromwell at Preston in 1648 the Scots clergy explained the disaster as the result of divine disapproval caused by the sinful behaviour of the soldiers. The Old Testament Israelites had done much the same.

Inevitably, the nine suggested categories overlap. There is too little surviving evidence of the background psychology of old wars to make precise judgments possible. But it would perhaps be fair to say that few if any so-called holy wars were totally without ulterior motives and equally that few if any 'ordinary' wars ever took place without some religious encouragement on one side or the other. In fact, it could be argued that almost every single war-leader until 1917, and several after that, boasted that God or gods were on their side. The unfortunate result for the human race has been a great deal of suffering, made worse by the fact that so many wars were copy-cat versions of ones that went before. One crusade followed another, just as one jihad followed another.

This habit of copy-cat wars suggests that there is perhaps a tenth mini-category, wars that were not religious wars at the time when they were fought but achieved emblematic significance afterwards, usually due to post-battle claims of divine intervention. The Roman Emperor Constantine's cross in the sky before Saxa Rubra almost falls into this category (v. Part 1, Chapter 4). So, does the Battle of Frigidus in 394 when the Emperor Theodosius attributed his unexpected victory over the Goths led by his pagan rival Eugenius to the effects of a divine wind whipping up the Slovenian sand in the faces of the enemy. This in turn recalls the divine winds or Kamikaze which in 1274 destroyed the fleet of the Mongols under Kublai Khan during his abortive attempt to conquer Japan.

This is also true of the situation where minor victories of the past are subsequently reinterpreted for propaganda purposes to boost morale, as with the Russian Orthodox hero Alexander Nevsky's skirmish against the Catholic Swedes on the River Neva in 1240; he was later made a saint and his exploits bruited to encourage the Muscovites against the Muslim Tartars. Similarly, the Battle of the Boyne in 1690 achieved a significance in later years which its actual participants would not have envisaged. The Saxon King Otto the Great's victory over the heathen Magyars at Lechfeld in 751 was subsequently attributed to his possession of the Holy Lance and this divine assistance for his victory boosted his credentials for becoming Holy Roman Emperor.

Of course all wars are started because of either greed or fear, or a mixture of both, but religion is almost always a component in both these motivations.

'Ballistic missile threat in-bound to Hawaii. Seek immediate shelter. This is not a drill.'
Hawaii ballistic missile alert, 13 January 2018

II *The characteristics of religious wars*

'The LORD is a man of war; The LORD is his name.'
Book of Exodus 15. 3 (King James Bible)

As we shall see many of the sectarian wars of religion had what seem in retrospect extremely trivial causes: minor disagreements over rites or terminology, the words of a prayer book or the number of fingers used for a blessing. Of the features that typify wars of religion several stand out. So often they took place between new sects allied to an oppressed underclass against old sects associated with wealth and exploitation. This was true of early Islam's internal wars, the Buddhist White Lotus, the Wars of the Reformation and many others. Often the new sects tended to be puritan in outlook, abstemious and strict, in contrast to their opponents who were accused of self-indulgence, corruption and ostentatious wealth. New sects or religions with no artistic heritage or inherited wealth attack older ones that have rich priests, costly symbolism, icons and idols. From Moses smashing the images of Baal via Mohammed in Mecca, to the Calvinists trashing cathedrals and the Taliban blowing up the great stone Buddhas of Afghanistan, iconoclasm has been a popular way of letting off steam. Many inter-religious conflicts involved widespread temple destruction and idol smashing.

A second common feature we can observe is the apocalyptic nature of many religious wars, for all four of the dominant religions had a tradition that their greatest prophet would at some point be reborn, the Jews and Christians waiting for a Messiah, the Muslims waiting for a true Mahdi and Buddhists for a Maitreya, a new Buddha. The fact that this visitation also involved the end of the world meant that the soldiers had nothing to lose by dying.

Thirdly, loyalties to a religion and to an ethnic group become inextricably involved and accentuate their differences with neighbouring states, so increase the likelihood of distrust, dislike turning to hatred and conflict. This has been particularly true of the Jews, the Armenians, the Kurds, the Irish, the Iranians, even the Confederate States of the USA.

Part of our review must also consider the influence of the holy texts of various religions in encouraging or condoning warfare, the history of one old war providing justification for a new one. The world's two most influential holy texts, the Bible (or more specifically the Old Testament) and the Koran both endorse the use of war as a means of protecting and expanding the faiths they represent. Similarly, the Hindu *Bhagavad Gita* blesses the fighting duties of the warrior class, as does the epic *Mahabharata*. The Sikh gurus reacted to persecution by changing their code to encourage armed resistance, Japanese Shinto undoubtedly championed an aggressive stance as did the bloodthirsty religion of the Aztecs in Mexico. Even Buddhism, perhaps the most pacific of all the great religions, produced cliques of warrior monks at various times in history, has for many centuries been enthusiastic about training in the martial arts and, as we shall see, encouraged several major wars.

This takes us to the much broader question of the extent to which religions helped shape codes of morality which themselves encouraged warlike attitudes. In the case of Islam there is no doubt that from the start its moral code did contain the obligation to fight for the faith, but in Christianity, Buddhism and Sikhism this was, as we shall see, not originally the case. All three started off as anti-violence religions but later acquired a more militant ethic. In Christianity there is little evidence of warlike attitudes until at least three centuries after its foundation, but then through the middle ages its moral code gradually came to admire the more aggressive virtues, courage and loyalty, alongside piety. In the sixth century the Archangel Michael was revered no longer as a healing spirit but as the leader of armies fighting against evil, and other military saints such as the belligerent George soon joined this specific pantheon. Soldiers who died in battle began to be equated with religious martyrs. By the high middle ages soldierly and spiritual values were coming together to create the idea of chivalry, a career path for thousands of virtuous warriors to seek glory by waging wars. Similar trends are visible among both Buddhists and Sikhs, whilst in Islam they have been revitalised by new generations adapting to new military opportunities.

It could therefore be suggested that religion provides much of the human infrastructure that makes war possible: the indoctrination that breeds a willingness to volunteer, the basic obedience, the willingness to make sacrifices, the belief that a society or a faith is worth fighting for. Without these not even the most autocratic of governments would be able to go to war. In the case of 1940s Japan, as Brian Victoria put it 'Zen served as a powerful foundation for the fanatical and suicidal spirit displayed by the Japanese Imperial Army.'

It is a truism that all wars are started by people who expect to win, an expectation usually based on a belief, possibly justified, in military superiority, but in the case of religious wars the decision is often less rational. The wars are started in an emotional rather than rational atmosphere, with the rightness of the cause considered rather than the number of battalions, so the preparations are often less adequate. A classic example would be the People's Crusade (v. Pt 2 Chapter 15).

Finally, one of the surprising side-effects of religions becoming involved in warfare is that they tend not to bless the idea of a 'fair fight', but instead preach total ruthlessness. The level of war-crimes and atrocities in religious wars is sometimes even worse than those where less fanaticism is involved. For example, the almost religion-free wars of Louis XIV and Marlborough in the eighteenth century were more gentlemanly affairs, where generals could surrender with honour to avoid unnecessary bloodshed. Genuine religious warfare is often characterised by suicidal levels of bravery and recklessness encouraged by the promise of an afterlife in paradise, and at the same time callous treatment of opponents who, as disbelievers, are regarded as beneath contempt and deserving of execution.

Christianity and Islam both have unedifying track-records in this respect, as have both of their two largest sectarian divisions, Catholic/Protestant and Sunni/Shiite. What is more, there is no evidence that such conflicts in the modern world are any less barbaric than, say, the Crusades or the Thirty Years War. To make matters worse, wars of religion, as we shall see, tend to be asymmetric, dysfunctional affairs with uncontrolled collateral damage. They achieve no satisfaction for either winners or losers, and since the losers never accept that they have lost it means that their wars tend to be self-perpetuating. Most war start-ups show signs of irrationality, but the wars between religions or between sects are usually the least rational of all.

Religion is one of the factors in life which make peoples different from each other, thus leading to irritation, dislike and disapproval, so creating an excuse or component reason for quarrelling or an excuse for leaders to indulge in conflict and aggression. This is particularly true of the vast number of places where history has left irredentist enclaves, people of one religion or sect left stranded on the wrong side of a border; Palestinians in Israel or Germans in Poland and Poles in Germany, Shiites and Christians in Syria, Protestants in Ireland, Armenian Christians in Turkey. These incompatible enclaves are the result of four sometimes interlinked causes: conquest spreading one religion into the region of another, followed perhaps by retreat leaving behind isolated pockets like the Muslims of Bosnia or Kashmir, or the Dutch Reformed Church in South Africa. Then there's migration or diaspora. Profit from trade took Muslims far east along the Old Silk Road or to ports like Mombassa, which became a Muslim enclave in otherwise mainly Christian Kenya. Finally, there is the effect of missionaries, which can often outlast the power of the conquering nation that deployed them. Thus we have the Baptist Christian region in Nagaland existing uneasily between Hindu India and Buddhist Myanmar, or the volatile mixture of Pentecostalists in once Catholic Guatemala.

Religious irredentism is almost as harmful as ethnic irredentism, so the world is littered with overlapping ethnic and religious fault-lines like the jagged frontier across sub-Saharan Africa from Mali to South Sudan, where the former conquests of Islam intersect with the later empire-building of the Christian Europeans. There is an even longer and equally dangerous religious fault-line stretching from Kosovo in the Balkans to Kashgar in China.

'...myriads of causes combined to bring it (the 1812 war) about and so there was no one cause for that occurrence but it had to occur because it had to.'

Leo Tolstoy, *War and Peace*

III *Why do religions so often support wars?*

Over the past three if not four millennia religions have more often encouraged wars than discouraged them. It is perhaps also true that in most of these wars religions played the subsidiary role, supporting political aggression as opposed to having politicians back genuine religious causes.

The reasons for both of these generalisations are not hard to seek. Aggressive wars are often fought for no reason except the aggrandisement of an individual or a tiny elite, and it suits them to have supernatural sanction. King Eannatum of Lagash contrived to obtain the blessing of his god Ningursu in 2450 BC, as is recorded in stone on the so-called Stela of Vultures now in the Louvre Museum. Ningursu promised him victory over the neighbouring city of Umma and he made sure the promise was validated. And since then there have been thousands of examples of brutal wars given encouragement by numerous state religions.

In the pre-modern era when virtually all wars were started by a single monarch, the link between church and state was obvious. Since there is no rational explanation for hereditary kingship there always had to be an irrational one – variations on the divine right of kings, a religious explanation as to why peoples accepted monarchs. Hence the muddling of divine and terrestrial monarchs. Jesus is referred to as King of the Jews, gods are referred to as kings in numerous cultures, just as kings and emperors assumed divine status or descent from gods. Caliphs are successors of Mohammed. Gods also sit on thrones and wear crowns whilst earthly monarchies were often described as sacred. Similarly, gods are often depicted as leaders of armies; the phrase Lord of Hosts or *Adonai Tzavaot* (army commanders) appears more than two hundred times in the Old Testament. Gods were seen as war-leaders, sometimes with a heavenly host of angels led by officer archangels. Samuel pronounced it a duty 'to go and destroy wicked peoples' and in the Book of Numbers 'God ordered the Israelites to take vengeance on the Midianites.' Understandably, such ideas were recycled and re-publicised by leading church philosophers like St Augustine of Hippo and St Thomas Aquinas, redefining the idea of the just war for each succeeding generation.

Religions were uniquely well placed to provide such backing for wars as in almost any society they have been the chief guardians and most vocal proponents of non-rational behaviour patterns. They have specialised in the creation and dissemination of unverifiable information such as the existence of an afterlife (especially a wonderful one for dead soldiers), the validity of royal dynasties descended from god, the idea that a people could be a chosen people, the receipt of information direct from gods, divine paternity, virgin birth, visions, judgemental infliction of natural disasters and so on.

For governments wanting to wage wars by far the most useful piece of unverifiable but pleasantly credible information was that the god or gods were on their side and they would win the war, a message which naturally often turned out to be invalid, for example for Kaiser Wilhelm II in 1918 when the Prussian motto 'Gott mit uns' was disproved. When it worked, however, it was a great benefit to belong to a chosen race or an empire with a manifest destiny, not to mention a divinely ordained ruler to whom his or her people were required to give absolute obedience even at the cost of their lives. It is no coincidence that gods were often referred to as kings or lords, thus part of a parallel supernatural elite replicating the earthly monarchs and aristocrats. This compliment was returned when the earthly monarchs were promoted as divinities themselves or at least given family trees of divine descent. The 'Gott mit uns' motto lasted in Germany from 1701 when adopted by the first king of Prussia until the Second World War, when it still appeared on the buckles of Wehrmacht soldiers. Its antecedents were in the Old Testament Immanuel, in the Gospel of St Matthew and in its Latin version 'Nobiscum Deus', used by the armies of the late Roman Empire. Its Dutch version 'God zi met ons' was the motto in the Eighty Years War and its Russian version 'S nami Bog' was that of the Russian Empire and of the right wing militia Aidar Battalion during the Ukraine war of 2014.

The key unverifiable message was for centuries the offer of post-mortal happiness for soldiers who died in battle; Valhalla. In addition, also useful was the ability to damn all enemies as at best deviants from the true religion or at worst total disbelievers who should be slaughtered or forced to accept the one true religion.

The other side of the coin was that it suited religions to have lay help in preserving their singularity, for any alien, unverifiable information was potentially very damaging to them. As soon as alternative versions of any creed started to spread it meant that at least one of them had to be untrue. Thus, for example, Christian Arians and Manichaeans who disagreed with the idea of the Trinity exposed the conflicting ideas of Jesus being divine or the Son of God, so they had to be persecuted to death. Similarly, to some Sunni Muslims, Shiites were a menace and no better than heathens.

It also often suited religions to avoid all forms of democratic input since it was essential that the absolute unverifiable truths had to be expounded only by the professionals who were the sole guardians of the divine source that had imparted these truths. Any form of deviation or alternative ideas would challenge the authenticity of the original creeds, which being by nature unverifiable were also more fragile when exposed to mockery or abuse. Religions therefore needed to see things in absolute terms and this fitted in well both with monarchy and the requirement to justify wars. The enemy must be seen as utterly in the wrong. Even minor discrepancies in rituals, dogmas, prayer books or hierarchies were enough to engender fierce opposition and violent persecution, so war was a natural enough outcome. The religious professionals were well used to proclaiming unverifiable messages of their own and easily brought these techniques to the aid of warmongering masters.

It has always been quite hard for clerics to oppose wars pursued by their political counterparts. It was said of Catholic bishops in the US that they dare not voice disapproval of the Saddam Hussein War 'to avoid even the appearance of being unpatriotic'. Similarly, the Nazi regime in Germany took considerable care in the recruitment of good preachers as padres for the Wehrmacht in the belief that it would help legitimise what Doris Bergen called its 'war of annihilation'. These army chaplains were 'caught between the word of man and of God'. Just as in Germany so throughout the world, army chaplains trapped in uniform and commissioned rank have played a key role in keeping god or gods on side.

In this context it has to be recognised that if there is any blame on religions for cooperating or encouraging wars it is the staff not the creed which in almost all cases deserves the criticism. It is obvious that established religions offer career opportunities, possible wealth and positions of power, which attract those whose motives are not necessarily spiritual. It was particularly true of the younger sons and sometimes daughters of aristocratic families who could be found a career suitable for their social status. Many popes were lawyers or diplomats by training rather than theologians. Many men from humbler backgrounds saw a church career as an opportunity for senior positions in government. Cardinals Wolsey, Richelieu and Mazarin are obvious examples. Sometimes it was just the ability to read and write which allowed clerics to reach positions of power in both church and state, so their attitudes to war and peace would be conditioned not by their religion but by their political aspirations.

It is clear therefore that religions are frequently an integral part of the infrastructure for wars. Because of legal training and communication skills clerics have over the centuries frequently been employed as diplomats negotiating treaties, helping to break them, sorting out the justifications for war. Religions have also often been important fund-raisers for wars, as in the case of the crusades, and it is doubtful if Edward III of England could have afforded his first invasion of France in 1337 if he had not taken over the war chest the church had collected ready for some future crusade. Leading churchmen also become bankers, such as the Frenchman Pope Clement VI (v. Pt 2 Chapter 16) who was the biggest single lender to the French crown during the Hundred Years War. King John of France transferred 10 per cent of all French church income for the war effort. It was also true of the

Templars, who provided not only their far-flung banking function but like other monastic orders also provided hospitality for armies on the move.

> '...the current (George Bush) administration's policy on war is not only morally justified but has been given divine sanction.'
>
> Dr Charles Stanley

IV The value of religious communicators

> 'Clergy in both the North and South (in 1861) found scriptural grounds to ardently support their respective sides.'
>
> James Moorhead, *Preaching the Holy War*

Religions need the most skilled communicators to survive and expand, partly because their messages are often complex, usually lack any verifiable evidence and frequently have to compete against equally experienced competitors. They are well used to appealing to the emotions as well as brains of their audiences, since their normal method of instruction relies on feelings rather than facts. They thus provide aggressive governments with very useful propaganda infrastructure. In addition, their pyramidal organisation enables them to create ground forces throughout their sphere of influence, priests in each parish advocating war. Because they are accustomed to promoting both love and hate they find it easy to polarise opinion.

Thus, the writers of the Old Testament and editors of the Koran have been adept at projecting the need sometimes to use violence. Fine orators like Pope Urban II with his 'Deus vult' sermon at Clairmont and St Bernard of Clairvaux with his 'sacrum bellum' argument for the Second Crusade had massive impacts. Others debated the morality of war on a longer term basis, as in the writings of St Augustine who used St Paul to argue that 'God had given the sword to governments for a good reason' and 'the wise man will wage just war' (*City of God*), while St Thomas Aquinas in his *Summa Theologica* defended the just war 'as punishment for an evil perpetrated'. Both Martin Luther and John Calvin, the two greatest promoters of the Protestant Reformation, chose to hit Catholicism where it hurt, in its relationship with God and monarchy, thus justifying armed rebellion against kings who chose to support the alleged corruptions of the Vatican. Thus German propagandists such as Thomas Rohr (1521–1582) a priest from Bavaria, encouraged armed attacks on Catholic rulers and Luther was cited by the pamphleteers of Magdeburg as justification for the Thirty Years War, one of the most brutal in world history. The Catholic Croats supporting the Holy Roman Empire were portrayed as cannibals. Significantly it was in 1622, four years after the start of the war, that the Bologna Jesuit Pope Gregory XV founded the *Congregatio de Propaganda Fide*, which provided for training of Counter-Reformation missionaries and incidentally introduced the word propaganda to several languages. Similarly, in France Calvin's writings were recycled to justify the Huguenot attacks on the Catholic regime while the philosophers of the Sorbonne responded by demonising the Huguenots, leading to the bitter and protracted French Wars of Religion.

The great value of religious communicators in war is that they reliably provided credible answers to key questions: is God on our side and likely to help, does the enemy deserve death, will dead soldiers go to heaven? In addition, religious leaders are more accustomed than ordinary politicians to asking their flocks to make personal sacrifices, even to suffer death, because such ideas play a part in most religions. They are also good at preaching austerity, since rejection of over-indulgence is also a typical theme in many religions. Clergy have long supported concepts like Lent and Ramadan or other periods of fasting so this can easily be adapted for a war situation. The churches during the American Civil War organised fast days to support the war effort. From the 1890s onwards Japanese Shinto used the shrine at Yasukuni for fallen warriors to invoke the idea that a common soldier could achieve divine status; and fifty years later kamikaze pilots were treated to a ceremonial cup of sake before making the ultimate sacrifice. From around 2004 the term radicalisation was recognised as describing a new technique of conversion and recruitment for religious violence, exploiting the credulity of vulnerable or disenchanted young people and the availability of social media. Many of its methods recall some of the indoctrination techniques used for the Crusades, for the Assassin brotherhood, the Jesuits, and many more recent military elites.

Similarly, clergy in many religions are used to dealing with apocalypses, millennial dies irae, Armageddons, so that wars and disaster seem more acceptable and natural. As Kant put it 'some philosophers believe that wars ennoble humanity.' Certainly, it is a reasonable overall conclusion that throughout history religions, even the most respected ones, have done more to encourage wars than to prevent them.

'The first six books of the Bible centre on the gracious saving acts of God in election deliverance, covenant and conquest.'
Jimmie Nelson, *South Western Journal of Theology*

PART ONE

THE ANCIENT WORLD

'I killed all the warriors in the city for the well-pleasing of Chemosh and Moab and I removed all the spoil and offered it before Chemosh ... but I did not kill the women and maidens for I devoted them to Ashtar Chemosh.'

The words of King Mesha of Moab inscribed on the Mesha Stele or Moabite Stone, dated 840BC, one of the oldest surviving inscriptions describing a war in which religion played a significant role.

I

THE EXAMPLE OF ISRAEL – JEHOVAH AGAINST BAAL

'The villages of Israel would not fight until I, Deborah, arose.
God chose new leaders when war was at the city gate.'
Song of Deborah

In the Old Testament the idea of aggressive religious war starts with Moses. The best estimate is that he lived in the fourteenth century BC. Whilst there were many other ancient cultures with similar attitudes, his rhetoric has retained its influence for three millennia thanks to being recycled in the Old Testament, long accepted throughout Europe as the ultimate sanction for violence against other faiths, believed or exploited by hundreds of regimes to justify gratuitous aggression.

Moses and his followers masterminded the covenant by which Jehovah guaranteed victory against non-believers so long as the Jewish people followed the instructions passed down from Mount Sinai. Thereafter Jehovah was also 'the Lord of Hosts' who inspired leaders like Joshua in the otherwise difficult conquest of the area called Canaan and endorsed genocide or ethnic cleansing of the 'promised land'. Thus, when Joshua undertook the eventually successful siege of Jericho 'they utterly destroyed all that was within the city, both man and woman, young and old, and ox and sheep and ass with the edge of the sword.' (Joshua 6. 21). Similarly, in Deuteronomy (20. 16), 'of the cities of these people which the Lord thy God doth give thee for an inheritance thou shalt save alive nothing that breatheth; but thou shalt destroy them, namely the Hittites, Amorites, Canaanites, and Jebusites as the Lord thy God hath commanded thee.' Thus, even allowing for some exaggeration in folk history there is absolutely no doubt about the strategy being applied, nor of the message for posterity. The slaughter of believers in other religions is portrayed as totally ethical. The faithful Israelites justified the use of violence in order to acquire their 'land of milk and honey', a materialistic more than a theological objective.

To amplify this concept the theme of Jehovah as a war god is frequently mentioned in Exodus (19. 5) and as a winner of battles in Deuteronomy (9. 4). Later in the Old Testament the concept is repeated in Isaiah (I. 24) – 'Therefore saith the Lord, the Lord of Hosts, the mighty one of Israel, Ah, I will ease me of mine adversaries and avenge me mine enemies ... and purge away thy dross ... and the destruction of the transgressors and sinners.' Later still in Amos (6. 14), 'I will raise up against you a nation, O House of Israel, saith the Lord God of Hosts; and they shall afflict you.' Not only is the meaning quite clear but the language in every case is highly emotive, so even those who regard the Bible, particularly the Old Testament, as historically unreliable can accept such unpleasant passages in it as credible evidence and appreciate its power as a potent piece of propaganda in favour both of war and religious persecution. There are other small details showing the divine warrant for warfare, like the habit of making sacrifices before battle, a custom shared with pagan religions such as the Greek and Roman, and similarly the prohibition on sex before battles, as famously in the case of Uriah and Bathsheba.

One particular Hebrew word which appears frequently in the Old Testament and the *Tanakh* is 'Herem' or 'Cherem', the translation and meaning of which have been argued over by scholars over the years but in English is usually given as 'utterly destroy'. There is no doubt that it encapsulated the basic Jewish belief that they should destroy anyone or anything that stood in the way of their strictly monotheistic religion plus their God-given entitlement to an attractive piece of territory. This was the period of the Milkhemet Mitzvah, war ordered by the Talmud and needing no new decision-making by the elders.

Given that the archaeological evidence of mass destruction in Canaan is very limited it is possible that the Bible may have exaggerated the belligerence of the early Israelites, as it was probably written at a time when the small, fragile state was threatened with invasion by outside super-powers such as the Babylonians and Assyrians. Perhaps its authors were more concerned to motivate the population than to provide a precisely accurate history. Thus they strove to make heroes out of great warriors like Joshua, emphasising their aggression so that the current generation might be inspired to fight back. Given the literal interpretation of these texts, they left a toxic inheritance to be exploited by aggressive elements throughout the next three millennia, not just the Christians but also Muslims, since they too recycled the ideals of the Old Testament. Phrases like 'the slaughter of the Amalekites' were regurgitated by the Puritans during the English Civil War, by Catholics at the siege of Magdeburg and by the Scottish Cameronians. Similarly, they were echoed by the pronouncements of Islamic jihad in the twenty-first century.

It should be said at this stage that even if at times the Israelites were genocidal, this was far from unusual in the era during which they were trying to establish their new state. From the days of Sargon of Akkad (*c.*2334-2284 BC) several of the empires of the Middle East had been accustomed to exterminate whole populations. King Sargon himself was born in Kish (south of where Baghdad now stands) and was aided by his patroness the goddess Ishtar or Astarte, who combined the roles of fertility and war, but he also had a separate war god Zababa who is equated with the biblical Nimrod. Astarte also figured as a war god in Canaan alongside the dreaded Baal, who became a focus of hate for the Jews.

The Assyrians enforced mass migration as their form of ethnic cleansing and backed their propaganda with claims that their chief god Ashtur helped their conquests of neighbouring nations whose own gods let their people down badly. Ashtur according to legend then adopted as his son the neighbouring god Ningirsu, the one who had helped Lagash to beat Umma, *c.*2450. Ningursu was also known as Ninursa and may have been the same as Nimrod. Thus, the rival gods of each region competed for supremacy in a parallel world to their earthly patrons. Burning of cities and salting of the land were standard practice and were blessed by local religions. Greed for more land happily coincided with the growth of their religion.

The Israelites, however, were special in so far as religion was a central platform of their state-building and absolutely unique in so far as their ethos was preserved in texts that survived many disasters to be an inspiration for nation-builders and sectarian warriors thousands of years later. It is a credible scenario that when Moses appointed Joshua to begin the conquest of 'the promised land' he was leading a very poorly equipped army, the equivalent of a modern guerrilla force, against states like Canaan, with men well-trained in chariot warfare and defended by ramparts; hence some of the unorthodoxy in Joshua's tactics, like the ambush at Ai following a feigned retreat and later his surprise attacks at night. So, given the heavy odds against success, a degree of intimidatory violence was a natural tactic. Even then there would probably have been no success at all but for the fact that at this point the two neighbouring super-powers, the Egyptians and Hittites, were both weakened by dynastic upsets. Yet despite the alleged exhortation by Moses to wipe out the previous inhabitants of Canaan, it seems that most of the conquered cities were left standing; only three, Jericho, Ai and Hazor, were razed, since it really made no sense for the Israelis to destroy the infrastructure of their new 'land of milk and honey'.

The problem with this relative clemency was that Israelites then intermarried with the defeated Canaanites and in significant numbers became infected with local paganism, to the disgust of their own monotheistic leaders. After all, Baal seemed to be a fairly respectable god, not all that different from their own except that he allowed himself to be portrayed in statues or images, so there was something to see. There came a succession of divinely authorised judges like Othniel and Ehud who blamed foreign attacks on Jehovah's angry reaction to this apostasy and used the threat of judgmental disasters to motivate a return to Mosaic strictness and bolster the will of the people to resist those attacks.

The Moabite Stone has backed up the accounts in the Old Testament, a stela dated to around 840 BC now in the Louvre Museum that was discovered in what is now Jordan in the nineteenth century. On it King Mesha of Moab boasted of his defeat of invading Israeli troops in terms very similar to those used in Deuteronomy, except that his Lord of Hosts was the Moabite god Chemosh, who had helped him to victory. Just as in the Old Testament there is the herem, or ban on defeated enemies, their extermination and the destruction of their cities.

Many of the hero-figures of the next era combined generalship with hatred of pagan practices and exhibited an underlying religious motivation for their military exploits. The figure of Gideon, the victor against the Midianite or Bedouin marauders and probably an amalgam of several local heroes, had controversially destroyed a popular image of Baal before his victory and deliberately took a reduced army so that it would prove that God deserved the credit for his success. Then he followed it up on divine instructions with a massacre. Similarly, Samson, the hero of resistance against the Philistines, notable for his condemnation of idol worship and alcohol, was seen as rescuing the Jews after a period when they were being punished by God for drifting back into idolatry. The Bible makes no attempt to minimise his brutality as a soldier.

Even when it was decided that Israel needed a more centralised monarchy, the selection of kings was by divine ordinance. Thus King Saul, who was under orders from Samuel, who in turn took his orders from God, all but ethnically cleansed the Amalekites, ending what had become 'the Lord's war against Amalek from generation to generation' *(Exodus* 17. 14). In fact, their extermination had been decreed even earlier *(Deuteronomy* 25. 16) but when Saul halted in the final stages and spared King Agad he was reprimanded by Samuel.

Saul was moody to the point of bipolarity and much less successful against the Philistines. He appeared to lose divine approval, so he was deposed (a common fate in the ancient world for kings who failed on this score) and was replaced by the more charismatic King David, who had proved his worth by slaughtering Philistines, famously bringing back 200 Philistine foreskins as a trophy, behaviour that would now be treated as a war crime. David successfully united his own tribe of Judah with the rest of the Israelites and then achieved major military success with the conquest of most of Canaan and the capture of Jerusalem, which he turned into the capital of his new dual kingdom. Both David and Saul relied on priests to advise them when it was the right moment to fight a battle and emphasised the divine source of their power, albeit the Bible makes no effort to hide their flaws, bipolarity in the case of Saul, sexual indiscretion and murder in the case of David.

David apparently with divine approval was again guilty of what today would be regarded as atrocities with his execution of two-thirds of the population of Moab and when, after his siege of Rabbah, 'he brought forth the people that were therein and put them under saws and under harrows of iron and under axes of iron and thus he did unto all the cities of children of Ammon' (II Samuel 12. 31).

Whether these atrocities were true or not is less important than the fact that the Books of Samuel were regarded as absolute truth by both Jews and later Christians, so when Oliver Cromwell completed his siege of Drogheda in 1646 he could refer to 'the righteous justice of God' when excusing his massacre of its Catholic population. Though the ethics of warfare embodied in the Old Testament were very much on a par with the other states in the middle east at that time, their real importance is not so much as a historical record but in the stubborn retention of their mythology which was exploited by both Christians and Muslims to justify war and sometimes ethnic cleansing in eras when that should have been less acceptable.

The war song of Deborah (Judges 4. 4) is also a highly emotive summons to arms, particularly as it came from a female leader who subsequently won a victory for the Israelites over Canaan in Esdraelon and scorned those who failed to help: 'Curse Meroz,' said the angel of God ... because they did not come to the aid of God.'

Outwith the canon of the Old Testament authorised for most Protestants and several other sects are the Apocrypha which lionised similar war heroics by leaders like Judith in the Assyrian/ Babylonian period and Judas Maccabeus in the years after the conquest of the Middle East by Alexander the Great. The Maccabee rebellion was provoked by the aggressive King Antiochus IV of Syria who, after twice capturing Jerusalem, attempted to stamp out Judaism: Mattathias, the ancestor of Judas, was ordered to sacrifice a pig to the Greek gods in 167 BC. Thus, even when a succession of super-powers – Babylon, Persia, Macedonia and

Rome – one after another crushed the prospects of Jewish independence, there were numerous forlorn rebellions ending with the destruction of Jerusalem by the Emperor Hadrian in AD 134 and the diaspora that followed.

The New Testament reflects much less warlike attitudes but is by no means pacifist, since that idea was introduced much later to Christianity by scholars like Tertullian, Origen and Cyprian. Jesus, while refusing, so far as we know, to support armed rebellion against the Romans did not wholly discount violence; in the Gospels (Matthew) he did not 'bring peace to the earth but a sword'. Similarly, Luke (3) describes John the Baptist as not disapproving of war and again Jesus (22. 35) telling his embattled apostles to sell their clothes and buy swords. In the same way the Book of Revelations supposedly written by John of Patmos spoke of 'the armies of heaven smiting the nations... Faithful on a white horse in righteousness he judges and makes war.' So it could certainly be used as an incitement to violence, particularly during periods of stress like the Black Death when the end of the world seemed an imminent prospect and millennialist hope offered the only chink of light. This picture of first-century Israel is backed up by the so-called *War Scroll* discovered with others by the Dead Sea, which describes the Sons of Light fighting the Sons of Darkness.

'The Canaanites were well aware of God's role in the conquest of Canaan.'
American commentary on the Book of Joshua

2

ANCIENT GODS OF WAR – EUROPE AND THE MIDDLE EAST

'The worship of Mithras, the Persian sun god was to be found wherever Roman troops were stationed … for he was especially the soldiers' god.'

R. H. Barrow, *The Romans*

As we have seen, what was special about the Jewish attitude to war was not just the very strong motivation of a single God but also the extraordinary fact that the remarkable triumph of this underdog nation was enshrined in a text that became The Book of numerous other nations for the following three thousand years, and also a key inspiration for the Koran, which recycled the Israelite concept of holy war as jihad. Other ancient religions may have contained nearly as potent an ethic of warfare but their holy texts were long since discredited or lost, so their subsequent influence has been much less significant. So, while we cannot apart from the conflicts of Israel identify any genuine religious wars in this period, we find that almost all wars were sponsored by religion. Yet even the Israelites had plenty of other motives for their armed migration out of Egypt.

It is evident that many of the ancient empires to varying degrees used their religion as a means of justifying conquest. Kings relied to a considerable extent on identifying themselves as chosen by a god or gods, if not on actually being divine themselves, and on this basis they went to war with their neighbours and built their empires. For example, Assurbanipal of Assyria (r. *c.669–631*) regarded himself as appointed by the god Ashur with a divine mission to establish a world empire, so any who rejected his claims were regarded not just as rebels but as heretics against whom all forms of atrocity could be accommodated. Ashur as their chief god was depicted on their monuments as an archer, since the bow was their prime weapon.

Certainly, the Assyrians showed no desire to convert the peoples they conquered to their religion, for they attributed their success to their own special divine sponsors and mocked their enemies for having inferior faiths. So, while they did not wage religious wars as such, they certainly used their religion as motivation for their armies and justification for the ravaging of their defeated foes. Ethnic cleansing, crop destruction and mass execution were all deployed.

It was probably the Egyptians who first had what might be called a national god, Horus, and significantly he was a god of war and protector of the people, a Sun god from whom were descended all the pharaohs who during their lives became the Sun's earthly embodiment and were his high priests. It was a formula for empire building and popular motivation shared by many civilizations, including the Aztecs, the Incas and the Japanese. In addition, like later civilizations the Egyptians had a mother goddess, Necth, who cared for warriors killed in battle and consoled both young soldiers and the bereaved. It worked well in helping the pharaohs to build up their empire by conquest, though occasionally they varied the theme, as when Thutmose III (*c.1479* BC), builder of the great temple at Karnak, declared the god Amun as the divine inspiration for his wars and identified himself with his god during his epic Megiddo campaign.

As with the Assyrians, there is no real evidence to suggest that the Egyptians waged religious warfare, but certainly the divine attributes of the pharaohs gave them encouragement to wage war when they wanted. It is significant that two of their most aggressive empire-builders, Thutmose III and Rameses II (1292–1213 BC) both paid close attention to glorifying their own status as gods on earth, Rameses in particular having huge statues of himself built, such as those at Abu Simbl.

The Persians under the new dynasty founded by Cyrus (576–530 BC) were dedicated followers of the god Mazda and boasted of his assistance in their conquests, but surprisingly were tolerant of non-Zoroastrians, as in their fair treatment of the Jews whom they allowed to return from captivity in Babylon and for whom they helped build a new temple in Jerusalem.

Overall the ancient empires made sure their wars were blessed by their gods but did not in the main fight wars specifically on their behalf. Their religions tended to be so complex and so basically similar that it was easier for conquered peoples to simply accept gods much like their own but with different names. Thus, famously, Zeus the chief god of the Greeks was painlessly identified as Jupiter, the chief god of the Romans, when the Romans triumphed. Rome also adopted new gods whenever it was socially or politically expedient, famously introducing the Magna Mater, Mother Goddess, when they needed a morale boost during a low point in the Carthaginian War in 217 BC.

The numerous city states of ancient Greece had no national religion and whilst the god Ares embodied the lust for war, no wars were started because of him and religious motivation in warfare was at best tangential. There was no real fanaticism except among fringe sects. The Parthenon in Athens may have been the finest temple ever built, but it was a display of artistic endeavour and civic opulence, not a real focus for any faith that had active adherents. So, whilst Athene gave superficial credibility to the Athenian Empire she was certainly not a prime motivator. Nevertheless, religion did play a significant role in the infrastructure of all wars among the ancient Greeks. In Crete the warriors did their ritual dances in the cave of Zeus on Mount Ida. The Spartan war system was very much based on the cult of the Dioskouri and the Spartans were notoriously superstitious about rites before battle; they refused to join the Athenians at Marathon because the moon was in its wrong phase. Similarly, the Delphic Oracle was regularly consulted by states to check that the gods were on their side.

The first Greek to begin to take religion seriously as an empire-building tool was Alexander the Great (356–324 BC) who as a youngster had been persuaded by his mother that he was the son not of his earthly father but of Zeus and was thus destined to be a world conqueror. So while he waged a series of successful wars his own motivation was semi-religious and he claimed that he was seeking vengeance for the burning of Greek temples by the Persians. His Macedonian troops had a tradition of marching between the two halves of a bisected dog to purify themselves for battle. After adding Persia and Egypt to his empire he proved his divine status by visiting the Oracle of Siwa in the North African desert, where his divinity was obligingly confirmed, and he began to make use of it to help cement his vast, otherwise unsustainable dominions. He died before this had much effect but his successors adopted the same strategy and after the fall of the Roman republic so did the Roman emperors, all of whom claimed divine descent until Christianity took over. However, the religious component in warfare remained at what might be called the tactical level in both the Greek and Roman civilizations. The Romans were extremely strong on pre- and post-battle rituals and every legion had its haruspex who supervised the procession of a goat, a boar and a bull round their camp before ritual sacrifice. The terrible defeat of the consul Camillus was held up as an example of the stupidity of a general who ignored the fact that the sacred chickens had not eaten their seed on the eve of battle. In 340 BC another consul, Decius Mus, was convinced that he must sacrifice himself for the gods to help him win a battle, so he ritually devoted himself to death and charged alone to certain death as the battle commenced. After any victory all Roman generals dressed up as Jupiter Capitolinus, the chief god, to take part in post-war ceremonials.

Equally superstitious were the Romans' most formidable opponents, the Carthaginians, who were fatalistic worshippers of their native Phoenician god Baal, the one so much derided in the Old Testament and after whom Hannibal – Hannibaal – (248-183 BC) was named. While the two Punic Wars were more about commercial control of the Mediterranean than competing religions there was clearly a strong religious undertone in the careers of the Barcid family, particularly their most able member Hannibal. He waged one of history's longest and most daring campaigns motivated by a psychotic hatred of Rome which dovetailed with his ancestral religion to provide exceptional levels of motivation. They led in the end to his nation's self-destruction and the deaths of 15,000 of his original army. In one battle alone, Cannae in 216 BC, he lost more than 5000 out of a force of 56,000, but had slaughtered 48,000 Romans, so he was delighted.

Yet even such victories meant the steady attrition of his own limited manpower, so that in the end his defeat was inevitable.

The Romans themselves retained their old uninspiring religion, which few took too seriously, though as among the Greeks there were flirtations with eastern cults like Magna Mater, Isis and later Mithras to help motivate the ordinary soldiers. The Romans in the early days did on the whole avoid religious warfare, as whenever they conquered another nation they sensibly assumed that these foreign gods were the same as their own simply described in a different language. Thus, all the Greek gods were conveniently found to be exactly the same as the Roman ones, Zeus was Jupiter, Aphrodite was Venus and so on, so there was no need for controversy.

In 27 BC however, as the Roman Republic came to an end religion began to play a new role in politics. Octavian (63 BC–AD 14), the nephew of Julius Caesar, was awarded the new name of Augustus, a word with divine connotations, and soon afterwards began styling himself as 'Son of the divine Caesar'. Thus, he and his successors were treated as living gods, a useful tool to help control a massive empire made up of many disparate conquered nations. It can be argued therefore that religion played a role in helping to motivate the armies wage wars to expand and defend the frontiers of one of the world's largest empires, and altars to the divine emperors were built in every provincial capital, but there were no genuinely religious wars or missions to convert the provinces to worshipping Jupiter.

Some of the conquered peoples did fall back on their own religions when they aimed to rebel. Famously in Roman Britain in AD 71 it was recorded by the Roman historian Tacitus that Queen Boudicca's army included a significant number of fanatical druids and their female acolytes who gave the legions considerable problems, until military discipline proved more effective than fanaticism.

Similarly, the religiously broad-minded Romans did have a problem coping with the fanatical monotheism of the Jews. The Roman province of Palestine was a regular source of religious tension, made worse when the Romans decided that their own emperors should be deified. When the unstable Emperor Caligula had a statue of himself put up in the Temple at Jerusalem – bad enough to have an actual god, let alone a deified human – there were signs of open rebellion. Caligula was murdered in Rome so the outbreak was delayed until AD 46, when leaders called Jacob and Simon staged an armed revolt that was quickly put down.

Twenty years later it broke out again as the so-called Great Revolt provoked by Romans despoiling the Temple and Greeks harassing the Jews. The Jews won the first battle, massacring several thousand Roman soldiers but soon split up into disputing factions, the Zealots, the Sicarii and the Sadducees, and were forced into submission by the new Emperor Vespasian's son Titus. He captured Jerusalem after a brutal siege in AD 70 and famously demolished the Temple. The last Jewish stronghold at Massada fell three years later when the surviving defenders committed suicide rather than be captured. Typically, these Jewish rebellions were asymmetric wars between a superpower with very little interest in religion except as a cosmetic prop for the imperial line and a small province of people hugely offended when they were compelled to see this cult introduced to their holy city.

A third Jewish rebellion against Roman rule followed in AD 115, and was known as the Kitos War. This time it was spread throughout the Middle East and Egypt by Jews feeling oppressed by the pagan Romans. Numerous Romans were slaughtered before it too was crushed. Then in 132 came the last great insurrection, this time provoked by the Emperor Hadrian who had banned circumcision and was replacing the ruins of the old temple with one dedicated to Roman gods. A charismatic leader appeared, Bar Kochba, who was acclaimed a Messiah by a majority of Jews but not by the Christian Jews. The result was not just destruction but the ethnic cleansing of the Jews from their homeland, their subsequent dispersal round the world, to be frequently forced out of one state after another when their differences caused unpopularity. It also caused the final split between the people of the Old and New Testaments and residual antipathy not just between European Christians and Jews but also with the other Semitic races of the Middle East.

Apart from Israel and Persia, most of the ancient nations had whole families of gods, often two or three generations. All tended to have specific gods of war, fertility and weather etc., so the names could be interchangeable. Major gods like Baal, Kali or Odin were portable and easily crossed national borders, so there was no point in persecutions or compulsory conversion. Among the polytheistic nations of this period there were remarkably similar superstitions and acts of propitiation or atonement practised by warriors before and after battle, reassuring themselves that they were winners, survivors and free of guilt. George Fraser in *The Golden Bough* describes many such rituals; the head-hunting people of central Celebes, for example, 'took the heads of their enemies and afterwards propitiated the souls of the slain in the temple.'

The ancient polytheistic religions were so similar in many respects that there was little motivation to conquer neighbouring peoples just in order to convert them, but the help of religions to inspire the troops and help pay for conquests was exploited when rulers chose to do so.

'Even war is part of God's gracious activity.'
Jimmie Nelson, sermon notes

'The Athenians believed that Pan came to their rescue in their battle with the Persians (at Marathon) so they founded a temple in his honour.'
Fragment of Simonides

3

ANCIENT GODS OF WAR – THE FAR EAST AND THE AMERICAS

'Indra the Vritra slayer, Fort Destroyer, scattered the Dasa hosts who dwelt in darkness.'

Hindu *Rig Veda*

Qin Si Huang (259–210 BC), the first ruler to unite China, worshipped Chi You the Chinese god of war and masterminded his aggressive conquests of the six other regions of China to create a political empire for his dynasty, not for religious reasons, albeit he sought divine blessing.

This was already available due to the widespread teachings of Confucius (551–479 BC) who though he basically disapproved of war as an inefficient method of settling disputes still gave his quasi-religious blessing to so-called just wars, which included any war waged by a righteous emperor. Thus, he advocated a punitive war to the Emperor of Lu against Qi on the grounds that its emperor had been murdered by an ambitious official. His basic theory was that emperors were sons of heaven and so automatically had the mandate of heaven – *tianming* – unless they became bad emperors. Since their remit came from the gods it covered the entire world, therefore they had the right when necessary to defend their rule of the entire world against any opponent who would not accept peaceful arbitration. He also blessed the use of force to wage war on any external rulers who were cruel to their subjects, for example by misusing their resources so that people starved. Confucius's whole emphasis was on the divine blessing available to all righteous rulers, whose moral quality would be passed down to their generals and from them onwards to the ordinary soldiers.

It could be argued that the Confucian ethic, which was endorsed by other sages such as Mencius, established the role of Chinese emperors in uniting what was for most of history the largest single nation, but also in restraining them on the whole from foolhardy campaigns beyond what became their natural borders.

Parallel to the teachings of Confucius came those of the Taoist master Zhang Daoling (c.AD 34–156) who developed his ideas as a faith-healer; his usual fee from patients was five pecks of rice. As the first of what came to be known as the Celestial Masters, he preached an ethic of avoiding illness and ensuring a good afterlife by avoiding overindulgence, particularly in sex. His followers were to become the chosen people living in a small theocratic state that he set up in the Hanzhong Valley north of Sichuan on the edges of the, at this time, weak Han Empire. The Taoist theme was the Great Peace or *Taiping* and its focus was on aiming for a pleasant afterlife rather than an extremely unpleasant hell. This inspired his even more ambitious successor Zhang Lu to raise an armed rebellion, the War of Five Pecks of Rice, the Yellow Turbans against the Han dynasty in 184, so that the new state could be extended to become Zhanghan. Thus the Tao, a fundamentally non-violent faith, did justify the use of force against an unsatisfactory regime and the new state survived seven years before being overrun and its people dispersed in AD 191. Total casualties have been estimated at between three and seven million including the usual collateral starvation that dogged Chinese wars. Apart from Israel, it was a unique example of a deeply felt religion being allied to an oppressed minority and provided a template for the many Buddhist-inspired rebellions that occurred later in Chinese history.

One of the two greatest benefits of religions for ancient empires which were often at war was that nearly all of them promised a marvellous afterlife for fallen warriors and all of them had a war god in some shape who would help them to win. In India, the Hindu Vedas promised heaven for soldiers killed in battle and praised the *dharma*, or duty of the warrior caste to fight, assuring them that the gods would help. The *Rig Veda* is a massive compilation of war poems reflecting the military ethos of the Indo-Aryan invaders as they conquered the original inhabitants of the Indian sub-continent. In the Battle of Telip (*Rig Veda* 7. 18) or the Battle of the Ten Kings, supposedly around 3500 BC, the Aryan god Indra helps King Sudas conquer the Dasyus. 'Renowned is Indra when conquering, and slaying, it is he who wins the cattle ... gold, horses, he breaks first in pieces.' In the hugely influential Hindu text the *Bhagavad Gita* Krishna explains to Arjuna that 'there is no greater good for any warrior than to fight a righteous war.' Yet the multiplicity of Hindu gods did not compete with each other militarily and India seems to have been immune from bona fide (if the phrase can be used in this context) religious wars until the arrival of Islam, just as China and Japan were largely immune until the arrival of Buddhism.

Of the so-called great religions Buddhism perhaps had the best reputation for encouraging peace, but the Buddha was himself involved in some fairly messy politics in the Kingdom of Magadha, which had become his biggest patron. His advice was sought by King Bimbisara on some of his wars of expansion that not only helped increase the Magadha empire but also the initial expansion of Buddhism. Buddhists often supported armed resistance, particularly Mahayana Buddhists. Perhaps the first example was in 2 BC when the King Datthagamini of Sri Lanka/Ceylon with Buddhist blessing successfully conducted a holy war against the Hindu Tamils of Chola, thus turning himself into a long-term icon of Sri Lankan independence and rejection of Tamil Hinduism. Then in AD 515 came the war inspired by the Buddhist monk Faqing against the Wei emperor in China, when he led an army of 50,000. Having promoted himself as a *Dasheng*, a potential reincarnation of the Buddha, he argued that the murder of barbarians or non-Buddhists did not constitute a sin and to wage war was part of a duty to pursue the cosmic battle against Mara.

The other early manifestation of violence in Buddhism was the promotion of unarmed combat. The development of martial arts training at the Shaolin Monastery began in 487 AD and the first significant fighting by Buddhist warrior monks seems to have been at Hulao in 621, albeit the cause was to eliminate two warlords, not to spread Buddhism.

One of the most remarkable events in ancient history was the dramatic conversion of the previously ruthless emperor Ashoka (*fl. c.*264–233 BC) who according to his own edicts carved in stone felt such extreme revulsion after his bloody defeat of the Kalinga – 100,000 killed outright, many more dead from wounds or starvation and 150,000 deported – that as 'the Beloved of the Gods' he would renounce war. However, in practical terms he did nothing to rectify the ethnic cleansing, nor apparently did he reduce the size of his army.

In early Japan it is hard to separate myth from reality but certainly the divine status of the Yamato emperors was established early in its history. The semi-legendary Emperor Ojin, supposedly in the third century AD, was identified with the war god Hachiman, an archer, and from the fifth century onwards Buddhism and Shinto joined forces in Japan to provide the military ethic for the class of warriors later known as samurai. While wars were not, so far as we know, caused by religion they were certainly sponsored by it and the two rival religions competed to share the credit.

The relationship of war and religion is even harder to analyse in the early civilizations of Central and South America. Little is known of Mayan wars but from before the Christian era they had a war god Xbalanque who took the form of a jaguar, and wars seem to have been preceded by elaborate rituals. Yucatec, or the war leader, had to spend five days in the temple before the start of a campaign. There may or may not have been a demand for prisoners of war to keep up the required tally of human sacrifice, but certainly human sacrifice was a feature of their religion and perhaps a useful tool for the intimidation both of their enemies and their subjects. The great pyramid Temple of the Sun at Palenque, in what is now Mexico, was dedicated to war and celebrated the life of the leader Pacal the Great (d. 683). In the same way the Toltecs from around the ninth century had a warlike god Quetzalcoatl, or the Feathered Serpent, whose high priest Our Lord One Red seems to have been a war leader. Further south in pre-Inca Peru the Mochica culture from around AD 100 seems to have encouraged ritual wars between elite groups of warriors as a source of victims for human sacrifice, as many centuries later did the Aztecs (v. Pt 2 Chapter 7).

There is at least literary evidence of one other war in ancient times caused, it seems, solely by religion and it may have been as early as 2000 BC, or perhaps later, round about the time of Moses. This, according to the *Gathas* – seventeen devotional hymns purportedly written by Zoroaster himself – was a war between King Vishtaspa (Hystapses according to the Greeks) of Balkh (an area in the north of what is now Afghanistan) against King Arjasp of Turan in the Persian-speaking area. Vishtaspa was a supporter of the prophet Zoroaster (Zarathustra) and having adopted his worship of Ahura Mazda and his code of ethics refused the orders of Arjasp to go back to the old religion of the Aryans. They fought a battle and according to the Zoroastrian text Vishtaspa came off best.

There is also some evidence that Zoroastrianism, perhaps the greatest of the ancient religions to more or less disappear (except in the Mumbai region) after the birth of Islam, was involved in another religious war more than a thousand years later, though this may be legend. Ardashir, a hereditary prince of Pars, waged a war in AD 224 to take control of all Persia and Mesopotamia from the Parthians, urged on by Tansar the high priest of what he regarded as orthodox Zoroastrianism. Thus an armed insurrection was masterminded by priests of one sect of Zoroastrianism against another. Having forcibly imposed their Mazda version of the faith on the entire region they began persecuting all who disagreed. Ardashir also set about the smashing of graven images. Some time later the new dynasty was involved in 274 in the execution of the prophet Mani (*fl. c.*216-274) who was trying to evolve a new hybrid religion using what he regarded as the best features of Christianity, Buddhism and the local Zoroastrianism. But Manichaeism did not suit the politics of either the Roman or Iranian empires and its followers were persecuted violently throughout the known world. It was to resurrect itself among the Bogomils of Bulgaria and the Cathars of southern France, leading to the same violent suppression.

In most ancient empires religion was a useful tool for power-brokers, a prime source of motivation and manipulation, a fall-back position when things went wrong, a way to lock-in loyalties and an aid in creating political conformity. Only really in the case of ancient Israel was war so predicated on an unbending doctrine, with its almost paranoid objection to idolatry and rigid rules for ceremonial and behaviour, that no compromise was possible. And only Israel left behind a hand-book which became required reading for the whole of Europe and in recycled form for the whole of the Islamic world.

'...the contest of cosmic forces of good and evil.'
Jamsheed Choksy, *Justifiable Force and Holy War in Zoroastrianism*

4

CONSTANTINE AND JULIAN – CHRISTIANS AGAINST PAGANS

In hoc signo vinces ('In this sign shalt thou conquer')
Attributed to the Emperor Constantine by Eusebius

'Vicisti, Galilaee.' (You have won, Galilean.')
Supposed last words of the Emperor Julian according to
Theodoret of Cyrus

The battle of Saxa Rubra or the Milvian Bridge on the Tiber near Rome in AD 312 marks the first act of war involving Christianity and is one of the most significant battles in all world history. At the time the young Emperor Constantine (274–337) shared his rule with three other emperors – the Tetrarchy – two of whom were strongly pagan whilst he himself was also pagan but tolerant of Christians, as was the fourth co-emperor Licinius. In fact, Constantine's father and predecessor Gallienus had issued an edict instructing tolerance of Christians, so the worst days of persecution were over and Christians now made up a sufficient minority of the empire's population for the politicians to consider looking for their support. As a young man Constantine had been made to witness the persecution of Christians by the obsessive Emperor Diocletian and perhaps on the strength of his reluctance to participate at that time he had been passed over for promotion, so his career had been in the balance.

For the ambitious Constantine his quarter share of the Roman Empire was not enough – his share was basically Gaul and western

Europe – and his army based in Gaul was too small to take on his rivals. So the Christians, particularly the Christian soldiers in his army, were useful allies, though he also had several legions which clung to the Mithraic sun god. Using these troops he built up his reputation by winning a series of battles against the Franks in 306–8.

According to near contemporary sources (Eusebius and Lactantius) Constantine along with other witnesses saw a cross in the sky a few days before the battle at Saxa Rubra as he commenced his attempt to conquer Italy and take it from his pagan rival Maxentius based in Rome. This convenient apparition did not in fact indicate Constantine's full-blooded commitment to Christianity, for the cross in the sky could have been interpreted as the more common cross of the Unconquered Sun – Sol Invictus – which many of Constantine's army from Gaul were accustomed to have as their emblem, so both his Christian and his sun-worshipping soldiers could have allowed themselves to be inspired by it. Similarly, the words allegedly appearing near the cross 'In hoc signo vinces' could apply either to the Christian god or the Mithraic sun, so the pagans were not offended. Naturally, Christian historians were in no doubt that it was a Christian message that Constantine saw in the sky; as Eusebius put it 'he saw with his own eyes in the heavens a trophy of the cross arising from the light of the sun,' but it is not too cynical to suggest that Constantine shrewdly kept his options open and decided which cross it was, Christian or Mithraic, well after the battle.

Either way it was a famous victory and though the casualties may not have been huge the death of a rival emperor was more than enough, so this single battle changed the whole course of European history and ranks in importance alongside Abu Badr (v. Pt2 Chapter 6) as one of the most important examples of a battle that is known as one of competing faiths. Though Constantine himself did not convert to Christianity until he was on his death-bed twenty-five years later, it suited him politically to position himself as tolerant of Christians, especially since one of his two surviving rivals, Maximin, based in the Middle East, made a point of championing the old religion. So as his campaign to mop up the rest of the Roman Empire proceeded it made sense to Constantine to embellish the legend of the Milvian Bridge/Saxa Rubra. Meanwhile, he also published the Edict of Milan, which granted Christians immunity from persecution, so the Milvian Bridge was a major step forward for the Christian religion.

In the end the job of eliminating Maximin was mainly achieved by his temporary ally Licinius, the co-emperor based in the Balkans. This conveniently left Constantine with one remaining rival, Licinius himself. The latter had shared Constantine's policy of tolerance to the Christians, but it did not save him. Constantine finally got rid of the last of his three rivals at the battle of Chrysopolis in 323.

Thus, having established himself as sole emperor by AD 325 and having warmed further towards the Christians he moved gradually towards adopting Christianity as the state religion of his empire, perceiving that it offered advantages in terms of its strong infrastructure to legitimise his hold on the purple. Yet it was another twelve years before he accepted baptism himself and his personal behaviour in those years was far from the Christian ideal; he had both his son Crispus and his wife executed in a fit of pique in 328.

Ironically, having begun his career as a champion of tolerance towards Christians he now insisted that his new religion adopt strict rules with no more deviations in liturgy or theology. He organised the pruning of the Bible to exclude books that displeased the church establishment and instigated persecution of all who disagreed. An emperor who refused baptism until just before he died in 337 was responsible for a radical re-shaping of Christianity to fit the pattern of his empire, and consolidated the infrastructure of both. With his impressive new title 'Apostolos' he acted as moderator at the Council of Nicaea in 325, which fixed many contentious doctrines like the Trinity with the threat of persecution for any who dared dispute the decisions. It was a classic example of putting an end to argument by the enforced adoption of an unverifiable doctrine, and it was later to cause several wars.

In considering how a theoretically peaceful religion like Christianity began to become more aggressive, we can see that the change of mood predates Constantine. It went back to men like the Carthaginian scholar Tertullian (c.160–220) who began spreading new doctrines about the elimination of heretics and attacking both heathens and Jews. Cyprian from the same city had similarly intolerant views, as did Origen in Egypt, both of them having suffered severe persecution themselves. All three disapproved of war but not of persecution.

Sixteen years after Constantine's death his grand-nephew Julian (331–363) took over the empire from his Christian cousin Constantius II and reversed his uncle's policy. Officially a Christian, but by preference an undercover pagan, he did not reveal his faith until he had begun his military coup d'état against Constantius II. Ten years earlier at the age of twenty this complex young man had secretly converted to Mithraism, the religion still popular among many soldiers, which had been Constantine's alternative choice before Saxa Rubra. More or less faced with the same choice as Constantine, Julian after supposedly 'wrestling with the Gods all night' professed his allegiance to the old religion in front of his rebel army at Sirmium on the Danube and won approval. So to some extent his subsequent battles were between pagan and Christian forces.

Once in power, however, Julian did not persecute either Christians or Jews. He was killed in battle against the Persians after only two years of replacing Christianity with paganism as the official religion of the empire. His attempt to reverse the rise of Christianity in the Roman Empire was a failure.

Meanwhile, having at long last captured an empire, Christianity had in turn been captured and was transformed, scarified and co-opted as yet another instrument of power. According to Edward Gibbon, Christianity deserved a significant portion of the blame for the decline and fall, but that is a little unfair, for the empire was already proving dysfunctional long before Constantine. However, his shift of the capital from Rome itself to the new city of Constantinople did contribute to the weakening of the western half of the Empire and was later to create one of the first serious splits in Christianity. He also perhaps unwittingly left behind a legend, the Legend of Sylvester, according to which he was allegedly cured of leprosy by Pope Sylvester and in return promised that the popes of Rome would be the masters of Christianity. This legend accompanied by the almost certainly forged Donation of Constantine was to be a prime cause for a series of wars 600 years later (v. Pt 2 Chapter 14).

Thirty years after the death of the Emperor Julian there was one final attempt to make war on behalf of the old Roman gods against the Christians. In 392 an ex-teacher Flavius Eugenius seized power in the western half of the Roman Empire and though himself a

Christian was persuaded by his supporters that the best way for him to maintain power was by restoring the old religion, partly because many of his troops were pagan mercenaries from Gaul and Germany. So the temples of Venus and Jupiter were re-opened and he went to war against the emperor of the eastern half of the Empire, Theodosius I (*c.*346–395), based in Constantinople. The Battle of Frigidus (in the Vipiva Valley in modern Slovenia) in 394 was the last confrontation between the old and new religions of Rome. After two days of heavy fighting in which Eugenius nearly scored a victory there came fierce winds which blew sand into the western army's eyes and deflected the arrows they had fired back into their own ranks. Theodosius came out the victor, claiming afterwards that it was divine intervention, an example of our possible category 10. Eugenius was executed and his chief general committed suicide. Sixteen years later in 410 Rome fell to the Goths, who were Arian (anti-Trinitarian) Christians.

There is one other remarkable example of a Christian war-maker in this period, Ezana (*fl* 320–60), King of Aksum, a substantial empire covering what are now Ethiopia, Eritrea, Somalia, parts of Sudan and Yemen. Our knowledge of him comes almost entirely from inscriptions in which he boasted of changing from allegiance to the war god Mahreb to fighting on behalf of 'The Lord of Heaven and Earth'. This began a long tradition of Christianity in Ethiopia. Ezana justified a number of aggressive wars, including an invasion of Arabia, in which he authorised plunder, intimidation and forced migration. The Aksumite Empire was involved in another largely religious war in 520 when King Kaleb sent an army to Yemen to depose the Jewish King Dhu Nuas who had been persecuting the local Christians. A third partly religious, partly commercial war came in 570 when the Aksumite leader of Yemen, Abraha, attempted to divert pilgrims from Mecca to Sana'a, but his army was defeated before it could reach Mecca. Despite this, Aksum remarkably gave asylum to young Mohammed when he had to escape from Mecca after he had been threatened with violence during his early years of promoting Islam (v. Pt 2 Chapter 6).

> 'Abraha's army was totally destroyed on its march by
> the Stones of Sjeel.'
>
> *Koran*

5

FROM ALARIC TO JUSTINIAN – ARIAN CHRISTIANS AGAINST TRINITARIAN CHRISTIANS

'He (Valens) insensibly hated those sectaries to whom he was an object of hatred.'
Edward Gibbon, *Decline and Fall of the Roman Empire*

One of the mercenary officers fighting for Theodosius at the Battle of Frigidus was a young Goth prince called Alaric, who sixteen years later played a major part in the fall of the Roman Empire. What tends to be forgotten is that the sack of Rome in 410 was at the hands of largely Christian Goths, as is evidenced by their sparing of the shrine of St Peter.

At Frigidus, where together Theodosius and Alaric had faced a heathen usurper, we find further complexities. For Alaric (370–410) and his Goths had been converted to Christianity during the reign of previous emperors such as Constantius and Valens. They had supported the Arian version of Christianity, which did not regard Jesus as the same as God or in any physical sense the son of God. In other words, they rejected the official Trinitarian doctrine created by the Nicene Conference and then dictated by Constantine. This was a serious split in Christianity, which had already led to bouts of persecution and incidents such as the 'accidental' burning of 80 bishops on a ship moored in Constantinople. Even the two brothers Valens and Valentinian, who were joint emperors, were on opposite sides in this controversy. Ironically, the Arian Christian Valens was defeated and killed with the loss of some 20,000 men at Adrianople (now Edirne in Turkey) in 375 by an army of Arian Christian Goths led by a recent convert, Fritigern.

Thus, despite their shared victory at the River Frigidus Theodosius, who was strictly Trinitarian/Nicene and had cleansed the church of Arians, must have regarded Alaric as a heretic. This perhaps accounts for the fact that Alaric did not receive the promotion in the Roman army which he expected after his huge contribution to the victory, but instead returned to his tribesmen who soon afterwards accepted him as their king. Alaric was therefore aware of the Old Testament history of the Jews and as a Goth identified with them looking for the promised land, in his case Italy.

In 410 AD the officially Catholic/Orthodox heart of the Roman Empire was overrun by groups of northern tribes, Goths, Visigoths, Ostrogoths and Vandals, who had largely been converted to Arian Christianity during the period between Constantine and Theodosius. In Italy Alaric died soon after his conquest and his Goths mainly settled in Gaul, so the Italians survived as proto-Catholics. However, in 476 Italy was conquered by another Arian Christian, Odoacer, who was ethnically a Hun, or Germanic. He was then in 493 himself defeated and killed by Theodoric the Great (455–526), leader of the Ostrogoths and another apparently fanatical Arian-Christian who made his capital in Ravenna. Initially tolerant of his 'Catholic' subjects, Theodoric began to persecute them towards the end of his reign, partly in retaliation for the persecution of Arians taking place in the Byzantine Empire. Meanwhile Alaric's illegitimate son Theodoric I, also an Arian Christian, expanded the Goths' kingdom of Gaul and is best remembered for his share in the defeat of Attila the Hun in 451.

The Visigoths who took over Spain and Portugal established an Arian Christian dynasty based in Toledo which was actively anti-Semitic and at times aggressively anti-Catholic, though it did not force its Catholic subjects to convert. The crisis came in the 580s when the commitedly Arian King Liuvigild was organising his son's succession. His elder son and designated heir, Hermenegild, unexpectedly converted from the Arian to the Catholic stance and rebelled against him. Liuvigild besieged and defeated his son in Seville, an example of a civil war caused by the strong feelings of opposition between Arian and Trinitarian beliefs; albeit their sectarian differences were doubtless exploited to advance their political ambitions. Hermenegild was murdered, probably on his father's orders, and replaced by his brother Reccared, who after the old king's death also converted to the Catholic side in 587. He had to suppress a number of Arian rebellions. The largest of these was in Septimania/Narbonne where the promoter was the fanatical Arian Bishop Atholoc. Ironically, the rebels summoned help from Guntram, the Catholic king of Burgundy, but the now Catholic Reccared defeated the joint Arian/Catholic rebels with considerable slaughter, another war largely caused by this sectarian divide within western Christianity. The Visigoth Spanish dynasty, now even more fanatically anti-Semitic, survived until overrun by the Muslims in 711.

Meanwhile Clovis I (465–511) had taken over as king of the Salian Franks in 481 and consolidated the new Merovingian dynasty by defeating the last Roman governor of Gaul and creating the new nation of France, with its capital at Soissons. Brought up as a pagan, then converted to Arian Christianity, he was under pressure from his wife Clotilde to change to Catholicism, something which might have undermined his position among his fellow Franks. However, it suited his long-term objective, which was to differentiate France from the other Arian Germanic tribes. So, in one of the most ingenious examples of retrospective religious warfare, he attributed his victory at the Battle of Tolbiac near Cologne to the Catholic Saint Remigius, thus providing justification for his own conversion and that of his Arian barons. The battle had been against the Alemanni confederation. He now controlled the Rhineland and was able to present himself and France as champions of Catholicism against the Arian Christian Goths to the east. The saint's victory also justified the creation of Reims (Remigius) as the spiritual centre of French monarchy. It was a classic example of retrospectively turning an act of tribal warfare into a religious war and exploiting it for political benefits.

The Vandals who took over the Roman province of Tunisia and what is now Algeria in 435 similarly established an Arian Christian dynasty based in Carthage and like the other three new monarchies ruled a largely Catholic population, but unlike them had a tendency to be less tolerant, regularly persecuting them. For example, their King Honeric forced the population of Libya to convert from Catholic to Arian in 480 and committed unknown atrocities against other Catholic adherents. Under King Humeric and his supplanter Gelimer, the persecution continued and it was perhaps this that prompted the new Byzantine Emperor Justinian in 527 to get rid of this heretical dynasty and make Tunisia once more part of the Eastern Roman Empire.

Justinian (482–565), based in Constantinople, had a lofty view of his own destiny as a world leader and champion of orthodoxy. In his own words 'Governing under the influence of God our empire which was delivered to us by His Heavenly Majesty we prosecute wars with success ... we do not put our trust in our soldiers, nor generals nor our own skill but rest all our hopes in the providence of the Supreme Trinity alone.' So when a Libyan bishop announced that he had had a vision asking Justinian to save the Christians of Libya from Arian oppression, he responded with alacrity.

The successful holy war against Tunisia and Libya gave the Emperor Justinia increased confidence and convinced him that he could bring back the whole of the old Roman Empire to the Nicene Creed. In 535 his chief general Belisarius retook Sicily from the Arian Ostrogoths but the rest of Italy took much longer and involved seeking mercenary help from the Lombards (then settled in what is now Romania) who as it happened had been converted to the orthodox, not the Arian version of Christianity. As Percy Ure put it, 'The fact that they were not Arians like the Goths and Vandals was a dominating factor in the history of the shaping of the western world.'

The disagreements about doctrines like the Trinity which had been imposed by Constantine after the Nicean Conference were thus the first cause or excuse for warfare between rival sects of Christianity. The conflicts were by no means as severe as the Reformation crisis, but did cost a large number of lives.

After his victories Justinian could now pose as 'Pantocrator', ruler of the world, and he regarded his war against the Sassanids of Persia as a holy mission. But the casualty list from his wars was a very long one, exacerbated by the bubonic plague, the Plague of

Justinian, that spread through the world from Constantinople in 541, in part disseminated by his continual troop movements and destruction of local infrastructures in areas that he attacked.

'At Constantinople on one occasion not a few Manichaeans after strict inquisition were executed in the emperor's (Justinian's) very presence, some by burning, others by drowning.'

F. Nau, R*evue de l'Orient,* 1897

PART TWO

THE MIDDLE AGES

'...it had now become clear that they (the non-Muslims) could be
made to listen only by force.'

Alfred Guillaume, *Islam*

6

MOHAMMED AND JIHAD – MUSLIMS AGAINST PAGANS

'Let them fight therefore for the religion of God, who part with the present life in exchange for what is to come ... for whether he be slain or victorious we will surely give him a great reward.'
Koran Chapter IV

Like the Jews after their flight from Egypt the first followers of Mohammed (570–632) were faced with overwhelming difficulties, to which the response was resorting to aggressive war. Initially Mohammed converted only a small, dedicated group of adherents and there was considerable opposition from the Meccan establishment. Apart from its role as a staging point on the lucrative caravan trade route to the north, Mecca's main source of income was from pilgrims visiting the sacred site of the Kaaba, at this time a place for venerating the old pagan gods of Arabia. Mohammed's rejection of these gods threatened the Meccans with a huge loss of business, so they reacted violently.

Mohammed initially lacked the manpower to make progress, but when he was asked to lead a rebel community in Medina he seized the chance. As one whose earlier career had been as a caravan manager he was skilled in arms and well used to repelling Bedouin raiders. Now he turned the tables and began raiding caravans himself, using the loot thus acquired to pay for his first little army. Even at this stage his situation as an underdog was similar to that described in the struggles of Moses and Joshua in the Old Testament, with which he was probably quite familiar, for his early career as the manager of camel caravans had seen him regularly travelling to Jewish and Greek cities en route to the ports of the Mediterranean.

It was almost by accident that Mohammed's policy of raiding caravans, *ghazr* or *razzia* as it became known in a French version of the Arabic, developed into jihad (literal translation 'effort') or holy war. For his first real military success came at Abu Badr as the result of a botched attack on a large caravan. The Meccans had upset his plans by rerouting the caravan, but his followers, frustrated by loss of expected booty, fought a larger force of Meccans with desperate bravery and achieved an astonishing victory, one that revealed the full potential of a small but highly energised and mobile force against uninspired opposition. It also provided firm evidence that Mohammed had Allah on his side; as written in the Koran: 'Allah helped you win at Abu Badr when you were a contemptible little force.' So almost overnight came the concept of jihad, battle both mental and physical against unbelief. As Alfred Guillaume put it, 'Idolaters whose very existence was an insult to the one true God would have to accept Islam or the sword; other monotheists would have to acknowledge their inferiority by paying a special tax.' Thus despite the fact that the battle of Abu Badr involved at most only a few hundred combatants it ranks alongside the Milvian Bridge/ Saxa Rubra as one of the most important battles in history.

It was in this atmosphere that Mohammed had pronounced many of the assertions in the Koran which justify holy war (the word used in the Koran is *qital*, not jihad). In the Koran we find exhortations very similar to those in the Old Testament, for example in Chapter IV: 'Fight therefore for the religion of God and oblige not any to what is difficult except thyself; however, excite the faithful to war, perhaps God will restrain the courage of the unbelievers.' This is the same promise as previously made by Moses that adherence to the faith would improve the odds in battle. At the same time the Koran is generous in its rewards for those who fight and hard on shirkers as in Chapter XLVIII '...whoso shall obey God and his apostle he shall lead him into gardens where rivers flow, but whoso shall turn back he will chastise him with grievous punishment ... he sent down on them tranquillity of mind and rewarded them with a speedy victory and many spoils which they took.' Hadith 2497: 'He who does not fight the idolaters utterly nor joins the warlike expedition will be smitten by Allah with a calamity.' Hadith 2462, for a woman who lost two sons in battle: 'You will get the reward of two martyrs because the people of the book have killed him.' These are emotive words which have inspired ISIS and other militant groups in the twenty-first century.

Mohammed waged his first wars against the superior forces of Mecca and gradually made steady progress in the battles that followed Abu Badr. Although he never actually brought the Meccans to their knees he was sufficiently close to that for them to agree in 630 to a compromise whereby the city kept its role as a pilgrimage destination but the Kaaba was now to be sacred to Allah instead of the pagan gods. In addition, Mohammed and his followers could return to Mecca and complete the conversion process, now made much easier by the fact that the livelihoods of the merchants and inn-keepers had been saved. In the meantime, he had fallen out with the local communities of Jews who in some cities he had punished severely for their resistance, and prayers were no longer said in the direction of Jerusalem, but Mecca instead. This was the first sign of an anti-Semitic strain in Islam that would resurface many years later.

Now that he had a successful, highly motivated, self-funding and highly mobile task force under his command Mohammed decided to use it, not disband it. Hence in the last few years of his life the holy war continued to mop up the remaining corners of the Arabian peninsula and start to expand westwards into Greek-held territory. Hence Hadith 2477 in which came the orders, 'Go to Syria for it is Allah's chosen land to which his best servants will be gathered,' adding Yemen and Iraq as the next two targets. This is amplified by Hadith 2478 with 'a section of my community will continue to fight and overcome their opponents till the last of them fight with Antichrist.' For motivation he offered 'women, cattle and sheep ... that will be the booty of the Muslims tomorrow (2495) and 'He who goes on Allah's path and dies or is killed ... is a martyr and will go to paradise' (2493).

The momentum thus created accelerated after his death. His successor the Caliph Abu Bakr (*fl* 632–634) had to suppress several variant versions of Islam, such as that headed by a rival prophet Musulman in the Yemen who had claimed to be equal to Mohammed and offered verse revelations supposedly from God. Mohammed had condemned him as a liar and he could not be allowed to survive. Some 10,000 of his followers were killed. There were similar false prophets that had to be eliminated in Oman, Yemen, Bahrein and the Hadramaut before Arabia was cleansed of deviant sects.

After the short series of civil wars known as the *Ridda* had eliminated all local opposition the Muslim armies resumed their rapid conquests in both directions, east and west. In the battle of Firaz on the Euphrates in 634 a Muslim force of around 20,000 defeated a joint Persian and Byzantine army with five times the number of men, resulting in the conquest of the area now known as Iraq. Then the battle of Yarmuk in 636 near the Golan Heights brought the conquest of Syria, taken from the Christian Greeks. Both battles were won by outnumbered forces commanded by the brilliant Khalid ibn al Walid, a fairly late convert to Islam. Between them these two battles accounted for nearly 100,000 fatalities and both demonstrated how the two declining superpowers of the region, Greco-Roman Byzantium and Sassanid Persia, were too weak and too unpopular to withstand a determined attack. The task begun at Firaz was then completed at Qaddissiya in 637 when Saad ibn ali Waqqas, a cousin of Mohammed's, convincingly defeated the Persians who had tried to drive out the new Muslim garrisons. An offer of peace if the Persians would convert to Islam was rejected, so a bloody four-day battle followed with some 35,000 Persian casualties. This led to the end of the Sassanid dynasty and the virtual end of their long-established and sophisticated religion, Zoroastrianism. It also led obliquely to Persia in due course becoming Shiite rather than Sunni, since the troops left to keep an eye on Persia from the new barrack towns of Kufa and Basrah were isolated from the new Muslim regime that shortly asserted itself in Damascus.

These three battles were even more historically significant in that they convinced the Arabs that they could if they wanted subdue the entire Middle East, if not the world. They had founded Basra and Kufa as advance military bases, just as they later founded Cairo in what became a new pattern of settlement. By 643 the Arabs were expanding rapidly beyond Egypt along the North African coast and in 655 added naval prowess to their portfolio when their new fleet defeated the Byzantines at the Battle of the Masts. The one serious problem, and it was hardly a setback, was the Plague of Emmaus in 639 that probably resulted from so many armies being cooped up in insanitary barrack towns. This may have cost up to a million lives, which could be defined as collateral damage from Muslim wars and troop movements.

Despite such progress the first cracks appeared a mere three decades after Mohammed's death, the beginnings of the Sunni/ Shiite split. It was back to civil war as the provincial governor of Syria, Muawiyya, refused to accept the authority of the fourth Caliph, Ali, Mohammed's son-in-law, and defeated him in battle at Siffin in 657 (70,000 casualties estimated). The Syrian army had been close to defeat but then as a last resort used the trick of putting Sunni Muslim slogans on their lances to undermine the confidence of Ali's army, thus paving the way for a non-priestly caliphate based in Damascus. This created a major rift in Islam between the politically proactive Sunnis represented by Damascus and the more spiritually minded Shiites, the supporters of Ali who embraced the concept of hereditary priest-kings, imams or Mahdis, and who could mainly be found in the Iraqi outposts of Kufa and Basrah.

The new militant but non-clerical dynasty of Damascus caliphs continued the rapid expansion of Islam by force of arms, not using compulsory conversion of captured nations, but accidentally encouraging it by tax penalties, a source of income that therefore soon dried up.

Thus by 686 Tunisia had been overrun and long-range squadrons had reached the Atlantic and Spain in the west. Turkestan fell in 692. Then after a change of dynasty (see below) came the remarkable victory over the Chinese at the River Chui by Talas in 752 in what is now Kyrgyzstan. Islam had conquered a swathe of three continents from the Pyrenees frontier of France in the west to the edge of China in the east. The warfare that created this huge empire was becoming much less of a genuine holy war.

What had begun under Mohammed as a war of the disinherited against the rich, of iconoclasts against idolaters, of the abstemious poor against the wealthy and self-indulgent, Muslim against pagan, had spread with huge rapidity. In his own lifetime Mohammed had not only crushed paganism in Arabia but many townships of diaspora Jews, and he had already threatened the Orthodox Christians of the Eastern Empire. Within a few years of his death his followers had almost wiped out Christianity in North Africa, and Syria but had also almost totally obliterated Zoroastrianism, the faith of the Persians which was to survive only in an enclave of western India. They had then begun to make inroads into Hinduism in India and clashed with the Buddhists of western China.

It is impossible to estimate at all accurately the number of casualties of this militant expansion of Islam. Many of the initial battles were won with shock tactics by small, highly mobile forces, so the numbers were perhaps quite modest. But the casualty rate in the bigger battles with the Byzantines and Persians began to escalate, and by the time the Muslims invaded India we begin to hear of massacres, so it is hard to believe that this period caused much less than a million lives lost. In addition to deaths during battle there was considerable mortality created by the plague that followed the first wave of conquests, notably the aforementioned Plague of Emmaus in 639, which cost the lives of several of Mohammed's closest allies based in the barracks at Emmaus.

Alongside the massive geographical conquests, Mohammed left a number of other potentially toxic legacies which encouraged sectarian war during subsequent years. The Koran and its supplementary hadiths formed a massively important document which retained its influence over many millions for the next 1400 years, advocating war against infidels in much the same way as the Old Testament's litany of slaughter did for Christians. The exhortation to 'fight the idolator utterly' (Koran 9. 36) was taken seriously by successions of aggressive regimes based in Damascus, Baghdad, Cairo, Delhi, Kabul, Beijing, Samarkand, Marrakesh and later Istanbul. Also taken seriously was the encouragement to grab booty, which applied particularly to the Arab raids on the Hindus of India. The poet al Katumi wrote: 'Our business is to make war on the enemy, on our neighbour and on our own brother, if there is no one else left.' The by-product of this was to create huge wealth among the Arab elites, which inevitably eroded most of the other value systems created by Islam.

The third potentially toxic legacy was lack of clear instructions about the succession, an ambiguity which had led to the first stages of the Sunni/Shiite split and was to cause numerous violent clashes over the following centuries.

'The Arabic word jihad is often translated as "holy war" but in purely linguistic terms it means "struggling" or "striving".'
Islamic Supreme Council of America

7

KARBALA – SHIITES AGAINST SUNNIS

'Allah will create a nation who will mourn Husayn till
the day of judgement.'

Mohammed

The basic quarrel between those later known as Sunnis and
Shiites could be traced back to the day Mohammed died and
when his son-in-law Ali (c.600–661) was too preoccupied with
grief and funeral arrangements to take part in the meetings to
decide the new leader. He therefore missed his chance to be
appointed the first caliph. His preoccupation meant that instead
of one of the family taking over as a hereditary imam the choice
fell on the more practical Abu Bakr who presided over the first
few years of rapid military expansion, the conquests of both
Syria and Persia.

As it turned out two more caliphs were appointed as successors
before Ali himself got his chance to become the fourth 'righteous
caliph' and first imam in 656. He was faced almost immediately
by an armed coalition headed by Mohammed's widow Aisha,
which he defeated in the Battle of the Camel near Basrah with
an estimated 10,000 casualties, the first major Muslim civil war.
A year later he clashed with his rival Muawiyya, governor of Syria,
whom he came close to defeating at Siffin near the Euphrates with
total casualties of around 70,000, the majority of them from the
Syrian force. By this time Ali's supporters were known as the Shia
Ali, or party of Ali, but were beginning to have disagreements and

confrontations with each other, as well as with the power-hungry Muawiyya. Caliph Ali's previously most fanatical supporters, known later as the Kharijites, became his enemies and it was one of their number who assassinated him after he had been in power for five years. In terms of categories the Siffin campaign should probably be classified not so much as a sectarian rift as a power struggle between two rival groups of the same religion.

Ali had designated his son Hassan as his successor or second imam but Muawiyya with his superior forces was now unstoppable; he declared himself caliph from his capital at Damascus, thus founding a dynasty of hereditary caliphs based in Syria, as opposed to the Shia insistence on hereditary imams based in Kufa. It was the now extremist Kharijites who declared that jihad was the Sixth Pillar of Islam.

Twenty years after the death of Ali, the Battle of Karbala in 681 was perhaps the most significant battle between two opposing sects of one religion in all world history. Not that it was a big battle, for Husayn, the second son of Ali and Fatima, so the Prophet's grandson and the third imam (his brother Hassan had died), could only muster a tiny army to face a major force sent from Damascus. Caliph Yazid, the son and heir of Muawiyya, had become an allegedly somewhat less than devout second caliph of the new dynasty. Husayn could have avoided the battle altogether and even afterwards could have easily escaped with his life, but instead he more or less chose martyrdom when most of his supposed supporters stayed at home in Basra or Kufa. This bequeathed not only a genuine hero to the Shiites, but also a lasting sense of guilt among the large numbers of his followers who had shirked the battle and remained at home. It also made the Caliph Yazid not only the villain of this event, the murderer of the Prophet's grandson, but a symbol of all that was wrong in a materialist-minded hereditary caliphate based in Damascus, compared with the first four Righteous Caliphs who had all avoided wealth and ostentation. On top of everything else, Caliph Yazid had a reputation as a drinker.

So, the Battle of Karbala fits into the category of a struggle for power between two rival sects of a single religion, though it was a totally asymmetric war between a well-equipped, powerful 'monarchy' and a tiny group of disorganised protesters who never stood any chance of supplanting the Damascus caliphs. Instead its enormous historical importance rests on two peculiar circumstances: the fact that Husayn's death was remembered as a form of saintly martyrdom and the fact that so many of his reluctant supporters not only felt guilt for deserting him but passed on this guilt to their descendants in a frenetically exaggerated form, which was to create deep-seated hatred and fanatical resistance that would keep resurrecting itself for the next thirteen centuries.

In political terms the Shiites failed to make any real inroads against Damascus, but in psychological terms Karbala was as significant as a major victory, for it provided motivation for Shiite communal guilt and solidarity for the next millennium and created serious fault-lines through Islam that are still causing disruption now, particularly the dangerous rivalry between Iran and Saudi Arabia representing the two most powerful states supporting the Shiite and Sunni causes.

A mere five years after Karbala in 686 came the almost equally significant and equally forlorn revolt of al-Mukhtar, also against the Ummayid caliphs in Damascus, and similar in so far as al-Mukhtar was a son of Ali, though by a wife other than Fatima, so he was a half-brother of Husayn, not really a grandson of Mohammed. Nevertheless, it was he who propagated the idea that descendants of Mohammed would reappear throughout the ages as Mahdis. Thus, a tradition was established of millennialist expectation, like the Second Coming of Christ, so that self-appointed mahdis appeared from time to time over the centuries, including the first of the Fatimids in Egypt and the famous Mahdi of Sudan, each of them with a mandate to use war to seize power.

It is less easy to calculate the level of purely religious motives in many of the inter-Arab wars of the next few centuries. Certainly, the Abbasids took advantage of Shiite sentiment when they began their rebellion against the Damascus Caliphs in 747. Their own credentials were somewhat oblique since they were descended not from Mohammed himself but from his uncle Abbas, but when Ali Abbas commenced his attack on Damascus in 747 at the end of Ramadan he won Shiite supporters from their heartland around Kufa and Basra. Thus, the Battle of the River Zab (a tributary of the Tigris) in 750, which ended the power of the Damascus caliphs, falls into the category of two rival dynasties vying for control of the same religion and the same sect, Sunni; albeit both sides were heavily politicised, and the Abbasid winners were somewhat cynically exploiting their tenuous connection with the Shiites. Once in power and having massacred almost every member of the old Damascus elite, Ali Abbas (now renamed as Caliph As-Saffah) abandoned his pretence of Mahdi status and pursued dynastic aggrandisement like a typical Sunni. This was even more the case with his more ruthless brother and successor Al Mansur, the founder of Baghdad, who purged all potential imams and Mahdis. He even had his most successful general executed in case he became a serious rival for power.

The Abbasid victory at the Zab was in the end an enormous disappointment for the Shiites, yet disappointment just served to fuel their extraordinary guilt complex and determination to survive. The first successful Shiite breakaway state was in Morocco where one of Caliph Ali's few surviving descendants, Idris, staged in 788 a near bloodless coup d'état and his short-lived Shiite dynasty was involved in wars against Sunni neighbours like Algeria, but these were expansionist rather than religious. Idris himself famously succumbed to Sunni revenge from Baghdad, allegedly in the form of poisoned tooth paste organised by Caliph Haroun as Rashid, the devious hero who features in some of the stories in *One Thousand and One Nights*.

The second more substantial Shiite success came in 909 when Said Ubaid (873–931) from Salamiya declared himself a new Mahdi on the basis of claimed descent from Husayn. With huge help from his mentor Ali Shi he staged an armed coup in Tunisia, ejecting the previous Sunni dynasty from Kairouan. His descendants the Fatimids later invaded Egypt and founded Cairo as a new Shiite capital in opposition to Sunni Baghdad. Meanwhile, the self-styled Caliph Al Mahdi had not only eliminated his all-important apostle Ali Shi but also turned on the extreme Shiite group the Kharijites who had aided his coup.

The Shiite credentials of the Fatimid dynasty which he founded were soon eroded by the demands of hereditary monarchy and the luxuries of the Cairo court. However, since in theory there should only be one true caliph or successor of Mohammed they did continue to challenge the other caliphs in Baghdad and this became even more complex when in 929 a third dynasty based in Cordoba, Spain, also began to use the title.

Thus, there were three caliphates waging intermittent frontier wars, Cordoba versus Mahdia (from 964 Cairo) for control of North Africa and Mahdia/Cairo versus Baghdad for control of Syria and the holy cities of Jerusalem and Mecca. It reached its peak when the Fatimid Caliph al Aziz captured Aleppo in 994 boasting that 'Gods grant victory to their armies through the holiness (*baraka*) of the men in charge.' So although there was a strong empire-building element to these wars there was also a keen awareness of the sectarian divide. For a period the Shiite Fatimids challenged the Sunni Abbasids for the world leadership of Islam and their empire at its peak stretched from North Africa through Syria as far as India.

Among the Shiites a number of extreme variants survived persecution. In 1090 the Ismaili sect of the Shiites began training their first cadres of suicide raiders, known subsequently as the Assassins, whose main objective was to exterminate Sunni heads-of-state, but were often diverted to the even more popular target of European crusaders such as The Lord Edward, the future Edward I of England, who narrowly escaped death at their hands. This remarkable sect set a precedent for the suicide bombers of the late twentieth century and survived in their mountain fortress of Alamut (in the Alborz region of western Iran) until it was destroyed by the Mongols.

Two other major campaigns of conquest could be termed as Shiite in style although both came from extremist sects that had developed among the Berber tribes of the Atlas Mountains and the Draa area between the Senegal and Niger rivers, which were out of reach of mainstream Sunni teaching. The first was led by Yahya ibn Abraham, who was in fact so hugely impressed by new Sunni teachings when he did the pilgrimage to Mecca that he founded a monastery or *rabat*, hence his followers were marabiteen or marabouts. He and his mentor Abdullah ibn Yasi (d. 1059) were so convinced of their correctness that they declared jihad, built up an army of mountain Berbers and captured Sijilmasa in 1055, which gave them access to the wealth of the cross-Sahara trade routes.

From this start they began to wage an acquisitive religious war both northwards and southwards, taking over the Ghana Empire to the south in 1075 and invading Tlemcen to the north where they founded the new city of Algiers. Their successors went on to found a new capital, Marrakesh, for the new dynasty and proceeded to invade Spain where they deposed the religiously lax local Sunni emirs by fatwa. Then under their geriatric but very able emir Yusuf ibn Tashfin they soundly defeated the Christian Spaniards under Alfonso VI at Sagrajas near Badajoz in 1086, killing half the Castilian army in the process. They absorbed all Spain south of the Tagus as well as the Balearic Islands into their Almoravid empire, which at its peak stretched from Andalusia to Ghana. Their wars had begun as religious in intent, a desire for purer Islam, but soon acquired commercial and imperial facets which later left them exposed to criticism from a fresh wave of fanatics.

A very similar pattern was followed by another inspired leader from the Atlas Mountains, Mohammed ibn Tumart (*c*.1080–1128), a wandering scholar who had absorbed new ideas in Baghdad before returning to Morocco where he began an attack on unveiled women and other breaches of Sharia law. In 1121 he announced that he was the new Mahdi and condemned the Almoravids as idolaters. He turned his followers into a tightly organised militant commune based at Tinmel in the High Atlas before commencing a prolonged guerrilla war in the Atlas Mountains. By 1149 his successors had taken over Marrakesh. They then ousted the Almoravids from Algeria, the Christian Portuguese from Ceuta and in 1195 beat the Castilian Christians under Alfonso VIII at Alarcos south of Toledo. Having completely supplanted the Almoravids they moved their capital to Seville where the tower of Giralda became a symbol of their success, the centre point of the Almohad Empire which lasted till 1248, when it was finally destroyed by the Christians at Las Navas de Tolosa. Both the Almoravid and Almohad wars were mainly against fellow Muslims, in effect one kind of apocalyptic sect against another, but between them they also held back the Iberian *reconquista* for some 200 years.

As previously mentioned, even more extreme than the mainstream Shiites were the ultra-violent Kharijites, originally supporters of the fourth righteous caliph, Ali, who then deserted him, were defeated in battle by him in 658 and retaliated by murdering him three years later. This persistently rebellious group believed that all Muslims outwith their own sect deserved to be killed. They caused havoc with their persistent armed rebellions but despite violent suppression survived in southern Iraq and parts of North Africa. Among a succession of civil wars, the most serious in northern Iraq lasted for thirty years (866-96) and cost a great number of lives on both sides.

Another deviant and rebellious version of Shiism is found in the Alawites, descendants of a sect in the Aleppo area which had been devoted to the eleventh Imam. They survived centuries of persecution in the mountains of Syria, including a determined attempted genocide by the Ottomans under Selim the Grim, until becoming the ruling class after the coup by Hafez al-Assad in 1970. Their aggressive stance helped cause the bitter civil war of 2010, which in turn provoked a Sunni/Shiite civil war in Iraq four years later (v. Pt 4. Chapter 40) and the proxy wars fought in Yemen and Palestine by Saudi Arabia and Iran.

Equally eccentric and at times violent were several other variants of Shiism, basically owing their bifurcation to the Seventh Imam and taking their generic name Ismailis from Ismail bin Jaffar around 765. They included the Zaidis, who waged numerous campaigns mainly in North Africa with Berber support and in the Yemen, and the Qarmathians who had their own Mahdi in 930 and waged war against the Abbasids, mainly from Bahrein.

Though for non-Muslims the differences between Sunnis and Shiites, as well as the differences between sub-groups of both, seem relatively minor, their strong mutual antipathy has if anything grown with the years and has fuelled violence and warfare on a par with that caused by the great Christian schisms and shows no signs of arriving at peaceful compromise. The sectarian element in their conflicts was part of the hate cultivation which matched secular antipathies based on race and economics, so these wars were often as much about power as religion.

'...they adopted the doctrine that there was an infallible Imam in every age to whom God entrusted the guidance of his servants.'
Alfred Guillaume, *Islam*

8

EMPEROR LEO AND THE ICONOCLASTS – ORTHODOX VERSUS CATHOLIC

'The issue of whether Christians were right to employ and pay
respect to images of Christ or the Virgin had gradually come to
the fore in the later years of the seventh century.'

John Haldon, *Byzantium: a History*

One of the by-products of the spread of Islam was a kind of
religious panic-attack in the Eastern Roman Empire based in
Constantinople. Many saw the Muslim contempt for graven
images as something which they should imitate. The great Muslim
attack on idolatry perhaps fuelled an underlying revulsion among
the Orthodox of the Byzantine establishment who felt that their
veneration of icons had got out of hand, particularly with the cult
of the Virgin Mary, and that it was contrary to Mosaic Law. Hence
in 726 the Emperor Leo III (680–741) who himself spoke Arabic
and had spent some of his childhood in a Muslim-occupied city,
set in motion a major change in the Orthodox Church that led to
the compulsory destruction of icons and statues, many of them
held in great affection by laity and clergy alike. The iconoclastic
reforms were very unpopular in many parts of the empire, most
particularly in Italy where there was an armed rebellion that had
massive consequences for the future of Europe.

The iconoclastic controversy led to persecution and almost civil
war in Greece and the Middle East but in Italy it provided an
excuse for Liutprand, the ambitious king of Lombardy, to wage

war as a supposed champion of those who loved their religious icons, among their number Pope Gregory II (669–731) in Rome. Riots in Constantinople had to be suppressed by force, perhaps exaggerated in some accounts, and a fleet was sent to put down a rebellion in Greece.

Leo's policies went much too far from the point of view of the Vatican, especially when he started raising the taxes in his Italian province to pay for his wars against the Muslims. In response Pope Gregory II encouraged an armed insurrection in the Exarchate of Ravenna and the response was two failed conspiracies to arrange his murder.

After this fiasco, yet another Byzantine fleet was sent to put down the rebellion, but the fleet was badly damaged by storms and Leo was too busy fighting Muslims to send a replacement. Nevertheless, Pope Gregory II took the drastic step of excommunicating the eastern iconoclasts including the Emperor Leo III himself, and then felt so threatened that he appealed for help to Charles Martel of the Franks. The Frankish leader had recently won the first major victory against Islam by defeating the Moors at Tours in 732, allegedly thanks to a miracle organised by Pope Gregory. This was itself seen as a significant defeat of Muslims by Christians, though in reality it was also much more a defeat of ethnic Saracens by Franks, a war between members of two religions who hated each other's faiths but were more concerned with territory.

As James Bryce observed, 'a course was now taken whose dangers no one then foresaw.' The Pope gave his blessing to a coup d'état in France by which Charles Martel's son Pipin the Short displaced the old dynasty of the Merovingians and made himself king. This was to endow the French monarchy with special religious credentials, which it clung to disastrously until 1789. It was also to create a precedent for popes having the power to appoint or depose both kings and later emperors, again with dangerous results, paralleled by the opposing belief that kings or emperors could appoint popes and bishops. Thirdly, it provided Pipin and his successors in France, later Germany and Austria, with an excuse to invade Italy on a regular basis for the next five hundred years. Thus the new relationship between the Vatican and the kings and emperors of Western Europe was to be responsible for a large number of invasions, armed interventions and real wars. These were not holy wars, simply struggles for control over a religion which was an important component of the political infrastructure and population control, including a virtual monopoly of literacy.

Initially this led in 753 to the famous trip across the Alps by Pope Stephen II to meet Pipin I. In response to his pleas Pipin twice obligingly invaded Italy to defeat the new king of Lombardy, Aistulf. This was followed by a similar appeal by Pope Adrian to Charlemagne, who also obliged by invading Lombardy under its next king, Desiderius in 773 (see next chapter), the first of a long series of armed interventions in Italy from north of the Alps, ostensibly to protect the papacy.

Thus, the revived Roman Empire was the indirect result of the iconoclastic controversy among the Greeks, which in turn was a by-product partly of the success of Islam in reviving the iconoclastic features of the Old Testament. The involvement between the papacy and its new lay equivalent, the imperial throne, was to cause a succession of wars and invasions of Italy, as the heads of church and state vied with each other to keep on top. This was to stunt the development of Italy as a nation state and also arguably that of Germany until after the fall of Napoleon. In the medium term the consequences of the iconoclasm conflict were the withdrawal of Byzantine governors from Italy, an increase in the independence of the papacy and the eventual declaration of the Great Schism in 1054, the second major split in Christianity.

Meanwhile an even more drastic example of Greek Orthodox violence was the massacre in Armenia ordered by the regent Empress Theodora in 840 of members of the Paulician sect, who rejected most of the Old Testament and some of the New. They made themselves even more unpopular with the establishment by condemning the court in Constantinople as materialistic and evil. Some 100,000 are estimated to have been killed.

The Byzantines had strategic as well as religious interests in mind when they invaded Bulgaria in 863 to persuade its leader Khan Boris to bring his nation into the Greek Orthodox, not the Roman Catholic, sphere of Christianity. There was minimal bloodshed as the pagan Bulgars were starving owing to crop failure and an earthquake, so Boris quickly made peace and joined his people to the Orthodox Church a year later.

For the next few centuries there was much less warfare between Catholics and Greek Orthodox than between many other sects, though as we shall see (v Pt 2 Chapter 17) there was to be more serious conflict between Russian Orthodox and Catholics, for they shared more disputed territories like Poland, Lithuania and the Ukraine. The one major example was the treacherous Latin attack on Constantinople in 1204, one of the worst by-products of the crusades and which resulted in the Parthenon in Athens being converted briefly into a Catholic church, until it later – for longer – became a mosque.

'Now whole towns and multitudes of people are in considerable agitation over this matter (iconoclasm).'
The Patriarch Germanus, 726

9

CHARLEMAGNE – CHRISTIANS AGAINST MUSLIMS AND PAGANS

'He (Charlemagne) appeared as the vice-regent of God on earth, as the vicar of Christ whose decisions were those of God.'
Walter Ullman, *Political Thought in the Middle Ages*

As we have seen the iconoclast struggle in Byzantium had caused warfare in Italy which resulted indirectly in the popes seeking help from the French leader Charles Martel against the Lombards in 739. This was just seven years after Martel's remarkable victory over the Muslims at Tours, one of the most important battles between two major religions. The Muslim invasion of Aquitaine had been led by Abd al Rahman, the Arab governor or *wali* of al Andalus. While his raid was motivated by desire for booty and marked by wilful destruction, there are also hints that he was a dedicated Muslim, for he had summoned recruits for his jihad from the radical elements in Yemen. Certainly, his defeat by Martel marked the end of Muslim attempts to conquer France and halted the north-western expansion of Islam at the Pyrenees. Ironically, Martel had been on the verge of being excommunicated by the church as he had commandeered considerable church properties to help him pay for a professional army, but equally, he had previously handed over many properties to the church.

A second appeal from the Vatican to the Franks came from Pope Adrian I in 774, who wanted to provide the currently unsustainable city of Rome with its own hinterland, a source of food and manpower. The whole affair climaxed in 796 with the attack on Pope Leo III by discontented Romans, which led to Charlemagne's capture of Rome and his subsequent coronation as the first Roman Emperor of the middle ages. The details of the new dual rule of popes and emperors were complicated by forgeries like the so-called Donation of Constantine. This allegedly gave the popes ecclesiastical supremacy over the emperors but there were counter-claims by both sides as to whether the emperor had really led the pope's horse, whether the emperor was the pope's sovereign or vice-versa, and which one of them appointed the other. Thus, the potential for conflict and the potential excuses for wars were numerous (v. Pt 2 Chapter 14). However, it was quite clear that without the military infrastructure of an empire like Charlemagne's it would be impossible for the papacy to assert its spiritual sovereignty over Europe including France, Britain and Germany, whilst the big empires could benefit in return by using a united Catholic church to boost their credibility and provide a valuable clerical infrastructure.

Charlemagne used the pretext of the burning of a church by pagan Saxons in 772 to begin a 36-year campaign of invasion and destruction that included eighteen battles. His divinely ordained and brutal conquest of the Saxons was followed up by their forced conversion led by St Boniface, who felled the sacred oak trees of their Druids and ordered the death penalty for all who refused to baptise their children or showed any other signs of rejecting the Christian church. In his own *Capitularies on the Region of Saxony* he decreed 'if any one of the race of Saxons hereafter conceals among them or shall have wished to hide himself unbaptised and shall have scorned to come to baptism and should have wished to remain a pagan let him be punished by death.' Just how genuine Charlemagne's faith was is impossible to calculate, but clearly he saw Christianity as a useful means of civilising people he regarded as barbarians and of providing infrastructure for subsequent control. The Carolingian Latin poem the *Paderborn Epic* observed, 'Terror is an aid to conversion … let them leap to accomplish what is compelled by God.'

It should also be stated that the extreme ruthlessness of Charlemagne's campaigns was at least partly dictated by the earlier outright refusal of the Saxons to listen to Christian missionaries and their great loyalty to their own religion. German historian Gerhard Seeliger noted that 'The ecclesiastical motive was particularly strong in the Saxon wars and the Saxons resisted ecclesiastical subjection as much as political.' Their belief in their god Odin was deeply entrenched and their conviction that he would welcome the fallen to Valhalla gave them desperate courage. Hence in many ways this was a two-sided religious war and when at last it finished the pope instructed the entire Christian world to rejoice at the victory.

Charlemagne also continued his efforts to drive back the Muslims from northern Spain, a war partly inspired by the need to protect France's Pyrenean frontier but also seen as a divinely sanctioned drive against the infidel. The minor French defeat at Roncevalles by the Basques was turned into the legend of Roland and Oliver, prototype crusading martyrs. The creation of a French county of Barcelona was to result in this region of Spain being more French than Spanish, to have its own hybrid Catalonian language and years later to look for independence from the rest of Spain.

The military involvement of Frankish and later German kings in the affairs of the Vatican continued. The Saxon Henry the Fowler had earned his spurs by conquering the heathen Slavs and Czechs in 928. His son Otto the Great (912–973) had received the blessing of the Teutonic church for his stunning victory (aided it was said by him possessing the Holy Lance) over the pagan Magyars at Lechfeld in 955, after which they were converted to Christianity. He then imitated Charlemagne by organising his divinely ordained coronation at Aachen as King of the Germans. He consolidated this kingship in 939 with a surprise victory near Xanten on the Rhine over Franconian and Saxon rebels.

In 951 Otto had responded to the usual threat against the Vatican from the Lombards and invaded Italy as soon as the allegedly corrupt young Pope John XII (930–964) promised the imperial crown as his reward. Thus King Otto was in 962 crowned Holy Roman Emperor in Rome, creating the first of Hitler's Three Reichs. The addition of the word 'Holy' to his title was extremely significant. He then had a mission to clean up the Vatican, which had become the plaything of a few corrupt and unscrupulous Roman families. Pope John died in suspicious circumstances and was briefly replaced by Benedict V who responded by encouraging the Lombards and even the heathen Magyars to rebel against Otto, so he deposed him and replaced him with his own choice of pontiff, his cousin, as Leo VIII, the first of the German popes. Otto massacred large numbers of the Roman population who refused to accept the new situation and two years later appointed another new pope, John XIII. Meanwhile the Poles accepted conversion to Roman Catholicism motivated by the fact that this deprived the German emperors of an excuse to invade them.

It must be said that the repeated invasions of Italy by three generations of German emperors, Otto I, Otto II and Otto III, were only marginally attributable to a desire to protect the Catholic Church, since the popes they chose were far from perfect, but equally the deaths of many German soldiers both in fighting and due to the malaria that plagued the area round Rome, would not have occurred but for the ambitions of the Vatican and the divine authority with which the popes claimed to give special status to the new breed of German emperors. Otto II became involved in trying to drive the Muslims out of Southern Italy, which had at least partial religious motivations. Abu Qasim, the Emir of Sicily, declared Jihad against him, and won an unexpected victory against the Germans at Stilo in Calabria. Otto II barely escaped with his life and died, probably of plague or malaria, still in his early twenties.

Young Otto III (king from age three in 983) regarded himself as 'An apostle of Jesus' in the Pauline tradition and nearly abandoned his throne to become a monk, but was groomed by Bishop Bernward of Hildesheim to take the role of divinely ordained ruler of the Christian world with the pope as his subsidiary ally. At the age of six he was taken with the army to reconquer the pagan Slavs and at least Brandenburg was regained for the Empire. Before he was twenty he invaded Italy to assert his authority in 996, only four years short of the millennium and the dreaded apocalypse, a concept which was very unsettling for all Christians. Like his father he chose a new pope, but unlike him made Rome the capital of his ambitious new theocracy and started to introduce elaborate ceremonials. At the age of twenty-two he died of smallpox or malaria during yet another perilous campaign to protect the papacy as part of his Holy Empire.

The argument as to whether the spiritual or temporal heads held pre-eminence and had the right to appoint the other was to cause sporadic outbreaks of war for the next century. Even Napoleon had to capture Rome in order to validate his right to become an Emperor, even if in his case he avoided the prefix Holy Roman. These wars were never due to any theological disagreement, only to a power struggle for control of the church infrastructure and wealth, which were obviously extremely valuable to both sides.

'The greater part of the religious and political system of the higher Middle Ages emerged out of the events and ideas of the Investiture Contest.'
Norman Cantor *The Civilization of the Middle Ages*

10

THE VIKINGS – PAGANS AGAINST CHRISTIANS

'Their (Norse women's) battle spells and combat rituals
complemented the men's physical acts of fighting in a
supernatural empowerment of aggression.'
Neil Price, *The Viking Way: Religion and
War in late Iron Age Scandinavia*

As Neil Price has shown, the early Vikings, before they were
christianised in the late tenth century, had one of the most
sophisticated spiritual constructs for warfare in human history.
Given their narrow coastal habitat, as Felipe Fernández-Armesto
points out, they were 'obliged to fight' in order to survive, for
their population grew faster than the limited agricultural space
and short summer season could provide for. They were also
handicapped during the Bronze Age since they had no tin.

For these reasons they were motivated to build the best sea-going
ships of the medieval era, become the best navigators – and develop
the most carefully targeted system of religious motivation that
could produce both intrepid sailors and highly motivated warriors.
Though they had no great desire to spread their own religion they
tailored it to be a major component in an aggressive programme
of overseas exploration and conquest.

The post-mortal rewards for both soldiers and sailors were
considerable. Of land warriors killed in battle, the *Einherjar*,
half would be ushered by the Valkyries into Odin's martial hall,
Valhalla, with its golden gates and roof of golden shields. The

other half would be chosen by the female war goddess Freyja to go to her field the *Fölkvangr.* Drowned seamen would be taken to yet another heaven. In addition, whilst still alive all warriors would be aided by the 'man-protecting god Thor relentlessly pursuing his foes'.

The background cosmogony included the great battle of Ragnörok in which the gods had killed all mankind except for one man and one woman who would restart the human race. All this was recorded in the *Edda,* old legends recycled in poetic form in the thirteenth century and sagas like the *Orkneyinga Saga* or the tales of iconic warriors like Eric Bloodaxe (885–954). The martial efforts of the men were backed up by the magical rituals of the women.

The Vikings conquered Iceland and Russia where they created new states, crossed the Atlantic, supplied mercenary troops for the Byzantines, and conquered and successfully settled in western France, where their Norman descendants pursued an equally aggressive trajectory as Christians, and in 1066 occupied the throne of England and of Sicily in 1072. However, in all these regions they soon abandoned their old religion and adopted the mindset of the conquered, using the benefits of their literate infrastructure to legitimise their own kingdoms. The old faith had usefully provided additional motivation for communities worried by the imbalance between population growth and food supply as well as a huge fondness for precious metals, so their wars were not religious but did have significant religious backing.

'Odin shot a spear, hurled it over the host that was still the first war in the world.'

Völuspa Edda

JIHAD IN INDIA AND THE FAR EAST – MUSLIMS AGAINST HINDUS AND BUDDHISTS

'Mughal generals erected towers of skulls from thousands of
rajput troops who resisted Akbar's early campaigns.'

Stephen Dale, *Islamic World*

The first real attack by Muslims on the Indian sub-continent came
when the brutal Al Hajjaj penetrated to the Indus River in 710.
It was to be the beginning of a prolonged antagonism between
Muslims and Hindus in India that was to last into the twenty-first
century and led to massacres during the partition of 1947/8. The
fact that Muslim invasions were mainly aimed at collecting booty
meant there was little consistent effort at conversion. The fault-
lines on the sub-continent have never been entirely remedied.

Al Hajjaj was followed by his cousin Mohammed ibn Qasim
(*fl* 695–715) who captured Debal near modern Karachi and
defeated King Dahar of Sind with great slaughter, executing all
enemy soldiers who survived his initial onslaughts. His motives
were far from purely religious for there was plenty of loot
available, but it set the precedent for subsequent invasions, as
there was minimal effort to convert the Indians to Islam. His own
reward was to be condemned to an unpleasant death by his jealous
Caliph Al Walid based in Damascus.

The next stage came in 977 when an ex-slave Turkish soldier,
Subuktigin, a fanatical Sunni Muslim serving the emir of Ghazni,
defeated the large Shahi kingdom the capital of which was Kabul,

helped by a sudden storm. His son took the then unheard of title of Sultan and made Ghazni the capital of a substantial Muslim empire stretching far into what is now Pakistan. He regarded it as a sacred but rewarding duty to wage holy war against the infidel Hindus and fellow Muslims if, like the Fatimids, they were quasi-Shiites. For sixteen years he led annual invasions of India from his summer base on the Helmand River, taking over Mutan, Lahore and the Punjab. His Ghaznavid dynasty appreciated the huge wealth they could amass simply by raiding nearby rajahs, collecting vast quantities of gold, elephants and slaves, regularly destroying Hindu temples and massacring the infidels who resisted. The wars were for loot rather than religion, but religion provided an excellent excuse.

In due course the Ghaznavids were seriously weakened by the inroads of the Mongols and their empire was taken over by Mohammed of Ghor (1149–1206) based in the Afghan mountains near Herat. He then pursued the same policy of intimidating Hindu rajahs by raids on Rajastan and Haryam, finally destroying Delhi in 1193, before choosing it as the site of his new capital. It was one of his ex-slave generals, Qutb-ud-din-Aybak, who founded the first formal Muslim state in north India and built in Delhi the remarkable Qutuk Minar, one of the tallest brick-built minarets in the world. From that time onwards until the Indian Mutiny or Indian Rebellion in 1857, large areas of India was ruled by a succession of Muslim dynasties, mostly emanating from Afghanistan and the north. However, there was neither mass conversion nor mass assimilation so that there was to be a lasting gap between a Muslim ruling class and a Hindu majority that created dangerous fissures that the later British conquest did little to erase.

As we shall see, the Muslims were also to come into conflict with a third religion, Sikhism, which they had been partially responsible for encouraging as a supposed compromise between Islam and Hinduism (v. Pt 3 Chapter 30). Of the Moguls, the Sultan Aurangzeb (1618–1707) was the most dedicated persecutor of both Hindus and Sikhs, destroying the temples of Varanese and Mathura and waging a number of expensive campaigns against Hindu areas. He also persecuted Shiites.

Firuz Shah Tughluq (1309–88) third in his dynasty of Delhi sultans, was a fanatical persecutor of Hindus, burning alive

Brahmin priests who refused to convert to Islam, using heavy taxation and intimidation to force conversion, and waging holy war in the Sind and other areas. In response Hindu warlords like Harihara (fl 1336–66), founder of the Vijanagaran state, championed Hindu resistance to the Muslims.

The rift between Sunni and Shiite soon migrated to India. In 1347 Aladdin Hassan, who had begun life as a Delhi barman and had 'by chance' discovered a trunk full of gold, founded the first Shiite dynasty in Southern India with its capital at Hasanabad, now Gulbarga, east of Mumbai. His successor Mohammed (d. 1373) waged jihad against neighbouring Hindu states and in 1367 is said to have slaughtered some 400,000 in one campaign, and overall was responsible for a million deaths. One of his successors Sultan Feroz (d. 1422) continued the ethnic cleansing and in the name of holy war raided Hindu villages to kidnap children of both sexes for his harem.

One of the most fanatical Muslim persecutors of Hindus was Sikander (d. 1473) the fifth ruler of a dynasty based at Srinagar in Kashmir who ethnically cleansed his kingdom by selling thousands of Hindus as slaves, driving many to suicide, destroying some 300 of their temples and melting down their gold images to raise money for his fine new mosque. At the same time, he insisted on Sharia law, forbade all games and generally earned the hatred of his surviving Hindu subjects. The forcible conversion of Hindus was continued by his son Zain al Abidin and one successor Malik Russa had a target of 2000 conversions per day. In 1518 there were massacres of Hindus who refused to convert to Islam. Forty years later the dynasty self-destructed and soon afterwards Kashmir was overrun by the Mongols. It still has a malignant Hindu/Muslim fault-line (v. Pt 4). As recently as 2009 the area of the Swat Valley was designated an area of Islamic extremism, favouring Sharia law and linked to the Taliban.

The Mysorean invasion of Kerala 1766–92 by the fanatical Hyder Ali was also motivated by religion as well as loot. He offered the conquered brahmins of Kerala a choice between conversion to Islam or death. There was thus a toxic legacy left by the Muslim conquerors of India who formed a ruling minority until the British took over in 1857 and preserved their safety, only to abandon them to their fate in 1947.

The Muslims had also left their mark further east, particularly with the remarkable campaign led by Ziyad bin Salik that climaxed in 751 with the five-day Battle of the River Talas, which lies in modern Kazakhstan. It was an extraordinary victory achieved against a royal Chinese force led by the Korean general Gao Xianzhi. Its long-term significance lay in the opening up of central Asia and the Old Silk Road to Muslim influence, which has been maintained ever since. It also involved the oppressed minority of Uighurs who were resisting Chinese oppression round Samarkand and have remained to the present day as a dissident religious and racial enclave enclosed within the frontiers of China and its dominant Han people. The battle allowed for subsequent two-way traffic, inventions like paper travelling west to the Middle East, whilst dynamic trader missionaries headed east with their religion.

The Muslim conquests in sub-Saharan Africa were mainly motivated by gold and many ambitious rulers chose to use Islam as a tool for expansion. Ahmad al Mansur, Sultan of Morocco, certainly wanted to collect more gold and to make himself Caliph, so he invaded the Songhai Empire in 1591 with an army of Spanish Moors. The conquest worked but the logistics of running the western Africa state from Morocco made it short-lived.

In summary, the spasmodic attacks and settlements of the Muslims in India and to a lesser extent China caused more long-term damage than their conquests in Europe, because there was neither mass conversion, nor mass assimilation, nor mass repatriation, so they left behind a dysfunctional patchwork of religious minorities unwilling to be subsumed and prone to violence for many centuries to follow. This was also true of Muslim forays into sub-Saharan Africa, which were later overlapped by European Christian colonies with resultant serious fault-lines.

'Skanda began his existence at a very early stage in Indian history. He seems to have become a popular war god who lived in forested hills, was fond of hunting and fighting with an apparent appetite for blood sacrifices.'
R. Pilai, *Indiayogi.com*

12

THE BUDDHISTS AND HINDUS
TAKE UP ARMS

'Kublai Khan asked the monk whether Buddhism offered a way
to world peace. Haiyun replied it did, but understanding
was required.'

John Man, *Kublai Khan*

Buddhism is in theory one of the world's least violent religions and
did not show any inclination for warfare until several hundred years
after its foundation. However, as it expanded throughout India it
became more politically involved, particularly after the dramatic
conversion of the Emperor Ashoka Maurya (304–232 BC) whose
empire covered most of the sub-continent except for the extreme
south. According to his own inscriptions Ashoka felt huge remorse
after conquering the Kalinga (in the area now known as Orissa)
and by his own confession killing 100,000 and deporting many
more. He announced that he was giving up war but does not
appear to have disbanded his army or to have repatriated the
surviving Kalingas. He did not clamp down on Hinduism or other
faiths, so his adoption of Buddhism may have been cosmetic.

As we have seen the first semi-legendary example of a Buddhist
ruler waging an allegedly sacred war was Dutthagamani attacking
the Tamil invaders of Sri Lanka in the second century BC. There
were many subsequent invasions by Hindu dynasties, climaxing in
the conquest of Sri Lanka by the Cholas of Tanjore in 1017.

In AD 402 came the first of six Buddhist-inspired rebellions in
China against the Tabgatch empire of the Wei dynasty. These lasted

on and off for over a century and in 515 a Buddhist monk called Faqing led an alleged 50,000 Buddhist adherents in a campaign against the Wei in north China.

The first example of monks training in martial arts is recorded in 487 at the Shaolin Monastery, which still stands with its famous Pagoda Forest on the mountain near the city of Zhengzhou by the Yellow River in Henan. As the pressures of persecution and the problems of banditry increased the Buddhists created a tradition of new forms of self-defence and almost bloodless forms of fighting using a staff as the main weapon.

The third great religion of India, Jainism, was also against all forms of violence, even the killing of animals, but unlike Buddhism did not become so politically involved. Jains were persecuted, particularly by Mahendravarman I (*fl* 600–25) who had begun life as a Jain himself. He aggressively built up the Pallava kingdom in what is now Tamil Nadu, sponsored the remarkable stone-cut temples and passed on his conquests to the even more aggressive Navasihmavarma, who persisted with persecution of Jains. It is ironic for this peaceable religion that the word 'Jain' comes from the distinctly confrontational Sanskrit word meaning 'victor'.

Meanwhile the Hindu Pallava dynasty looked for expansion outside India, which was bedevilled by interdynastic warfare. Thus Jayavarman II (770–835) declared himself a god-king and lord of the universe while he conquered the Khmer to carve out a new Hindu empire in what is now Cambodia. By 1150 they had built at Angkor Wat a massive state temple dedicated to the Hindu god Vishnu. Most of the kings had actively persecuted Khmer Buddhists, causing dangerous flashpoints in their empire. Jayavarman VII (1125–1219), an ex-general who had defeated a Cham invasion in 1178 and extended the kingdom into parts of what are now Viet Nam and Malaysia was one of the first to change religions to Buddhism and built Angkor Thom as a Buddhist temple. Ironically this remarkable new branch of the Pallava dynasty started to go into decline when it succumbed to internal pressures and converted Angkor Wat from a Hindu to a Buddhist temple.

Back in China the founder of the Sui dynasty, general Yang Jian, in 581 proclaimed himself emperor on the grounds that he was a Buddhist ruler using his armies to defend the Buddhist faith.

Buddhist participation in a major battle came at Hulao in 621 when they fought against an attempted usurpation by a general of the Sui dynasty, Wang Shi, which resulted in his defeat and death so that the area was taken over by the Tang. This was part of a series of rebellions against the Sui dynasty from 610 onwards that were partly inspired by the idea of the *Maitreya*, a second coming of the Buddha, similar to the Mahdis of Islam and the Second Coming of the Christian Messiah. However as with most wars there were plenty of grievances against the Sui emperors apart from religion.

There was a short intermission in the Tang dynasty when the ex-concubine Wu Zetian (*fl* 690–705) plotted her way into becoming China's only regnant empress. She was a convinced Buddhist who employed Buddhist monks as her chief ministers and made Buddhism the state religion above Taoism and Confucianism. She used her Buddhist iconography to enhance her own image, at the same time clamping down with concomitant violence on all opposition until corruption scandals finally led to her deposition.

The Shaolin monks and other neighbouring Buddhists staged another rebellion in 719, this time against the Tang dynasty, which in 841 was followed by a massive government clamp-down on Buddhism as an intrusive foreign religion, despite the fact that it had provided them with useful infrastructure for education and trade. Some 250,000 monks and nuns were expelled from their monasteries, 4000 of which were closed down, leaving an unstable force of Buddhist mendicants to cause trouble and eventually form the focus for further political rebellions.

Buddhist monks helped the resistance movement against Mongol conquests from 1215 onwards. The captured Buddhist monk Haiyun succeeded in partially converting Kublai Khan (*fl* 1260-1294) to Buddhism around 1251 soon after his final defeat of the Song dynasty. As a result, Kublai Khan began serious persecution of the Chinese Muslims. This strengthened Kublai's own conviction as a Mongol leader and grandson of Genghis that the Mongols were destined to conquer the entire world. In his case specifically this still meant the conquest of all China, Korea, Viet Nam and Japan. The rest of China and Korea soon fell under his new dynasty, the Yuan, but as we shall see his invasions of Japan were to fail (v. Pt 3 Chapter 23).

By 1352 the Mongol emperors of the Yuan dynasty were losing their grip. The most significant Buddhist monk in Chinese history and the most warlike, Zhu Yuanzhang (1328–98), was ejected from his monastery by the Yuan militia, the troops of the descendants of Kublai Khan who had by this time ruled China for nearly a century. Like many Chinese Buddhist monks he was accustomed to begging for a living, in fact he had probably only become a monk to avoid starvation, but this time he joined up with a rebel group known as the Red Turbans, linked also to the White Lotus Society, a revival of the *Maitreya* cult of millennialist Buddhism which looked forward to a new world and the second coming of a new leader. Within three years Zhu was the leader of the group and had a significant army of dissatisfied peasant soldiers. He soon afterwards captured the city of Nanjing from the imperial forces.

Ten years later he drove the last Yuan emperor out of his capital at Beijing and took over the throne as founder of the Ming dynasty, changing his name to Taizu. From that time onwards, he was by no means exclusively Buddhist, but used both the Tao and Confucianism to bolster his power. He had waged war ruthlessly to win the throne and showed similar mercilessness in power, eliminating all those who, to his paranoid mentality, showed signs of resisting his omnipotence. Perhaps half a million died in consequence. It had been a major coup d'état inspired by Buddhism and achieved with a war which ended 80 years of Mongol rule. The Ming dynasty founded by the ex-monk Zhu was to last nearly three centuries, until 1644.

Significantly, the White Lotus Society reappeared in 1796 to head an armed resurrection against the Manchus, another alien dynasty, and some 100,000 adherents kept up a guerrilla war for eight years until they were eventually suppressed. Another branch of this Millennialist Buddhist sect, the Eight Trigrams, took up the challenge in 1813 with similar numbers and stormed the Forbidden City before also being violently suppressed.

Apart from Taizu a significant number of other eastern rulers who converted to Buddhism were far from averse to aggressive warfare. In India itself Harshavardhana (c.590-647) defeated the Chalakya and built up an extended kingdom round the Punjab.

Anawrahta Minsaw (1014–77), founder of the Pagan Empire based in Burma, won his throne by killing his predecessor in single combat, then extended his nation over a large part of south east Asia by force. He had inherited an infrastructure dominated by powerful but corrupt Buddhist monasteries belonging to the local Ari sect, but was persuaded that the Theravada variant of Buddhism would enable him to improve the situation considerably. He therefore cleared out the Ari monks and replaced them with Theravada, justifying his conquest of neigbouring Thaton (now in southern Myanmar) by his desire to procure a copy of the Theravada Buddhist Canon.

In Thailand Buddhist monks were regularly involved in political rebellions from 1688 onwards when there was a strong reaction against French attempts to convert the king to Catholicism.

Meanwhile Buddhist militancy had also spread to Japan. In 949 the monk Ryogen began arming the massive monastery of Enryakuji built some 2,700 feet up on Mount Hiei as a rival to the Tendai Monastery founded to protect the imperial court at Kyoto from bad spirits. Both houses became notorious for unpredictable, misdirected violence; as one emperor put it 'It would be easier for me to change the course of the Kamo River than to succeed against these Sohei (warrior monks)' who lived in 'fortified cathedrals'. In 1121 and 1141 the Sohei monks burned down Mii dera Temple at the foot of Mount Hiei. For some six hundred years they were described as 'a formidable enemy armed with their distinctive long-bladed *naginata*' and they also quickly adapted to firearms.

The two rival monasteries frequently fought each other and during the Genpei War of 1180–1185 fought on opposite sides. From the 1340s to the 1360s they staged rebellions against various shoguns, resenting the favouritism offered to the new Zen sect that had played a prominent role in organising defence against the Mongol invasions of 1276. Then a new sect of warrior monks, the *Ikko Ikki* (Jodo Shinsu/True Pure Land), mounted an attack on the samurai regime in 1488 until they were finally defeated by the future Tokugawa shogun at the Battle of Azukizaka in 1564. Then in 1571 it took a force of 30,000 under Oda Nobunaga (1546–1616) to overwhelm Enryakuji, after which it was rebuilt to serve the Tokugawa shoguns. After Nobunaga's siege of the other Ikko monasteries their fortress was burned down, along with 20,000 warrior monks. The militant tradition continued and in both 1904 and 1914 Zen Buddhist monks helped fight the Russians. Thus, there was a thousand-year history of Buddhist warrior monks in Japan acting as the monastic equivalent of the lay samurai. As we shall see (Pt 3 Chapter 21) a large number of the members of the Japanese war cabinet which authorised the Pearl Harbor attack were practising Buddhists. Even in Tibet the Dalai Lamas in the sixteenth century were often forced to put down armed rebellions by deviant Buddhist sects.

In recent times militant Buddhism in Thailand supported the army dictatorship from 2004 and in Sri Lanka as we shall see the war against the Tamils. (See Pt 4 Chapter 39) Similarly, the Buddhist military regime in Myanmar persecuted the Rohingya Muslims.

> 'The mercy of Buddha should be recompensed even by
> pounding flesh to pieces.'
> Buddhist pamphlet quoted in Joseph Kitagawa,
> *Religion in Japanese History*

13

RECONQUISTA

'What was lost in seven years it took seven hundred to regain.'
J. H. Elliot, *Imperial Spain*

The Berber/Arab invasion of Spain in 711 had been the first of a series of invasions of European Christian territories by expanding Islam and while the invaders were mainly interested in plunder and acquisition rather than religious conversion, there was a strong religious as well as patriotic motivation for the Europeans when they began to turn back the tide. This was true in Spain, Portugal, Southern Italy and Russia, all of which had been conquered by Muslim forces, as much later were Greece, the Balkans, the Black Sea states and most of Hungary.

The original Muslim conquest of Spain in 711 was very far from genuine jihad, for its leader Tariq ibn Ziyad was a very recent convert to Islam, his Berber troops were mostly neither Christian nor Muslim and his main objective was plunder, made easier by the fact that the Visigoth rulers were all at each other's throats. The Arian versus Trinitarian controversy of Christianity had contributed to their internal antipathies.

The beginning of the Reconquista of Spain was traditionally dated to 718 or 722 when the beleaguered Visigoth prince Pelayo ambushed a small Muslim army at Covadonga to begin the liberation of Asturia. It was really a very minor affair but was given huge symbolic significance as the first Christian defeat of Muslims in Spain. At about the same time the Saracen invasion of

France begun in 719 was, as we have seen, halted in a much larger battle by the Frankish leader Charles Martel near Tours. However, the Spanish Reconquista, which lasted more than 700 years, was initially not much of a holy war any more than the original conquest by the Muslims, for it consisted mainly of sporadic local rebellions, often with the connivance of local Muslim emirs. The impoverished Christians in the north were simply raiding the hugely rich Muslim areas for booty or blackmail, whilst the Christians living in Muslim areas frequently converted to Islam and enjoyed the civilised comforts provided by cities like Cordoba too much to think of rebelling. The only flicker of Christian dynamism came around 800 when the supposed bones of St James/Iago were discovered and authenticated at a distance by Charlemagne, so that pilgrimage to Compostela became a serious focus for national fervour; but it was a slow-burning fuse.

It was not until around 300 years had passed that French Cluniac monks in the 1030s began taking over the hitherto corrupt Spanish church and the tiny Christian kingdoms in northern Spain began to get some religious motivation for the reconquest. This process was accelerated when Ferdinand I of Castile began importing French bishops. The demand for a holy war was not, however, welcomed by those impoverished Christian rulers of the north who survived on blackmail money from the plutocratic emirs. Then in 1085 came a significant breakthrough when Alfonso VI of Aragon captured Toledo, but this was a short-lived success for it was now the turn of the dysfunctional emirs of Andalus to be overrun by a new jihad from Africa, the Almoravids (v. Pt 2 Chapter 7).

With encouragement from Pope Gregory VII the Spanish knights were exempted from going on Crusades to the Holy Land so that they could concentrate on their own holy war. New Spanish orders of celibate knights were formed, the Orders of Santiago and Calatrava, but progress remained sporadic. Even the iconic figure of El Cid, Rodrigo Diaz, spent some of his career as a mercenary fighting for Islamic emirs and his capture of Valencia from the Almoravids in 1094 was with the help of local Muslims.

Worse was to follow when the strongly Muslim Almoravids were themselves wiped out in 1148 by an even more fanatical dynasty from the Atlas Mountains, the Almohads (v Pt 2 Chapter 7), who threatened death to all their Spanish subjects who did not convert to Islam and made Seville their new capital. It was not until the Almohads began to lose momentum that Alfonso VIII at last achieved a major victory at Las Navas de Tolosa in 1212, and the Reconquista began to deserve its name. The capture of Seville followed in 1248, leaving only Granada as a surviving Muslim emirate, which lasted till 1492.

By this time, now that the Christians were winning, there was much more talk of holy war against infidels and the residual hate of the Christian forces led to the ethnic cleansing of Muslims, Jews and so-called heretics that is associated with the Spanish Inquisition and the infamous *auto da fe*. As we shall see the energy thus generated also helped fuel the extraordinary conquests of Mexico and Peru (v Pt 3 Chapter 22) and the fanaticism of Cardinal Tomás Torquemada, head of the Spanish Inquisition, was at least partly a by-product of the Reconquista. Meanwhile the fighting had become more brutal and Geraldo san Pavor became a national hero in 1165 for his prowess in decapitating Moors.

Portugal's Reconquista had started later, largely because it was part of one of the Spanish kingdoms until 1147. A number of ex-crusaders and other adventurers had come to its aid, and one of them, Henry of Burgundy, married a Spanish princess. It was their son Afonso who won the first major battle against the Muslims with Portuguese troops, Ourique, in 1147, allegedly with some help from St James/Iago. As a result of this he not only established his credentials as a hero of the Reconquista but was also able with the Pope's blessing to declare Portugal an independent kingdom, so his campaigns were just as much political as religious, though very much publicised as a holy war, which he continued successfully until his death in 1185.

The same was also probably true of his grandson Alfonso VIII of Castile, who with the encouragement of Pope Innocent III won the even more dramatic victory of Las Navas de Tolosa in 1212 (near Jaen in Andalusia) against the aggressive Almohad Moors, which not only secured the freedom of Portugal but also of most of the rest of the Iberian peninsula. Alfonso was aided by two other kings, Sancho of Navarre and Pedro II of Aragon, as well as the Knights Templar and the two Spanish knightly orders. Typically, the fighting was brutal.

If the Reconquistas of Spain and Portugal had been messy, that of Sicily was even more so. For a start the main inhabitants of Sicily were Greek Orthodox as former subjects of the Byzantine Empire, since around 902 living a peacefully prosperous life under a succession of Muslim emirates. In the 1020s Pope Benedict VIII encouraged fortune-seeking Norman immigrants to fight both the Greek Orthodox Empire and the Saracens for control of Sicily, but in 1038 it was the Greeks who tried to oust the Saracens. Then the still land-hungry Normans, whose motives were not at all religious, defeated the Holy Roman Empire in battle and made a prisoner of Pope Leo IX. It was not until 1061 that the Norman adventurer Robert Guiscard was bribed by the French Pope Nicholas with the promise of a dukedom for capturing Sicily from the Muslims. This time the invasion was successful but even so, the Normans won by playing off one Muslim emirate against another. They also ousted the Muslims from Malta in 1127.

The Christian reconquest in Russia was also highly complex, with Saints Sergius and Basil playing the role of Saint Iago and Ivan the Terrible as the Christian hero, covered in Chapter 17. The reconquest of Hungary and the Balkans by the Holy League was even later (v. Pt 3 Chapter 28).

One of the most successful, albeit short-lived, reconquistas in the east was led by the general and in due course Emperor Nicephoros Phocas (912–969). After the death of his wife and son he came under the influence of the monk Athanasius of Athos and helped him found the Greater Lavra Monastery on Mount Athos. Deeply devoted to the Greek Orthodox Church and the ascetic life-style he waged holy war to recapture Crete from the Muslims in 961 and later supervised the recapture of Cyprus. Just as with western Christianity, the Orthodox adjusted its version of the just war.

The Reconquistas did a lot to make war an acceptable occupation for Christians, and one story was recycled in the eleventh century as the *Chanson de Roland*, an epic for public performance that romanticised the heroic martyrdom of Charlemagne's favourite paladins, Roland and Oliver, as they retreated after fighting the Moors in Spain in 778. In fact, their deaths at Roncevalles were probably caused by Basques, not Muslims, but the fictional version was to have a huge influence, helping to define and glorifying the chivalric virtues that supposedly characterised the medieval passion to wage war. It paralleled the other hugely popular legend of King Arthur and the quest for the Holy Grail, which began circulating in the French Vulgate cycle. Dutch historian Johan Huizinga wrote that 'piety and virtue have to be the essence of a knight's life,' and he quotes the *Jouvencel*: 'it is a joyous thing is war ... so valiantly exposing his body to execute and accomplish the command of our Creator'' The idea of chivalry blessed by Christianity encouraged the search for military glory in all wars, holy or otherwise.

'For my Cid the Champion that God keeps from evil/When we part today we are joined in this world or the next.'

Cantar de Mio Cid

14

INVESTITURE WARS – CATHOLIC VERSUS CATHOLIC

'Who does not know that kings and rulers sprang from men
who were ignorant of God.'

Pope Gregory VII

The rival claims of the popes and Holy Roman Emperors to invest each other, particularly the occasions when popes actually chose to depose monarchs, led to a number of wars. There had already been hints of this with the invasions of Italy by Charlemagne and the three Ottos (Pt 2 v. Chapter 9). Basically, the popes quite often needed the military support of the emperors to keep the local Italian factions at bay, whilst the emperors needed the papal blessing to provide credibility for their position of superiority to other kings and princes in Germany. The pope's ability to excommunicate disobedient royals proved a useful method for one royal to undermine a rival royal. The papacy's ownership of significant Italian territory made it a target for lay land-grabbers.

The worst example came due to the prolonged stand-off between Pope Gregory VII (1020–1085) and the Emperor Henry IV. During his minority Henry's regents had interfered with papal appointments of bishops and Gregory retaliated by excommunicating and deposing the emperor in 1076. Henry simultaneously deposed the pope, writing to him as 'the monk Hildebrand, Henry by the grace of God with all my bishops say to you come down, come down and be damned through all the ages.'

The on-going destabilisation in the Holy Roman Empire due to this mutual self-destruction had already led to a civil war in Germany and the battle of Langensalza (in Thuringia) in 1075, where the imperial forces routed the Saxon rebels. Among the rebels against the emperor was Siegfried, who was both Archbishop and Prince-Elector of Mainz (d. 1084), thus combining church and political office in a form that lasted in Germany until Napoleon. Siegfried participated in the theoretical deposition of the emperor and crowned his would-be replacement, thus encouraging the civil war. Fortune see-sawed between Pope Gregory and Henry IV. Henry at one time was in such a weak position that he had to beg forgiveness wearing a hair shirt in the snows of Canossa in 1079. This became an emblematic image, the humbled emperor on his knees in the snow, as this civil war developed into what became known as the Great Saxon Revolt of 1077–88. Pope Gregory even chose a replacement emperor, Rudolf (Henry had appointed a replacement pope) who defeated Henry at the Battle of Elster in 1080 but died in the process, thus granting Henry a temporary reprieve. In due course, as might be expected, the military allies of the Vatican would not support Gregory forever and it was he who lost the contest in the end after the loss of many lives.

Other monarchs at least theoretically deposed by popes included King John of England by Innocent III in 1212, Emperor Frederick II by Innocent IV in 1245, Philip IV of France by Boniface VIII in 1296, Ferdinand of Naples by Innocent VIII in 1485, and Queen Elizabeth of England by Pius V in 1570, the half Protestant Henri IV of France in 1587, then finally Napoleon by Pius VII in 1809. Each of these attempted depositions or excommunications resulted in or contributed to some form of armed confrontation. In King John's case it led to an invasion of Flanders by the French, later to his failed war against France and the fact that it was a papally blessed 'Godly Army' of barons that forced him to sign Magna Carta. Similarly, in the final stages of the civil war it was an 'Army of God and Holy Church' under Robert Fitzwalter that took to the field. Pope Innocent III (1160–1216) encouraged the war against King John for the usual reason of disagreements over the appointment of archbishops, but his wider war strategy was shown by his advocacy of the brutal Albigensian Crusade of 1205 and the diversion of the Fourth Crusade to capture Constantinople, a body blow to the Greek Orthodox Church (see next chapter). In the same way popes manipulated numerous dynastic wars to achieve their own version of a balance of power, which enabled them at times to defy all attempts at secular control of the church.

In the case of King Ferdinand of Naples who was excommunicated for refusing to pay extra dues to the Vatican, the pope followed this up by offering his Neapolitan throne to the kings of France. Charles VIII (1470–1498) took up the offer and invaded Italy in 1494, a campaign that cost some 13,000 direct casualties and many more due to the usual malaria problem and the newer one of syphilis. This was followed by the League of Cambrai War 1508–16, orchestrated by the Spanish Pope Alexander VI Borgia (1431–1503) to help his bastard son Cesare Borgia to take over the Romagna and continued by the next pope, the belligerent Julius II. The League of Cognac War of 1526–30 between the Holy Roman Emperor Charles V and Pope Clement VII included the brutal sack of Rome by imperial mercenaries in 1527. The Pope had become entangled with the French League of Cognac and a group of Italian cities.

Among other papal wars that were territorial rather than religious was the Salt War or Ferrara War of 1482–4 between Pope Sixtus IV and the Duke of Ferrara, and the Urbino war of 1517 between the Papal States and the Duchy of Urbino. From the German Reformation onwards popes were involved in further local wars such as the other Salt War of 1540 against Perugia and the wars of Castro in 1649, which included the destruction of Castro on the orders of Pope Innocent X. Pope Clement VII, as Swiss historian Jakob Burckhardt put it, 'hoped to root out Luther's doctrines not with arguments but by the Spanish sword ... the impending bloodshed would carry away the souls of thousands to hell.'

In the case of the excommunication of Queen Elizabeth I (v. Pt 3 Chapter 21) her theoretical deposition by the pope allowed Philip II of Spain (1527–98) carte blanche to plan an attack with his Armada in 1588.

The German Holy Roman Emperor Frederick II (1194–1250) whom Pope Innocent IV castigated as a 'friend of Babylon's sultan' and against whom he provoked an armed uprising which led, among others, to the bloody massacre of Altavilla in 1246, was theoretically deposed but retaliated. At the same time the Pope stirred up rebellion against Frederick among the prince-bishops of Germany, which similarly caused armed confrontations. Several of the imperial electors were princely archbishops, combining ecclesiastical and political power in their regions, such as Siegfried Prince /Archbishop of Mainz (1356-1403), who, as we have seen, led his own army to aid the Saxon rebels against the struggling Emperor Henry IV.

It is impossible to quantify the casualties caused by the numerous wars and rebellions attributable to the papal-royal confrontations over investitures, territory and money, but they were undoubtedly significant. The territorial acquisitiveness of the papacy also frequently brought it into conflict with rival city-states like Florence and Milan.

The French monarchy also resented papal authority and provoked wars as a result. Philip IV of France's (1268–1314) confrontation with Boniface VIII persisted until a French army attacked the papal palace at Anagni and captured the Pope in 1303 causing widespread outrage, not least to the poet Dante. It was a particularly demeaning period for the Vatican when the rival French papacy was set up in Avignon in 1305, referred to by Luther and others as 'the Babylonian captivity'. One of the wars of this period was the so-called War of the Eight Saints 1375–8 in which Gregory XI (1329–1378) a Frenchman who was the last of the popes based in Avignon organised an attack on Florence and Milan, employing as his chief *condottiero* the ruthless English mercenary Sir John Hawkwood. Gregory XI condoned burning at the stake to discourage the heretic Lollards.

The nadir of the investiture dilemma for the Vatican came nearly half a millennium later when it was resurrected by Napoleon. When still a general employed by the French Republic Bonaparte had made his name as the successful invader of Italy in 1796, driving out the Austrians. As a side show to this campaign he twice invaded the Papal States, the French having a grudge against the elderly Pope Pius VI for the consistent backing he had given to Austria and the other powers in their war to restore the Bourbons to Paris. In addition, there was a vendetta due to the murder of a French diplomat, Ugo Bassville, in Rome back in 1793. Bonaparte thus occupied the papal town of Bologna without any serious fighting and Pius soon sued for peace, letting the French have Avignon back and surrendering Bologna and the other papal towns. However, in the following year another Frenchman was murdered in Rome and this was an excuse to send General Berthier to occupy the Holy City. The Pope was arrested and died in French captivity soon afterwards, while much Vatican booty, including a diamond-studded papal tiara, found its way back to Paris.

The now successful war leader was preparing to transform himself from servant of a republic to leader of a monarchical state. It is perhaps significant that during his 1799 campaign in Egypt Napoleon noted the power of Islam and started warming to the idea of religion as a useful tool for social control. As First Consul he wanted the recently atheist republic to welcome back the Catholic priests so that he could make use of the church to bolster his revival of the monarchy. The Concordat of 1801 saw France return to the papal fold.

Personal relations between the new emperor and the new Pope, Pius VII, remained strained, for Napoleon was now posing as the Second Charlemagne in the tradition of the self-made, self-crowning emperors. In 1808 Napoleon once more sent his troops to occupy Rome, the Papal States were transferred to the new puppet kingdom of Italy and a year later he was excommunicated. While none of Napoleon's major campaigns can be classified as religious wars, several of his minor campaigns had significant religious issues.

'The Teutonic Emperor was the shadow of the Pope, cast on the secular world. The Eastern Patriarch was the shadow of the emperor cast on the spiritual world.'
James Bryce, *The Holy Roman Empire*

15

CRUSADES TO THE HOLY LAND – CHRISTIAN VERSUS MUSLIM

'Effectively he (Pope Urban II) had set a precedent which made
the promulgation of crusades a papal prerogative, one
which it would in time abuse.'
David Whitton, *Oxford History of Medieval Europe*

There is no real doubt that the religious motivation for the First Crusade was considerable but Pope Urban II (1035–1099) was in addition greatly concerned to divert the belligerency of the Normans away from Italy, where they threatened the papal estates. For the later crusades, religion was often a convenient excuse for less worthy motives, and this was even true of the later stages of the First Crusade.

The Crusading movement was initially very much the brain-child of the French Pope Urban II, who in 1095 responded to an appeal from the Byzantine emperor for western help to protect the large numbers of pilgrims visiting the Holy Land. This followed the disastrous battle of Manzikert in 1071, when the Byzantine army under the Emperor Romanos IV Diogenes was badly defeated by the new Sunni Muslim leader Alp Arslan, founder of the Seljuk dynasty. This battle, as Gibbon points out, marked the beginning of the end for the Greek Orthodox Roman Empire, and a new period of proactive jihad from the energetic Seljuk Turks. When therefore the Byzantine Christians asked for help from the Catholic West, they did so with no inkling of just how much additional damage they would suffer from the armies that were sent to help them.

Urban II's famous appeal at Clermont for knightly volunteers was presaged by the new slogan 'Deus vult' (God wills it) and evoked an immediate response throughout western Europe. Yet even this was made easier by the fact that there were already precedents for driving back the infidels, for Charlemagne's attack on the Spanish Saracens and his paladins' glorious defeat at Roncevalles, as mentioned earlier, had been enshrined in folk lore and romantic literature. From the mid-eleventh century popes had begun giving special privileges to men who went to fight the infidels in Spain right up the end of the fifteenth century. The Clermont sermon was to provide a religious blessing for warfare that cost large numbers of lives and provided career opportunities for numerous landless or almost landless knights who could carve out new territories for themselves in the Middle East. It was then to resurrect itself in the brutal conquests of Central and South America by the Spaniards.

It was Pope Urban II who rechristened the 'bellum justum' as the 'bellum sacrum'. In fact, the Spaniards' capture of Toledo from the Moors in 1085 had been a major inspiration to Urban before Clermont, as had the earlier conquest of Muslim-held Sicily in 1072 by the Norman Robert Guiscard. He had been sponsored by the controversial French Pope Nicholas II, who regarded the previously despised Norman mercenaries as the most likely prospect for reconquering the island. The building of Pisa's new cathedral in 1063 had been paid for by gold looted from the emirs of Palermo, so Muslims were becoming an easier and highly profitable target.

Papal indulgences had removed the guilt from warfare long before the First Crusade. Zoe Oldenbourg observes that the result of placing soldiers fighting Muslims in Spain 'directly in the service of the church' was that 'murder, under its noble name of war had long enjoyed a strong prejudice in its favour.'

The First Crusade began well enough with the victory of Doryleum in 1097 when the Frankish heavy cavalry proved highly effective against the lighter troops of the Seljuks. Of the roughly 100,000 participating, some 15,000 were killed, 70 per cent of them Turks. Significantly, the Christian infantry were commanded by the papal legate Adhemar le Puy. However, the siege of Antioch which followed came close to disaster; Bohemond of Toulouse managed its capture by trickery and allowed a massacre of the Muslim inhabitants but was then in turn besieged by the Turks, who came close to starving the Crusaders out. It was at this point that Peter Bartholomew claimed to have a vision of the hiding place of the Holy Lance, an example of our Category 9: when all else fails contrive a miracle. The unfortunate Bartholomew was forced to endure horrendous trial-by-ordeal to persuade the Crusaders that he was genuine. With this inspiration the Crusaders won another victory and Bohemond was rewarded with a princedom, Antioch. A year later came the final triumph when the Crusaders captured Jerusalem in 1099 with the aid of yet another vision, this time the ghost of the recently dead Adhemar le Puy, who had ordered the Crusaders to follow the example of Joshua in the siege of Jericho. They suffered considerable losses themselves, around 10,000 dead or wounded and around 40,000 Muslim and Jewish citizens were slaughtered in the aftermath. This allowed the creation of a new Christian kingdom which lasted on and off in Jerusalem for two hundred years and provided the encouragement for future crusades.

What was especially remarkable about the First Crusade was that not only the knightly warrior class, which was already well disposed to war but also huge crowds of civilians throughout Europe were motivated by the preaching of men like Peter the Hermit (*c.*1050–1115), to abandon their homes and head for Palestine. While Urban II had quite deliberately set in motion the recruitment of trained warriors to take up the cross, he was only indirectly to blame for the irresponsible and unworldly rantings of preachers like Peter, which led to an ill-equipped, undisciplined mass of at least 40,000 brain-washed innocents – perhaps as many as 100,000 – marching thousands of miles to a pointless death.

Peter the Hermit had numerous other 'holy men' as his aides, some of them genuine like Walter Sans-Avoir (d. 1096), some of them psychopathic frauds like the rabidly anti-Semitic Emich of Leisingen. Between them they recruited substantial numbers of naive and totally inexperienced peasants who abandoned their homes and set off eastwards, living off the land and frequently causing mayhem in the areas through which they passed, taking out their frustrations particularly on the luckless Jews whom they blamed as deicides for the death of their saviour. At Semlin in Hungary they were reported to have killed 4,000 of the locals and the population of Belgrade fled to the hills on their approach.

While the size of their army made them a formidable infestation for civilian populations, they were neither properly equipped nor trained to cope with the Turks. Thus, when those who had survived the journey made it at last across the Hellespont into Turkish territory they were massacred by the troops of Sultan Kilij Arslan.

The official crusaders had perhaps been slightly fewer in number but much better able to fight. Estimates of the numbers varied between 50,000 and 300,000, but realistically it is probable that there were no more than 10,000 knights supported by 70,000 infantry or other troops. In terms of fighting power they included many battle-hardened Normans who could easily outfight the more lightly armed though highly professional Turks. They were also highly motivated, both by their religious mission and in due course by the prospect of loot or of acquiring new kingdoms for themselves. Apart from the papal blessing which guaranteed swift passage to heaven if they died, they had no other rules of engagement or chain of command than feudal loyalty. There was no commander-in-chief, no kings, just a group of talented barons and princely tearaways like Robert of Normandy, Godfrey of Bouillon and his brother Baldwin, the ambitious Bohemond of Taranto and Raymond of St Giles, hence despite initial successes the crusaders lost momentum after a split decision on the storming of Antioch.

The image of the First Crusade was marred by the massacres of civilians after the captures of both Antioch and Jerusalem, where the Jews had helped the Muslims defend the city against the invaders. It was then followed by the land-grabbing establishment of Norman principalities in Antioch, Edessa and Jerusalem itself. These principalities soon became notorious for overtaxing and exploiting their largely Christian subjects. The surviving Crusaders who returned home in 1096 joined in massacring Jews in the Rhineland. Steven Runciman in his *History of the Crusades* observed that 'the high ideals were besmirched by cruelty, greed... From the Muslim point of view it created a long-running sore that was to encourage centuries of new jihad.' Amin Maalouf wrote:

'In July 1096 Kilij Arslan learned that an enormous throng of Franj (French) was en route to Constantinople... nothing good could come of the arrival.'

The success of the First Crusade in at least capturing Jerusalem meant that there was no requirement for another major expedition for the following half century, but the movement did continue at a reduced level. Sigurd I King of Norway was the first royal to lead a crusade and there were other small follow-up crusades such as that of Bohemond in 1101 and the Venetians in 1122. Significant also was the founding of the Knights Templar in 1129, for now celibate warriors were granted priestly status, the standard indulgence and extra privileges. They were programmed to fight with suicidal courage, as at the victorious Battle of Montgisard (probably near Ramla in modern Israel) in 1177, led by the teenage leper King Baldwin.

The First Crusade eventually had the effect of provoking the Muslims to mount a response. It was in 1105 that the Damascus scholar wrote his *Book of Jihad*, which re-emphasised the duty of all Muslims to expand their faith 'al jihad al akbar, al jihad al ashgar'.

The official Second Crusade of 1147–9 started with renewed spiritual fervour as its chief sponsors were the highly respected French Cistercian monk Bernard of Clairvaux (1090-1153) who became a major long-term advocate of the 'just war' theory, and Pope Eugene III. It was provoked by the resurgence of Muslim activity by a new dynasty based in Mosul whose founder Zengi captured Edessa (now Sanliurfa in southern Turkey) in 1144. It was supported by two kings, Louis VII of France and Conrad III of Germany. However, it was ineffective from a military point of view as it suffered serious losses on the way to Jerusalem and was then outmanoeuvred by Zengi's son Nur ad-Din at Damascus after the various leaders disagreed on strategy. Nothing was achieved and the surviving Crusaders went home. That same year the Genoese had mixed religion and commerce to capture the Spanish ports of Almeria and Tortosa from the Moors and a year earlier the Portuguese Christians had won back Lisbon.

The Third Crusade of 1189 was more effective, as it was a response to the newly united Turkish state now led by two highly competent Kurdish princes. The fanatically Sunni Nur ad-Din, who had already outwitted the Second Crusade, was a dedicated jihadist whose ambition had been to recover Jerusalem and the Al-Aqsa Mosque from the infidels.

His successor Saladin (1137–1193) succeeded where he had failed. He established his credentials by conquering Egypt and purging it of Shiites, emphasising that his Mujahideen were willing to court martyrdom to regain their lost lands. Having proclaimed himself sultan of both Egypt and Syria he united the previously disaffected local emirs to defeat the Christian army under King Guy of Jerusalem at Hattin near Tiberias in 1187 with the loss of 17,000 Crusaders killed or captured. He followed this up by recapturing the holy city for Islam, a major provocation to the European Christians.

Thus the Third Crusade was proposed by Pope Gregory VIII and supported by three kings, Richard I of England, Philip II of France and Frederick I, Barbarossa, the Holy Roman Emperor, but it too was marred by massacres and bedevilled by lack of coherent leadership after Barbarossa's death, then badly hit by infectious diseases. It achieved a compromise arrangement for pilgrims to visit Jerusalem but the human cost was very high, including the Christian massacre of the surrendering inhabitants of Acre. As a by-product it provided an excuse for a civil war in Germany, where the emperor was accused of a breach of crusading laws by imprisoning a fellow Crusader, Richard I of England.

The Fourth Crusade of 1202/4 was a ruthless misuse of the sacrum bellum in which the cash-strapped Crusaders treacherously agreed to capture Constantinople from their Christian allies in return for the offer of a free sea passage with the Venetian fleet, led by the blind and geriatric Doge Dandolo. Dandolo, who had a profound grudge against the Greeks, more or less bet the Venice treasury on the Crusade as an investment. It resulted in the Normans taking over the Greek Empire and exploiting it for their own and the Venetian merchants' advantage. This was a piece of opportunist empire-snatching very thinly veiled by its original religious objectives. It was also a betrayal of the Greek Orthodox empire based in Constantinople, which had long mistrusted the motives of the western crusaders and now had their suspicions amply justified. It was, however, a huge boost to the papacy under Innocent III, who had supported the idea and could now assert primacy over the entire Christian world. The Greeks were to remain under Norman control for the next eighty years and even when they were ejected the Byzantine Empire was left in such a weakened condition that its final collapse and Ottoman conquest was inevitable.

Ten years after the Latin capture of Constantinople came the so-called Children's Crusade of 1212. It was reminiscent of the days of Peter the Hermit, but this time huge crowds of teenagers were bewitched by messianic preaching. Some thousands of them made it as far as the ports of Marseilles and Genoa where most of them were rounded up and sold as slaves.

The Fifth Crusade inspired by Pope Innocent III just before his death in 1216 involved an attack on Egypt but achieved little. Similarly, the Sixth Crusade in 1228 was an occasion for Frederick II to fulfil his vows as a Crusader, but he wisely spent his time in useful negotiations to regain access for pilgrims to Jerusalem rather than pointless fighting. This apparent religious forbearance must be balanced against the fact that since through his second wife Isabella of Brienne he had a tenuous claim to the kingdom of Jerusalem, Frederick had himself crowned as its new king as soon as he had retaken the city.

The last two major crusades both involved the pious French King Louis IX, following the recapture of Jerusalem by the Turks in 1244. In the Seventh, having amassed a huge army at enormous cost, he landed on the Nile delta and was initially successful but lost momentum and allowed his force to be dissipated by disease. He himself was captured at Damietta and eventually ransomed at vast expense. In the Eighth Crusade in 1270 he invaded Tunisia and died of disease. He achieved little except posthumously to endow the Capet dynasty with a lasting image of divine approval. The crusade by Prince, later King, Edward I of England a year later was the last token gesture towards saving the Holy Land and he abandoned it on the news of his father's death.

Overall the anti-Muslim Crusades of 1095–1270 may have cost as many as a million lives in battle or from disease, achieved few if any of their long-term objectives, exposed a level of hypocrisy in the Catholic establishment, provided an excuse for ethnically cleansing the Jews in many cities and left lasting resentment among the Muslims which still survives and resurfaces today. The fact that they stimulated trade and resulted in a transfer of useful knowledge and technologies from east to west was small compensation and never any part of the original motivation.

One of the legacies of the crusades was the foundation of the new knightly orders which blended the medieval monastic format with the concept of trained mercenaries. These orders such as the Hospitallers and Templars provided what was in effect a standing army for backing up volunteer Crusaders throughout this period. They were also brilliant fund raisers and could afford to maintain horses and equipment for the heavy cavalry that played a major part in battles such as Montgisard 1177 and, though it was a bad defeat, at Hattin, the battle of the Horns in 1187. Because unlike most Crusaders they stayed on in the Middle East they were able to provide garrisons for towns and castles after the other Crusaders had returned home. In particular they held on to difficult outposts like Smyrna in 1374, Rhodes, which they had captured in 1317 and later Malta. There was for example a Hospitaller garrison at Bodrum inside Ottoman territory in 1494. Overall therefore, the various knightly orders helped to encourage and prolong the crusading wars. They even started wars on their own, as in the invasion of Armenia to fend off the Mamluks in 1298. Some of this could be described as beneficial, for example the Hospitallers' attacks on the Barbary pirates and their contribution to the Reconquista, but their imitation by the Teutonic Knights with their aggressive conquest of heathen Prussia is more suspect.

It is also significant that the Templars in particular became so good at banking and fund raising that they made many otherwise unlikely crusades possible from their fund-raising headquarters in Paris, which permanently paid for the upkeep of 4000 expensive warhorses. Certainly, they provided the funds for Louis VII in the Second Crusade, for Henry II of England for some of his wars, and for Philip II of France until he stole their entire war chest in 1312 and the order was abolished by the Avignon-based Pope Clement V. He had just preached a new crusade in 1308, aimed at the Egyptian Mamluk regime, but having attracted some 40,000 untrained volunteers he could arrange no transport for them and they drifted away malnourished and impoverished. In the end he sent a small Hospitaller expedition that captured Rhodes.

On the other side of the crusading wars the Muslims also had their version of monastic soldiers, specifically the so-called

Assassins founded at Alamut by Hassan Sabbah in 1094. They were members of the Nizari Ismaili sect of Shiism who took as their first target the Sunni Seljuk Turks but soon shifted to waging terrorist campaigns against the Crusaders.

The format of the anti-Muslim crusade was resurrected in 1396 with the Crusade of Nicopolis led by King Sigmund of Hungary, which began an attempted roll-back of the Ottoman conquests in Europe that was to take until the 1890s to complete (v. Pt 3 Chapter 28). A Christian force of around 10,000 of men from Hungary, Bulgaria, France, Germany, Burgundy and Wallachia fought against a much larger (at least 20,000) Ottoman army that included 1500 Serbs who since Kosovo had become Turkish subjects. Losses on both sides were considerable but the Crusaders were almost totally destroyed and as a result the Bulgarian Empire collapsed.

There were two further attempts to revive Middle Eastern crusading. In 1454 Philip the Good, Duke of Burgundy (1396–1467), reacted to the Turkish capture of Constantinople the previous year by holding a feast at his capital in Lille and persuading his guests to take a vow to rescue the eastern Christians. The second was the attempt by Pope Pius II (1405–1464) to launch a crusade against the Ottomans in 1459. He died before it could be finalised, but he had been a major motivator for two serious Christian revolts, one by the Albanian leader Skanderbeg (Iskander Bey or George Castrioti 1403–1468) who became something of a Christian hero despite having spent several years as a Muslim fighting for the Ottoman army. The other was in Romania led by the later notorious Count Vlad III Dracula the Impaler whose battle-plan in 1462 included an attempt to assassinate the Sultan Mehmet II, the so-called 'Night Attack'. Despite being a defender of the Orthodox Church, he was much admired by the pope, though there were some misgivings when he was later credited with having 20,000 Muslim prisoners impaled.

Meanwhile succeeding Popes organised or supported the seven wars of Venice against the Ottomans, all of which involved blessing Venetian trading interests in the Mediterranean but also attempting to force back Islam from formerly Christian territories. The First, in 1463–79, was over the Greek island of Euboea, the Second or Morean War 1499–1503 led to the conquest of southern

Greece, the Third of 1537–40 added most of the Greek islands. The Fourth of 1570–73 began when the Holy League fleet lost Cyprus but under Don John of Austria beat the Turks in a major sea battle at Lepanto (v. Pt 3 Chapter 28), the Fifth of 1645–9 marked the brutal conquest of Crete by the Ottomans, the Sixth (or Second Morean) War 1688–99 involved the Knights of Malta and led to the Venetians taking over Dalmatia and some parts of Greece. The Seventh and last, or Holy League of 1714, climaxed with the naval victory of Matapan against the Turks but also the loss of the last Greek islands to the Turks. So, while these seven partially religious wars between rival sea powers caused some ebb and flow of influence, the overall rolling back of Islam was in the end minimal and short-lived and in the case of Venice, religion played very much a secondary role to commerce.

The overall losses attributable to the Crusades may, as we have seen, have been close to a million, not including collateral damage such as the waves of anti-Semitic genocide but including the total waste of lives involved in the various amateur People's Crusades, as well as disease and hunger. They left behind long-term mutual distrust and hatred of the two combatant religions to come to the fore on many subsequent occasions. They also provided seasoned holy warriors to provide recruits for the – at times – lethargic reconquistas back in Europe.

> '...the crusades were one long act of intolerance in
> the name of God.'
> Steven Runciman, *A History of the Crusades*

16

THE OTHER CRUSADES – MOSTLY CHRISTIANS VERSUS CHRISTIANS

'The knight errant, fantastic and useless, will always
be poor and without ties as the first Templars had been.'
J. Huizinga, *Waning of the Middle Ages*

Even before the First Crusade there were already abuses of
the concept of just wars blessed by the Catholic Church. Pope
Alexander II had in 1066 given his blessing for William of
Normandy to invade England, mainly because he wanted to
encourage the new breed of Norman knights who were fighting to
win back new areas like southern Italy from Islam. William made
a pilgrimage to endorse his religious credentials and was ably
supported by his half-brother the fighting bishop, Odo of Bayeux,
one of a number of clerics who donned armour in the supposedly
righteous cause, but who fought with a mace instead of a sword as
priests were forbidden to shed blood. Even their opponent Harold
boosted his Christian image by going on a pilgrimage before
Hastings. It didn't help.

The systematic abuse of the crusading ideal outside Palestine
began seriously when the German Hospitallers first appeared in
1143, modelled on the other crusading orders like the Templars.
The first northern, non-Muslim crusade, the Wendish Crusade
of 1147, was directed against supposedly pagan Slavs or Wends
and blessed by Bernard of Clairvaux as a follow-up to the
Second Crusade. It was led by Saxon nobles with the excuse

of converting pagan Slavs but was in fact little more than a deliberate expansion of German territory. This was reinforced when the Teutonic Knights were founded as a similar order in 1190, originally to manage a field hospital at Acre where they bought a castle at Monfort/Starkenberg. In 1211 they expanded their activities to Hungary, where they fought the Cumans to prevent them taking over Burzenland. They backed the German Emperor Frederick II when he became King of Jerusalem and were rewarded by the right to fight the pagan Baltic Prussians from a base in Chelmno. The Order's conquest of Prussia led to considerable bloodshed but was later to be of huge importance in the development of Germany as the monastic state became the nucleus of Prussia, which in due course became the lead state in Germany. The Germans also has an internal crusade known as the Stedinger Crusade 1232–1234, when the Bishop of Bremen authorised the massacre of 'heretical' Saxon peasants for their reluctance to accede to his financial demands.

The foundation of the Livonian Sword Brothers and their crusade in 1202 inaugurated a drive by them to help the Teutonic Knights to conquer Prussia and the regions now known as Latvia, Lithuania and Estonia, turning them into German enclaves with the excuse that they had been previously pagan. In due course the popes extended their blessing to the Teutonic Knights for an attack on the Orthodox Christians of western Russia, until they were halted by Alexander Nevsky in the Battle on the Ice in 1242, but not before they had amassed substantial territories, characterised by ethnic cleansing, collateral plagues and repopulation by Christian Germans. This was nevertheless a bad period for the German knights as in 1241 they had supported the Poles against an invasion by the Mongols and were heavily defeated at Liegnitz (Legnica) where virtually an entire army of 30,000, mainly Christian peasants, was wiped out. The Teutonic Knights were also defeated in the so-called Priests War that lasted thirteen years, from 1467 to 1479, when they became involved in electing the Bishop of Warmia in defiance of King Casimir of Poland, another example of the investiture crisis.

The brutality of the Livonian Knights, whose efforts to win territory from the Russian Orthodox Church were frequently endorsed by the papacy, was horribly exposed in the 1470s when they burned the town of Kobyle (east of Krakow in southern Poland) along with some 3000 of its inhabitants, so this became a stimulus for the retaliatory efforts of Orthodoxy against Catholicism under Ivan III of Muscovy, the first Russian to copy the title Caesar or tsar from the Byzantines and the first to refer to Moscow as the Third Rome.

Pope Honorius III who had endorsed the Fifth Crusade and the attack on the Cathars (see below) presided over the concoction of a document justifying the annexation of Culmerland/Chelmno (later the site of a Nazi concentration camp). A significant portion of the lands acquired by the Catholic Knights – East Prussia – was in fact handed over to the Hohenzollern dynasty of Brandenburg by its last Grand Master, who happened to be a Hohenzollern and had seen the benefits of listening to Martin Luther. As an ex-celibate knight turned Protestant, he thus gained a wife and a dukedom. Brandenburg was thus propelled to greatness as the ambitious new state of Prussia, under a dynasty whose motto was 'Gott mit Uns', and became exponentially more ambitious until its downfall in 1918. It is estimated that the Teutonic Crusades blessed by several popes may have cost as many as 100,000 lives, not including consequential starvation or disease and in the longer term led to the irredentist spread of ethnic Germans round the Baltic, which provided one of the excuses for Hitler's war in 1939.

Not to be outdone, the Swedes launched three so-called Crusades (1150–1239) to conquer the allegedly heathen tribes of what is now Finland, adding to Sweden's territory. The first was allegedly inspired by King Eric VII the Holy (*fl* 1150-1160), who was meant to be canonised by the Vatican for his efforts in first conquering then converting the Finns but was murdered by one of his rivals in 1160, giving him martyr status. He shared this with his chief backer in the crusade, an English monk called Henry who had migrated to Sweden along with a colleague, John Breakspear, who subsequently became Pope Adrian IV. As Bishop of Uppsala Henry took responsibility for the conversion of the Finns, was himself murdered and canonised as a martyred hero of the Catholic Church.

The Second Swedish Crusade in around 1248 was led by Burger Karl. The Third in 1293 involved an invasion of Karelia and the founding of Vyborg Castle as the Swedes consolidated their control of what was later called Finland, a conquest that lasted for several hundred years.

There had been an even more flagrant misuse of crusadism. The papal crusade against Markward, the German regent of Sicily, in 1199, was a purely political affair orchestrated by the Vatican, which ended when Markward died three years later. The Vatican's claim to rule Sicily was the cause also of the Aragonese Crusade of 1284 when Pope Martin V tried to depose King Peter III of Aragon for interfering there, and encouraged an invasion by the French. Among its consequences were the massacre at Elne in Roussillon, the destruction of a French fleet and a French army decimated by dysentery. Pope Boniface VIII (d. 1303) also sent politically motivated crusades against the Aragonese dynasty in Sicily and engineered the transfer of Naples to the French, thus encouraging a French involvement in Italy which ended up with the papacy moving to Avignon.

Closer to home Boniface's even more blatant misuse of the crusading ideal was his crusade in 1300 against his rivals in Rome, the Colonna family, which included three cardinals and which resulted in the destruction of Palestrina.

In France in 1208 the Albigensian Crusade was ordered by the papal Inquisition under Pope Innocent III and spear-headed by the fanatically ruthless Simon de Montfort, who led the siege of Béziers with some 20,000 massacred. As the papal delegate Arnaud Amalric of Citeau put it, 'So did God's vengeance give vent to its wondrous rage.' Then followed the mass burning of so-called heretics, the peace-loving Cathars of Languedoc. They did not accept the divinity of Christ nor the authority of the pope, they believed that matter was evil, sharing many of their somewhat puritanical ideas with the Bogomils of Dalmatia, so disapproved of by the establishment that the Dominican Order of monks was set up to try to make them more orthodox, but having failed to do so by peaceful means resorted to force.

Four years after Béziers in 1213 came the Battle of Muret (near Toulouse) when the Cathar supporter Raymond of Toulouse along with Catalan troops under the prominent ex-Crusader King Peter II of Aragon was defeated by de Montfort with estimated losses around 20,000. Total casualties of the Albigensian Crusade may have been as high as 200,000 and while uprooting heresy was the main motivation it also became part of building a centralised monarchy in France.

In 1212 came the important Spanish victory of Las Navas de Tolosa over the Moors (Chapter 13). Even the English had two internal crusades, both against their kings, John in 1215 and Henry III in 1264, so the crusading umbrella was being used to cover general attempts at regime change when this suited papal policy.

As noted earlier the Fourth Crusade in 1204 had been diverted from its proper objectives in the Holy Land to capture the Byzantine Empire for Venice and the Normans. This had obvious attractions for Pope Innocent III as it provided the opportunity to absorb the Greek Orthodox Church and assert worldwide Catholic supremacy. That the Latin Empire only lasted fifty years before the Greeks seized back Constantinople was a great disappointment and not surprisingly there were two attempted crusades to get it back again, in 1261 and 1281, the last one instigated by Martin V.

There were a number of peasant crusades; in 1309 when there were spontaneous rebellions of peasants that spread through Europe but eventually petered out, and this happened again in 1320.

The Despenser's Crusade of 1383 was led by Henry le Despenser (1341–1406), known as the 'Fighting Bishop of Norwich', an attempt to undermine the alternative papacy based at Avignon but in reality to support a Flemish rebellion against the French. Christopher Tyerman considers that 'for all its canonical propriety it was the Hundred Years War thinly disguised.' Yet the Hundred Years War (1338–1453) itself did have significant religious undercurrents, as when the French expedition to reinstate King David II of Scotland and thus create a second front against England in 1335 was preached by Pierre Roger, Archbishop of Rouen, who soon afterwards became Pope Clement VI in Avignon. As such he provided a large portion of the funds needed by the French crown to fight the English. However, to his credit he did try his best to persuade the French that the Jews were not to blame for the Black Death. The rival bishops of France and England preached against each other and kept the war going. The French cardinals also defied the Germans' wish to make Ludwig of Bavaria their king, reasserting the necessity for all royal coronations to be blessed officially by the pope, thus making it difficult for Ludwig to take the English side against the French. Subsequently, since the French supported the French anti-Pope Clement at Avignon, it was only natural that the English would not, but instead supported Pope

Urban VI based in Rome. Thus in 1383 the city of Ghent began the campaign and Bishop le Despenser, promising that those who died would be martyrs, took English troops 'waving the Banner of the Holy Cross' to its aid by besieging Ypres, leading to significant casualties. Among the last official crusades were the five authorised to eliminate the Hussite heretics in Bohemia 1419–34 (see next chapter).

Apart from the abuse of the crusading ideal the other residual effect of crusading was the quasi-spritual development of the concept of chivalry, which gave its practitioners the belief that God would bless their ambitions. This was particularly true of Edward III, who adopted 'Dieu et mon droit' as his motto and applied it to his God-given right to take over the crown of France as well as that of England, Wales and Scotland. The Hundred Years War that he instigated was far from being a holy war, but both sides certainly claimed that God was on their side. Edward deliberately encouraged the cult of St George and organised the English priesthood to preach about his war-effort from their pulpits, partly because he was desperate for money to help fund it. In fact, if he had not purloined the war chest that the church had been gathering for the next crusade it is doubtful if he could have afforded his preliminary attack. Similarly, the French went to war for 'God and Saint Denis' in what became a long and brutal contest. By the time of his death in 1376 Edward was referred to by the chronicler Walsingham as 'a divinely inspired instrument of English salvation' the equal of King David in the Old Testament.

The prolonged nature of the war and the fact that England's main strategy was to lay waste huge tracts of France in an effort both to humiliate the French king and force him to take to the field, meant that the standards of military behaviour rapidly declined and the collateral damage for non-combatants was horribly severe. In vain had the French fighting the English at Crecy relied on their appeals to 'God and St Denis', whilst the English used their church pulpits to preach the benefits and glories of war, prayed for their armies and rang bells to celebrate victories. So as the French kept losing both face and battles they were eventually confronted with a new side to religion – as a last resort when all else has failed. As Stephen Richey put it, 'only a regime in the final straits of desperation would pay attention to an illiterate farm girl who claimed the voice of God was instructing her to take charge.' Even so, Joan of Arc (1412–31) had great difficulty in persuading the as yet uncrowned Charles VII (Joan insisted on referring to him still as the Dauphin despite the fact that his father was dead) to let her join the relief force at the siege of Orleans. Yet single-handed she turned the war into a semi-religious one to save 'the holy kingdom of France'; and it worked.

The ambivalent career patterns of French bishops who were often the younger sons of nobility, chosen for their family background rather than interest in the church, is shown by three of the Bishops of Beauvais. Jean de Marigny was a leading supporter of the French cause against the English and led an army against them in 1340 after which he was promoted to Archbishop of Rouen. Philippe d'Alencon (d. 1397) was also pro-French and a supporter of Robert of Geneva, the future anti-Pope Clement VII, who as a papal legate during the so-called War of Eight Saints hired mercenaries from the English condottiero John Hawkwood and used them to massacre the population (5–8000 people) of the town of Cesena in Forli, which was trying to withdraw from the Papal States. Our third bishop of Beauvais, Bernard de Chevron (1413–20), was by contrast strongly pro-English and played a leading part in the trial for witchcraft of Joan of Arc.

There were some attempted crusades after the Ottoman Turks began to make serious inroads into Christian Europe. The Albanian mercenary George Castriot or Skanderbeg (1405–68) had converted to Islam when he joined the Turkish army in 1443 but changed sides at the Battle of Nish twenty years later and converted back to Christianity. He then became a hero figure for Pope Pius II who pronounced that Albania was the bulwark of Christianity (*Antemurale Christianitatis*) and suggested that Skanderbeg's rebellion against the Ottomans be supported as a crusade. Pius died a year later but Skanderbeg remained a Christian hero.

The same idea of a Balkan bulwark was revived in 1519 by Pope Leo X (1475–1521) when after a massive reshuffle of cardinals he proposed a crusade against the Sultan Selim I to be led by the Croats and he announced that Croatia was now the bulwark of Christianity. This initiated what became known as the Hundred Year Croat-Ottoman War, the climax of which was the Battle of

Sisak in 1593 when a joint army from the Holy Roman Empire, the dukes of Austria, Carinthia and Styria effectively held back the Ottoman advance into the northern Balkans. It also boosted the credentials of the Croats as bastions of Catholicism when the Thirty Years War began in 1618.

> 'Pope Clement VI was one of the principal financers
> of the war effort.'
> Jonathan Sumption, *The Hundred Years War*

17

ORTHODOX VERSUS UNORTHODOX CATHOLICS AND MUSLIMS

'Those supporting icons were persecuted vigorously.'
Harlie Gallatin, *History of Christianity*

In most respects neither the Greek nor Russian Orthodox faiths were ever quite so obsessed with heresy as their western counterparts. There are fewer wars in Eastern Europe that can be attributed primarily to religious motives. However, there were periods of controversy and persecution.

As we have seen the efforts of the Greek Emperor Leo III to reform the Orthodox Church by reducing its reliance on icons had caused several minor wars and effectively seen the end of Byzantine Italy, which had remained defiantly iconophile with the full support of the papacy.

In the case of Russian Orthodoxy it must be remembered that virtually all of what is now Russia had been conquered and ruled by the Muslim Mongols or Tartars for over 150 years since the Russians' defeat by the Golden Horde at the River Kalka in 1223, followed by the capture of the capital Kiev. The Russians themselves were meanwhile split among a number of rival states, of which Moscow was not yet the most prominent. This lasted effectively until 1380 when Grand Prince Dmitrii Donskoy of Moscow received the blessing of the highly respected monk (later Saint) Sergius for a joint attack on the Muslims and defeated the Tartar Blue and Golden Hordes at Kulikovo Field on the

River Don. So the Russians had their own form of reconquista, Moscow became the leading state and it was the Muscovite princes, later tsars, who completed the expulsion of the Tartars from most of Russia.

Moscow's rival the city of Novgorod with Alexander Nevsky in charge had its epic battle in 1242 against the Catholic Germans on the frozen ice of Lake Peipus, driving them back down the Baltic. This represented inter-Christian competition between the Catholic Lithuanians and the Orthodox Russians. In fact, the Lithuanians had for a while been doing a better job than the Russians in driving out the southern Tartars, whilst Novgorod had done a better job than Moscow in driving back the Catholic Livonian knights.

For all the intervening 150 years the humiliated princelings of a divided Russia had paid tribute to their Tartar masters in the Crimea, and Moscow had grown to be an important town simply because it was a convenient collection point for all the tribute money. Moscow replaced Kiev as the seat of the Patriarch in 1325 and in 1472 its Grand Prince married a Byzantine princess so that Moscow could start to pose as the capital of the Orthodox world and its prince assume the title of Caesar or Tsar, a title with similar religious significance as Holy Roman Emperor.

As the Russian reconquista neared completion in 1550 the pro-Muscovite Metropolitan Makarii blessed the troops led by the young Tsar Ivan IV Groznii the Terrible (1530–1584) as they headed off to besiege the then major Muslim city of Kazan. So on this occasion Ivan was able to claim that he was waging a holy war and the Muscovite Orthodox church followed up with a largely unsuccessful effort to convert the conquered Tartars to Christianity.

As the small state of Muscovy made the breakthroughs that allowed it to start referring to its expanded territory as Russia, under Ivan III and Ivan IV, the effort was very much a holy war and Russia became Holy Russia. In addition, with the fall of Constantinople in 1453 Moscow had begun to take very seriously its role as the Third Rome and centre for the Orthodox Church. The so-called 'Legend of the White Cowl' gave the new tsars legitimacy. (The story was that the White Cowl was given by Constantine to Pope Sylvester I and by divine intervention was eventually transferred to Novgorod in the mid-fourteenth century.)

Religion also played a part in the conquest and colonising efforts of two independent groups. The fiercely Orthodox Ukrainian Cossacks under Yermak Timofeyich (1532–1582) took it upon themselves to invade the so-called Sultans of Siberia and won a major battle at Qashlik in 1582, thus beginning serious Orthodox inroads beyond the Urals. Parallel to this, the devoutly Orthodox Stroganov family developed the salt and fur trades eastwards with remarkable success, their founder Anikey Stroganov (1488–1570) choosing like his father before him to become a monk in his old age.

In fighting the Catholic Knights of Livonia Ivan III had religion as an additional motivation, just as Ivan IV did later in his capture of Kazan from the Muslim Tartars in 1550. The by then departed Saint Sergius had left behind him a famous vision in which the Catholic Lithuanians appeared to him as the 'evil forces' of the devil, inhabitants of 'Satanic Lithuania'. Furthermore, the later war against Poland was very much about preventing the eastward spread of Catholicism, which had already made inroads into the Ukraine. The threat that the Polish Catholic Sigismund would become the tsar of Muscovy in 1611 provoked the rebellion against Polish domination. At that point the patriarch Hermogen urged the Russians to fight a holy war against the Catholics. Thus, both the first two Romanov tsars, Mikhail and Alexis, regarded themselves as having a divine mission to repel Catholicism. 'War took on the character of a crusade for both sides. This made it easier to justify cruelty' (Philip Longworth).

The Third Rome concept did however bring problems, for the patriarch Nikon in 1653 took it upon himself to bring the ritual and dogma of the Russian church back into line with the Greek version, trying to eliminate alleged bad habits acquired by the often illiterate Russian priests. This resulted in a prolonged rebellion by those who clung to the old Russian ways, the *raskolniki*, and to serious persecution. It took a siege lasting eight years (1668–76) for the tsarist musketeers (*streltsi*) to subdue the massive, heavily fortified Solovetsky Monastery on the White Sea, so this was a religious civil war between two branches of Russian orthodoxy, the Moscow patriarch and the Old Believers. It was a war that was to persist for some years as the *raskolniki* would rather die than compromise. They shared in the Cossack rebellion on the

Volga led by Stenka Razin in 1670 after his followers had helped the defence of the Solovetsky archipelago. They also supported the Moscow uprising of 1682 when the old tsar's daughter Sophia seized power as regent for her two little brothers, one of them the future Peter the Great.

After the removal of Sophia from power and the punishment of her supporters Peter I (1675–1725), as Tsar and 'the Defender of Orthodoxy' began an even more radical reform of the Russian Church to make it more responsive to his idea of a westernised super-power, importing better educated clergy from the Ukraine and Belarus. Significantly, Peter's longest and most arduous war was against the Lutheran Protestant Swedes under the hyperactive Charles XII, so he was well supported by the patriarchs and finally defeated the Swedes at Poltava.

It was no coincidence that when Tsar Alexander I (1777–1823) began to restore Russian military confidence after the fall of Moscow to the French in 1812, it was described as a Holy Alliance. Similarly, it was his brother Nicholas I who very much identified autocracy with Orthodoxy and who began the second major persecution of all non-Orthodox sects in Russia as part of his plans for russification of his empire. This included a clamp-down on the *raskolniki* but also on the empire's largest religious minority, the Catholics in Poland and the Ukraine. Protestants in the Baltic states were less badly treated as they were a good source of army officers.

Poland itself staged a rebellion in 1830 after Alexander's death and it naturally adopted both a nationalist and religious stance; the radical nationalists formed an uneasy alliance with the Catholic hierarchy. Once the rebellion was crushed Nicholas orchestrated an attempt through new schools to russify the illiterate Polish peasants, but the native clergy managed to hold off the effects of this brain-washing.

There was an ongoing drive against Islam, for as the Russian Empire clawed its way southwards it also absorbed Muslim enclaves. As early as 1785 the Chechen leaders declared jihad against Russia. The deeply religious Grigory Potemkin (he had spent several years in a monastery) who led the conquest of the Crimea for Catherine the Great was passionate about the idea of freeing the Orthodox Armenians and Georgians from

Ottoman control. As he wrote to his mistress, the empress, Christ was on his side and would aid his efforts.

The regular Russian campaigns to organise compulsory conversion of the Muslim subjects caused deep resentment, as for example when Peter the Great insisted that all Tartar landowners should be baptised or lose their lands. Both the Batyrsha (1710-1765) holy war and the Pugachev revolts (1753 and 1773) in the Volga region were fuelled by the feeling of persecution among the Muslims. Similarly, the inroads made into Muslim territories that by this time were either parts of the Ottoman Empire or its client states provoked the sultans to declare jihad against the Russians. When the able General Count von Munch in 1736 devastated the Muslim enclave of the Crimea, the Turks responded with a *ghazavat* (holy war). The Russians had reasons for their campaign that were beyond any religious motivation, for the Crimean Tatars had long been involved in the kidnapping of Christians for the slave trade and also provided some of the elite mercenaries for the Ottoman sultans. Thus both sides waged a vaguely holy war that lasted from around 1444 until 1918. Potemkin, the ex-monk, certainly viewed his Orchakov campaign of 1788 as a crusade, one legitimately concluded with a massacre of Muslims. The friction and bitterness would be revived in the 1980s with the collapse of the Soviet Union and the problem of surviving Muslim enclaves in southern Russia like Chechnya, which had waged its own jihad since 1785 (v. Pt 4 Chapter 43).

For the Russians the war known in the west as the Crimean War of 1854–6 was known as The Holy War, as it had been provoked by a conflict between the Orthodox and Catholic Churches in Jerusalem over the rights of pilgrims to access the Holy Land – much the same as the mainspring of the First Crusade. Its real causes, however, were much more to do with Russian plans to win control of the Bosphorus and thus threaten French and British interests in the Mediterranean.

The subsequent extension of the Russian Empire as it conquered a series of Muslim regions including those now known as Uzbekistan, Kazakhstan, Kyrgyzstan and Turkmenistan in the late nineteenth century had only tenuous religious connotations so far as the Russians were concerned, since their motives were almost entirely economic, and no real effort was made at conversion, but they did have serious long-term effects on Muslim attitudes and on the ethnic balance of the future Soviet Union. By 1900 the main emphasis of Russian religious strategy was in supporting their land-grabbing efforts in China and in using the Jews as scapegoats for the incapacity of the government to reform itself.

'It was at the end of 1851. On a cold November evening Hadji Murat was riding into the hostile Chechen village of Mahket where the pressed dung fires were emitting their fragrant smoke.'

Leo Tolstoy, *Hadji Murat*

18

TIMUR – MUSLIMS VERSUS MUSLIMS, HINDUS AND BUDDHISTS

'Timur, Sword of Islam, conqueror of the world'.
Justin Marozzi, *Tamerlane – Sword of Islam*

While the conquests of Genghis Khan and his Mongol hordes had virtually no element of religion in them (he was famously tolerant of all religions) the same could not be said of the subsequent fight-back against the Mongols. In particular this was true of the battle of Ain Jalut near Gaza in 1260 when the Mamluk (ex-slave soldier) general Baibars led his ex-slave soldiers against 20,000 Mongols and achieved the first ever defeat of a Mongol army. Reputedly the sultan had urged his men to fight for Islam and the battle was historically important not just because it proved that the Mongols were not invincible but also because the Mamluks, being mostly ex-slaves brought to Egypt from the north, were Sunni Muslims. This sealed their takeover from the previous Fatimid dynasty, which had been basically Shiite. From that time onwards Egypt was fairly solidly Sunni.

The other three key battles that began to curtail the Mongol expansion were achieved by the representatives of three different religions: Shinto, Buddhism and Russian Orthodox. The Shinto-inspired Japanese repulsion of Kublai Khan's invading force helped by the god-sent gale or typhoon, kamikaze, was in 1272–81 (v. Pt 3 Chapter 23); the Buddhist monk Zhu Yuanzhang's (later Emperor Hongwu) defeat of the Mongol Yuan dynasty when he captured

Nanjing was in 1361 (v Pt 2 Chapter 12); and the Orthodox Russian Dmitrii Donskoy's defeat of the Tartar Blue Horde and their Catholic allies from Lithuania at Kulikovo (Tula on the Don) was in 1380, helped by some warrior Russian Orthodox monks and the blessing of Saint Sergei (v. previous Chapter).

However, soon afterwards the Mongols produced a new champion, Timur. Perhaps the most ferocious of all Muslim warriors and allegedly a descendant of Genghis Khan, the part Mongol, part Turk, Timur Leng or Timur the Lame or Tamberlane (1337–1405) sought omens from the Koran as he planned an invasion against the infidels of China. Whether his love of Islam drove him to massacres of both pagans and non-Sunni Muslims or whether it was just an excuse to indulge his natural addiction to violence it is impossible to judge.

His first important victory had been on the Terek River in 1395 when he defeated the rival Mongol Golden Horde with whom he was competing as to who should sack the richest cities in Persia. After a very hard fight he allegedly fell down and prayed to Allah.

His invasion of India in 1397 had initially been directed against fellow Muslims who were already engaged in a dynastic civil war and with the excuse that their Sultan Nasruddin Mahmud was being too tolerant of the Hindus. Among weapons used for his capture of Delhi were catapult- propelled liquid fire-bombs. His subsequent massacres after the siege were directed mainly against non-Muslims, for he seems to have developed a pathological hatred of 'the idolatrous Hindus'. He had 100,000 of them executed, as he recorded in his own memoirs, and he already had had the same number of captive slaves executed because there was no space for them. So far as sparing the other inhabitants of Delhi was concerned he commented, 'Although I was desirous of sparing them I could not for it was the will of God that this calamity should befall the city.' Total casualties may have been as high as 1,000,000.

Two years later he attacked and defeated the Egyptian Mamluks at Aleppo. Despite the fact that they were fellow Sunnis he authorised the usual massacre, at least 20,000, and left his trademark pile of skulls.

It is evident that there are numerous contradictions and uncertainties when trying to analyse whether Timur was the fanatical Sunni Muslim portrayed in his own memoirs or whether militant Islam was just a useful tool for a compulsive and utterly ruthless empire-builder, whose three decades of campaigning have been estimated to have cost up to 17 million lives.

There are complexities about his ethnic origin. He was born of Turkic mountain stock south of Samarkand in what is now Uzbekistan, but it was then under the control of the Chagatai Mongols whose style he adopted, learning to speak Turkish, Mongol and Persian. Having been kidnapped by the local Mongols as a child of nine and wounded during a later alleged sheep-stealing episode, he then clawed his way to the top of his own tribe before becoming such a successful commander that he had virtual rule over the Chagatai with the assumed title of emir, not khan, since he was not of royal blood.

At some point he decided it was his destiny to wage *ghaza* or holy war, but his true religious stance is hard to decipher. His key adviser was a Sunni scholar Abdul Jabbar Khwarezm and he appears at times to have had a genuine antipathy for Shiites and for lapsed Sunnis, but his closest friend was a Sufi holy man, Sayyid Baraka, so close that they were buried in the same tomb. He thus contrived to combine the ruthlessness and drive of Genghis Khan with the aura of an Islamic mystic, ordained by God to conquer the world and thus motivate his armies thousands of miles from home. In 1398 a passage in the Koran was interpreted as an instruction for him to conquer China.

His campaigns covered huge distances, involved exceptional qualities as a general and a staggering level of mass brutality. His defeats of the Ottoman Turks, the Mamluks of Egypt and the Sultanate of Delhi were all against major dynasties of the Sunni persuasion, whilst only Persia among his victims was Shiite, hence perhaps his worst atrocity was at Ispahan, the pyramid of 70,000 skulls. His main credentials as a ghazi or holy warrior came from his defeat of the Christian Knights Hospitaller at Smyrna and his massacres of Hindus. Had he ever succeeded in conquering China that might have added another religion to his list of victims.

His final triumph was the crushing of the Ottomans, also fellow Sunni Muslims, but he regarded them as corrupted by power and empire and killed some 30,000 of them at the battle of Ankara in 1402. He captured the previously all-conquering Sultan Bayezid who died soon afterwards, yet whereas the Ottoman Empire soon recovered under a succession of new sultans, Timur's overstretched empire vanished within two generations of his death.

Having built up his image as a good patron of sufis and builder of fine mosques and created credibility for himself as a brilliant commander, he may have exploited his new credentials as 'the sword of Islam' to satisfy his own vanity as an empire builder. His empire was, however, too massive to be sustainable and like the similar creations of Alexander the Great and Genghis Khan soon began to disintegrate, though the Moguls in India today are his genetic descendants.

'If tyrannies war's justice ye refute
I execute, enjoined me from above
To scourge the pride of such as heaven abhors'
Christopher Marlowe, *Tamburlaine*

19

CATHOLICS VERSUS HUSSITES, LOLLARDS, ANABAPTISTS AND TABORITES

'In the eyes of the radical Taborites all their opponents were sinners and must be exterminated.'
Norman Cohn, *The Pursuit of the Millennium*

The burning at the stake in 1415 of the would-be church reformer and precursor of Luther and Calvin, Jan Hus, provoked his followers to rebel and led to a war, euphemistically labelled as a series of five crusades, that lasted from 1419 to 1434. Huss with his emotive preaching had created a passionate dislike of the Catholic hierarchy, already unpopular for corruption and excessive financial demands. The militancy of the Hussites is shown in their Battle Hymn 'Ye who are warriors of God' and they were willing to fight to the death, but they soon succumbed to imperial troops, 'Crusaders' authorised by a papal bull endorsing the slaughter of anti-papal heretics. One of the achievements of the Hussite soldiers was to develop a new style of fighting, the laager or wagenburg/fortified wagon, a primitive form of horse-powered tank, which was copied by the Hungarians in their battles against the Turks.

Their role was taken over by the even more extreme Taborites, who were brilliantly led by the fanatical Jan Zizka (1360–1424), motivated by a strong belief in the Second Coming and the millennium, 'the end of time'. Zizka was an obsessive disciplinarian, ruthless and technologically astute. He was an experienced soldier and fought at the great Battle of Tannenberg, which resulted in the heavy defeat of the Teutonic Knights. A major military innovator, he pioneered the use of pistols in warfare as well as creative use of gunpowder. The terms pistol and howitzer are derived from the Czech words *pistala* and *howiecz*. It has to be said that the Taborites were also motivated by a strong antipathy to the Germans and the middle classes in Bohemia, but they also had the backing of radical priests like John Capek of Prague University, who wrote 'Accursed be the man who withholds his sword from shedding the blood of enemies of Christ. Every believer must wash his hands in blood.' Zizka won several victories including at Kutna Hora (now in the Czech republic) in 1421, but in the end the Taborite and Hussite forces were defeated and massacred at Lipany near Cisky Brod in 1434. (Moderate Hussites, the Utraquists, fought on the side of the Hussite and Bohemian nobility against the radicals.)

Under the pressures of all-out war the idealism of the Taborites had begun to deteriorate. Having abolished feudalism they then ended up robbing the peasants to feed their army. As extremists they then persecuted other extremists, as when they burned as heretics seventy-five Adamites, members of a proto-communist, sometimes nudist sect even more radical than themselves, who believed they were avenging angels destined to cleanse the world by slaughter. The Taborites also waged a holy war against the Pikarti Adamites, a variant of the Bohemian Adamites. The eccentric sectarianism meant that none of these anti-Roman sects managed to create a united front and they soon succumbed to pressure.

In England there might have been a similar religious civil war in 1381 as the Peasant's Revolt of that year was undoubtedly inspired by the rebel priest John Ball, who had been inspired by John Wycliffe and his followers, the barefoot Lollards. There were of course plenty of economic causes for the uprising in this period just after the Black Death. In the end the rebels were appeased by the empty promises of the teenage King Richard II and in due course the leaders of the rebellion were executed. This was not the only time that priests, not only Christian priests, took up arms on behalf of oppressed peasantry.

'Thenceforth alongside or in combination with the major campaigns waged under Ziska many campaigns occurred which were simply robbers' raids.'
Norman Cohn, *The Pursuit of the Millennium*

20

CATHOLICS AND PROTESTANTS VERSUS WITCHES AND JEWS

'...it was believed that the continued sterility of many years was caused by witches through the malice of the Devil.'

W. Rummel, *Hexenverfolgungen*

It was not a war in the conventional sense but from the mid-fifteenth century there was a coordinated attack on substantial numbers of so-called witches, which was numerically equivalent in casualty terms to a major war. It coincided with the later stages of the Black Death and the advent of printing, but also with the general disruption created by the Reformation. Particularly influential was the publication at Speyer in 1487 of the *Malleus Maleficarum (Hammer of Witches)* written by two rather devious and over-imaginative hacks from the fringes of the Inquisition, the Dominican monks Sprenger and Kramer. They provided a Europe-wide audience with an apparently credible hand-book that became one of the first best-sellers of the Guttenberg era. Ironically, having been spawned by Catholics it was soon repudiated by the Vatican and became hugely influential among Protestants.

There was nothing new about persecuting witches. The Old Testament included a condemnation of sorcerers and soothsayers (Deuteronomy), the Romans executed witches and at times of crisis, plagues or natural disasters it was standard practice in many societies throughout the world to look around for scapegoats among the more eccentric or unconventional members of sects or simply of society. Accusations of witchcraft went along with the suppression of the Cathars, Joan of Arc had conveniently been executed as a witch in 1429 and there had been hints of witchcraft linked to sodomy in the treatment of the Templars in 1220. On the whole, the Vatican condemned witch-hunts and poured scorn on the scaremongering among the illiterate that gave rise to it. The Council of Paderborn outlawed witch-hunts in 785 and Pope Gregory VII prohibited them in his letter to the Danes in 1080. Yet occasionally, popes supported them, as did Pope John XXII in 1320 and Pope Innocent VIII, who was persuaded to back the campaign of the two Dominicans Sprenger and Kramer in 1483.

One of the few prominent Catholic churchmen to stir up witch-hunts was the Franciscan friar Bernardino of Sienna ((d. 1444) and it was in his time and that of the other witch publicist Johann Nider (d. 1438) that there came, perhaps coincidentally, in 1428 one of the first apparently spontaneous outbreaks of witch fever in Valais, then a French town, now in Switzerland. There was a similar outbreak in Briancon.

The virus spread slowly but built up momentum in the 1540s when it spread to England. Then in 1563 came the first of the major outbreaks in southern Germany at Wiesensteig in the wake of another best-seller, *Of the Tricks of the Demons*, which was translated into several languages. Some of the worst examples in Catholic territory were those at Trier from 1587 (executions 1000) Fulda in 1603 (executions 250) Wurzburg from 1626 onwards (executions 900) and Bamberg at the same time (executions 600). The characteristics of these atrocities were spurious evidence, confession after torture, ducking, and execution by burning. (Total executions in Germany were around 26,000, France 5000, Switzerland 400, and eastern Europe 10,000.)

Protestant examples included York in England from 1567 and East Anglia thanks to the infamous witch-hunter Matthew Hopkins (total executions in England over 1000) and Fife and East Lothian in Scotland from 1590 (total executions in Scotland probably up to 1000) when witch-hunting was encouraged by the paranoid King James VI. Scotland had another outbreak of witch fever in the 1640s when the Church of Scotland became obsessed with punishing all forms of sin and elderly women experimenting with herbal remedies might find themselves being investigated by the prickers and often executed. Similarly, Denmark and

Torsaker in Sweden had outbreaks from 1675 (total executions in Scandinavia around 1600).

Overall estimates of burnings once soared to a million-plus but are now more conservatively reckoned to be between 35,000 and 80,000. Basically, it was a heady mixture of ill-informed religious prejudice, superstition and general resentment.

One of the other persecutions of minorities was the renewed attack on the Jews, which in some areas was a virtual war. After the Reconquista of Spain and Portugal was completed in 1492, there came an obsessive desire for ethnic cleansing against both Jews and Muslims, characterised by enforced conversion to Christianity followed by rigid tests, torture, execution or compulsory emigration. This led to a further Jewish diaspora, since the Jews formed a significant portion of Spain's population and a similar forcing out of the Moors. Martin Luther condoned a renewal of the anti-Semitism in Germany which had been rife during the Crusades and the Hundred Years War period, when Jews had been blamed for the Black Death.

'The hammer of witches which destroyeth witches and their heresy as with a two-edged sword.'
Kramer and Sprenger, *Malleus Maleficarum*

'... that priest whose name was Martin Luther – may his body and soul be bound up in hell – who wrote many heretical books in which he said that whoever would help the Jews was doomed to perdition.'
Rabbi Josel of Rosheim

PART THREE

THE EARLY MODERN PERIOD

'The Thirty Years War [was] a catastrophe which plunged a large area of central Europe into an abyss of barbarism and misery.'

H. A. L. Fisher, *History of Europe*

21

THE REFORMATION –
CATHOLICS VERSUS
PROTESTANTS

'Both Philip (II) and his soldiers looked upon it (the Armada,
1588) as a religious crusade undertaken by a Catholic army
against a people whom Philip persistently
described as rebels and heretics.'

John Elliott, *Imperial Spain*

The first major rebellion attributable to the Reformation was the
German Peasants' War of 1524–5. Even before Luther started
preaching, tracts had been appearing such as *The Book of
a Hundred Chapters* in 1501, which demanded religious and
economic freedoms for the Germans. In 1517 Martin Luther
launched his scathing attack on the indulgences by nailing his
Ninety-Five Theses to the door at Wittenberg, which attracted
immediate support at all levels. In 1522 came the so-called
Knights' Revolt, partly inspired by the new preaching but with
other motivations attributable to a struggling baronial class. Two
years later the Peasants' War was the largest anywhere in Europe
before the French Revolution and eventually boasted as many as
300,000 fighting men in the field. Though Luther himself was
reluctant to support such aggression and later condemned it,
other preachers like Thomas Münster were supportive. It spread
from the Black Forest to the Danube and soon degenerated, the
Massacre of Weinsberg by the peasants in 1521 being an example,
when seventy or so nobles were forced to run the gauntlet of pikes,

a form of execution. This gave the authorities a justification for similar atrocities. In the end some 100,000 rebels were killed with very minor casualties among the landsknecht. However, we must recognise that a mixture of economic resentments fuelled dislike of the Catholic establishment, which had become associated with wealth and corruption.

Ten years after the Peasants' War came the occupation of Münster by the Anabaptists in 1534. Again, religion and economic pressures came together; once prosperous Anabaptist merchants had fled persecution by the Spaniards in the Netherlands and suffered a temporary slump in the textile trade, so they sought asylum behind the walls of Münster. They came under the leadership of two extraordinary men. The first, Jan Matthys of Harlem, unlike previous Anabaptists, was not a pacifist but 'taught that the righteous must themselves take up the sword and actively prepare the way for the Millennium by wielding it against the unrighteous' (Norman Cohn). He and his successor John Bockelson (1509–1536) turned Münster into a fortified egalitarian Utopia that soon degenerated into a dictatorship under John, who roused the populace to hysteria with his rantings and supposed visions of himself as the new Messiah. He eventually abolished all private property except his own, and encouraged polygamy and compulsory rebaptism. In response the local bishop recruited troops from the Rhineland and began a siege of the city, waiting for the population to starve. Many starved to death or were massacred after marching out to surrender. John was tortured to death.

While Luther had been lukewarm about the use of war to help the Protestant cause, the teachings of John Calvin (1509–1564), or at least the way they were interpreted by his fanatical propagandists, were more aggressive. Calvin approved the Just or Godly War in his *Institutes* 'such even the Holy Spirit in many passages of Scripture declares to be lawful.' Soon there was bitter rivalry between the two main Protestant sects, the Lutherans taking over bishoprics as a going concern in the North, the Calvinists rejecting bishops altogether, promising hell-fire and communion in a wooden mug. Lutherans responded with 'The Calvinist dragon is pregnant with all the horrors of Mohammedanism.' Thus, with Lutherans, Anabaptists and

Calvinists all actively spreading their word against each other as well as against the Catholic establishment, Germany was in ferment. Religion became a focus for the independent-minded of all classes, whilst the Hapsburg emperors became identified with oppressive Catholicism. In addition, there were more extreme reformers like the Swiss Pastor Ulrich Zwingli (1484–1531) who was particularly strong against idolatry, spoke out against fasting during Lent and disapproved of Luther. Something of a Swiss nationalist, he started a food blockade against the Catholic cantons that developed into a war in 1531 and led to his death in battle near Zurich. Similarly, there was the belligerent radical Nicholas Storch and the other Zwickau prophets, who were condemned by Luther as schwärmer (dreamers) and who retaliated with mob violence in Wittenberg.

In Germany Luther's ideas had continued to win support from senior establishment figures such as John Frederick, who became sole Elector of Saxony in 1542 and leader of the Schmalkaldic League of Protestant princes. For the previous twenty years the Emperor Charles V had underestimated the threat posed by Luther since his effort to seek common ground back in 1521 at the Diet of Worms, and he had been too preoccupied with other affairs, leaving Germany to his brother Ferdinand to look after. As a king of Spain who initially could not speak Spanish he had had problems from the start of his reign, combining the almost impossible role of controlling both the newly united territories of Spain, his birthplace Flanders and Burgundy and the Vienna-based Holy Roman Empire. As a teenage king in Castile he had been faced with the Comuneros Rebellion, an expression of Spanish disgust at having to accept a new king of German and Burgundian ancestry who could not speak their language. Though not a religious rebellion, it was latterly led by a churchman, Antonia de Acuna, the warrior Bishop of Zamora. His amateur militia was defeated at the Battle of Villalar in 1521.

It was in the tradition even of Catholic clergy sometimes to support popular movements or oppose the imperial power; just one of the many problems Charles V had to tackle during his complex reign. Having been preoccupied with his wars with the French and the Turks it was not until the 1540s that Charles brought Germany to the top of his agenda. He had also had a minor scare when reports came in of a few Lutheran groups in Spain itself. Then to add to his to-do list there had been the Council of Trent and serious efforts to reform the Catholic Church.

At the Battle of Mühlberg in 1547 the Catholic princes of Germany aided by Spanish troops and Hungarian cavalry and led (despite an attack of gout) by the Emperor Charles V routed the Protestants of the Schmalkaldic League. The casualties seem to have been a mere 7000 but among them were several princes of small Protestant statelets and several others were captured, including John Frederick of Saxony, whose ambitious brother Maurice had been on the Catholic side and now took over all his sibling's territories. While it was a resounding victory for the imperial side and a severe blow to the Protestants, it made little lasting difference except perhaps to help consolidate the fault lines between those German statelets that were mainly Catholic and those which were mainly Protestant. The harsh persecution of Protestants that came after the battle simply served to stiffen resistance. As we shall see, the violence was to continue until the holocaust of 1618–48, the Thirty Years War, which also in the end provided no resolution. If apportioning blame, it might be fair to suggest that it was 60 per cent politico-economic and 40 per cent religious, but religion was the starting point and the edges were blurred.

The build-up of sectarian violence in France began with Henri II's (1519-1559) campaign of persecution against the Huguenots in Paris and southern France during 1534 after Calvinist missionaries had concentrated their efforts in those regions. A series of burnings at the stake simply added to the hostility and 10,000 sought asylum in Geneva where they were further radicalised, ready for their return to cause trouble in France. The conflict was often within and not between communities, as when the Calvinist peasants of the Baron de Fumel rebelled and killed him when he forbade them to attend their own church services. In 1562 came the massacre of Calvinists at Vassy by the Catholic leaders, the Guises, and ten years later the eruption of violence in Paris on St Bartholomew's Day.

The Calvinists persecuted by the last Valois kings were lucky to have a number of able professional soldiers on their side, several of them undoubtedly sincere Huguenots. Among these were Louis Prince of Condé who was killed at Jarnac, and Gaspard de Coligny, murdered during the massacre of St Bartholomew. Slightly less sincere were the father and son Bourbons, Antoine, who changed sides at least twice and his son, the future Henri IV, who certainly favoured Calvinism – but famously not if it cost him his capital ('Paris is worth a mass.').

Eight French Wars of Religion 1562–95 were disastrous and inconclusive, costing an estimated 800,000 lives, the destruction of nine cities and huge debt. Despite numerous victories by both sides there was never a definite result. The Battle of Dreux in 1552 was a Catholic victory with some 8000 deaths. Before Jarnac in 1569 Pope Pius V wrote that 'his enemies should be massacred and totally exterminated' and his wishes came close to fulfilment there, but still the Huguenots came back for more. Ironically, after the so-called war of The Three Henris, the last Valois king, Henri III, champion of the Catholic side, was murdered by an extremist Catholic, a Dominican friar 'doing the work of the Lord'. He was succeeded without violence by his legitimate heir and arch-rival Henri IV (1553–1610) who on and off had led the Protestant or Huguenot faction and was excommunicated by Pope Sixtus VI in 1587 during one of his many lapses. The third Henri was the Duc de Guise who in 1576 founded the extreme French Catholic League that intended to wipe out Protestantism in France.

The new king, having won several key battles before his accession and two against the Catholic League after it, Arques and Ivry, could subsequently never quite eliminate the Catholics or capture their greatest stronghold, Paris, so in the end as a realist he changed religions, thus reuniting France and its capital as a Catholic nation. Tolerance for Protestants was guaranteed for the time being by the Edict of Nantes.

Even after that there was continued bloodshed in the name of religion, for Spain had supported die-hard Catholics with an invasion from the south in 1594 and pockets of dissatisfied Huguenots survived in towns like La Rochelle, which underwent a prolonged siege by Richelieu's troops begun in 1627 (v. Pt 3 Chapter 25). One of Henri IV's senior ministers, Pomponne de Bellièvre, suggested somewhat naively that the Protestants and

Catholics should give up fighting each other and join forces against the Muslims in a new Crusade.

The third main area for post-Reformation religious conflict was in the Netherlands. The Eighty Years War 1568–1648 melded the ideas of religious and political independence and was provoked by the persecution inflicted by Spanish governors, particularly the Duke of Alba, installed by Philip II (1527–1598). The problems really began after the abdication of the Emperor Charles V. He had experimented with drastic persecution of Protestants in his early years. He had some 1300 executed between 1523 and 1566 but began to temper his zeal as he grew older. His son Philip II who took over the Spanish and Netherlands regions of the Empire was more fanatical and renewed the death penalty for heretics, and at the same time reorganised the Catholic hierarchy in the Netherlands, to the disgust of the locals. Driven not just by their religious views but also hatred of the heavy taxation imposed by Spain and the brutality of the Spanish army-of-occupation, the Dutch felt driven to extremes. With a wide mix of Lutherans, Calvinists and Anabaptists they were far from united, but in 1566 the *Beeldenstorm*, a mass destruction of Catholic churches and their images by enraged mobs, presaged the outbreak of real fighting. A small Calvinist army was defeated and the survivors executed at Oosterweel the next year. At this point Alba took over and began a ruthless crackdown, whilst almost at the same time young William the Silent of Orange (1533–1584), who had previously been a government official, resigned and went into exile, positioning himself as a future rebel leader.

Initially the rebel forces were untrained volunteers, nicknamed *Geuzen* (Beggars) or more famously *Wassergeuzen* (Sea Beggars), one of whose slogans was *Liver Turks dan Paaps* –better Turks (Muslim Ottomans) than Catholics. But as the long war developed it became increasingly a conflict of mercenaries on both sides and long sieges rather than set-piece battles. The subsequent sacking of several cities by the Spaniards simply made the Dutch more defiant. The war was marked by brutality and economic devastation. It was the Antwerp area that suffered most, owing to a Dutch blockade of the river, whilst Amsterdam began to thrive, helped by an influx of able Anabaptist entrepreneurs, thus paving the way for the Golden Age of Holland. Any estimate of total casualties is difficult and figures vary from 240,000 to 1,400,000. The result was the survival of Protestantism in the northern part of the Netherlands and of Catholicism in the south, the area now known as Belgium. It was a war provoked by religious feelings and religious persecution but with a strong admixture of nationalism. Had the Spaniards not been so obsessively anti-Protestant, the Dutch might have tolerated the other aspects of Spanish rule.

In England, Robert Earl of Leicester (1532–1588), a prominent favourite of Queen Elizabeth's, was, unlike her, a fervent Puritan. He was such an admirer of the Dutch revolt against the Spanish Catholics that he mortgaged his estates to pay for a private army that he led to the Netherlands to join in the fighting. He was aided by another well-respected English Puritan, Philip Sidney, who was killed fighting the Spaniards at Zutphen in 1586. Leicester became a close friend of William of Orange, claiming that he was involved 'for God's care and her Majesty's'. Elizabeth was in the end far from pleased, particularly when he was offered the post of governor general of the United Provinces; the last thing she wanted was for England to be involved in a war with Spain. But by that time Philip II had made his mind up that England would have to be subdued if he wanted to keep Holland. For Philip of Spain one of the main reasons for attacking the English was the fact that they were hindering his efforts to suppress Protestantism in Holland. His brief marriage to Elizabeth's sister, the rigidly Catholic Queen Mary, should have solved all his problems, for if he had fathered a child with her he could have added England to his empire. But she had died and his plans had come to nothing.

It was becoming apparent that Spain was losing the battle against international Protestantism and a plan had been put forward by the Marquis of Santa Cruz in 1583 to build a special fleet for an invasion of England 'that would bring the *Dutch* to their knees' at a cost of under 4 million ducats. Spanish priests were encouraged to motivate the populace with a return to the crusading zeal of the reconquista. The Jesuit priest Ribadeneyra wrote 'Every pretext for a just and holy war is to be found in this campaign.' The sinking by gunfire or storms of some fifty ships of the 130-strong Armada can be blamed ultimately on a heady mix of religious fanaticism and imperialism. For the English it was a boost for the self-confidence of the new Anglican version of Lutheranism and the Calvinist minority. For the Dutch it was an opportunity to embark on creating a Protestant overseas empire to balance the huge extension of Catholicism in the Americas.

In Britain itself the wars of the Reformation period were relatively minor. The deposition and expulsion of Mary Queen of Scots involved one full-scale battle at Langside in 1568 and the main causes were her unfashionable adherence to Catholicism and the fanatical preaching of the Calvinists. But there were other factors such as the rumours that she had been involved in the murder of her second husband, Henry Darnley, and had married a third husband with indecent haste. For the Scottish Calvinists, Langside was part of a holy war.

In England there were a number of serious armed confrontations, but none of them dignified with the title of war. The Lincolnshire Rising of 1536 led by a monk and a cobbler was specifically in response to the dissolution of the monasteries by Henry VIII and his break with the Pope in Rome, but there were also underlying economic issues. It involved up to 40,000 rebels but they were dissuaded from further action by the authorities and later their leaders were executed. Similarly, the Pilgrimage of Grace centred on York under the leadership of a prominent lawyer called Aske, again around 40,000 joined him and again they were appeased temporarily, allowing time for dispersal and the subsequent execution of over 200 of their leaders including Aske, several ex-abbots and some local barons. The third of this series was Bigod's Catholic rebellion in Northumberland, with a similar outcome including the burning of one woman at the stake.

The incipient civil war of 1553 between supporters of Lady Jane Grey and Mary Tudor undoubtedly had religion as a significant factor, as did Wyatt's rebellion of 1554, which was essentially a protest by Protestants against the religious policies of Queen Mary, particularly her marriage to Philip II of Spain and a possible integration of England into the Spanish Empire. Wyatt gathered an army at Rochester and marched on London, but there it was dispersed and some 90 of the leaders were executed.

The future Queen Elizabeth, at this time a prisoner, nearly suffered the same fate. The Northern Earls' Rebellion of 1569 was by contrast a Catholic initiative attempting to depose Queen Elizabeth, who had been excommunicated by Pope Pius V, and to replace her with Mary Queen of Scots. At least 600 of the rebels were subsequently executed.

Ireland also had its share of religious clashes at this time though there were underlying political ambitions as well. The Fitzgerald or Geraldine Rebellion of 1534 had been against the religious and political policies of Henry VIII. Fitzgerald failed to capture Dublin Castle, he lost the backing of the church and the rebellion fizzled out. The same family were behind the two Desmond Rebellions of 1569–3 and 1579–83, which had encouragement from the pope and which resulted in a scorched earth suppression by the English and an estimated death toll in Munster from famine of some 30,000, as well as a plague that ravaged Cork.

The aftermath of this ethnic cleansing in Ireland was an influx of English Protestant land holders or 'plantations'. In the north Tyrone's Rebellion or the Nine Years War 1594–1603 was more political than religious, but still had Catholicism as a unifying motive. Led by the ambitious Hugh O'Neill it kept an army of 18,000 English soldiers occupied for nearly a decade at huge expense and cost the lives of some 30,000, mostly due to disease. Irish deaths were probably around twice that number including between 25,000 and 40,000 during the Ulster famine of 1602–3 caused by scorched earth tactics. As in Munster, when a peace was arranged, this time by James I, it was followed by repopulation with Protestant immigrants mainly from Scotland, with the declared objective of 'rooting out papism'. Ireland was turned into a bi-sectarian island with religious fault-lines that have lasted for more than 400 years.

There was one other significant military by-product of the Reformation. Martin Luther was a powerful publicist at the dawn of the print era and the fact that he recycled medieval anti-Semitism in his *On the Jews and their Lies* published in 1543 had lasting impact. Describing them as 'full of the devil's faeces', he said that all Jews were heretics and recommended they be turned into agricultural slaves or driven out of Germany. It was a text that was to regain credence after 1918 as the Germans looked around for someone to blame for their defeat. This tied in precisely with Hitler's objectives.

One of the stranger by-products of the French wars of religion was the war between Huguenot emigrants and Catholic Portuguese in Brazil. John Calvin himself was involved in 1557 in recommending the establishment of a Calvinist colony in Brazil and the building of Fort Coligny on a small island off what soon afterwards became the town of Rio de Janeiro. The Portuguese governor of Brazil, Man de Sa, reacted by attacking the island with a large fleet and driving out the French Protestants in 1567. There was a later intrusion in Brazil by the French in 1612, this time blessed by the Capuchin friars. Three years later they were defeated and expelled by the Portuguese.

'The wars of religion erupted in a society long divided by social hierarchy and deference.'

Mark Holt, *French Wars of Religion*

21

THE NEW WORLD – CATHOLICS VERSUS AZTECS, INCAS AND OTHERS

'Aztec war was very ceremonial and fought in a spirit quite
different from the realistic calculation of European strife.'
G. C. Valliant, *The Aztecs of Mexico*

In 1518 when Hernando Cortes set sail for Mexico it was just
twenty-six years since the final act of the Reconquista, the capture
of Granada from the Muslims in 1492, so the dream of glorious
battles against infidels was still strong in the memory. As William
Prescott put it in his majestic and fairly unbiased *Conquest of
Mexico*, once Columbus had opened up the sea route to the
Americas 'there was nothing that the Spanish government had
more to heart than the conversion of the Indians... the sword was
a good argument when the tongue failed... the Spanish cavalier
felt he had a high mission to accomplish as a soldier of the cross.'

In fact, Cortes had specific orders from the Emperor Charles V
(who just seven years later massacred half the population of
Rome) to bear in mind above all things – even the search for
gold – that 'the object that the Spanish monarch had most at
heart was the conversion of the Indians.' Thus Cortes, who was
an insecure adventurer desperate to make a fortune for himself,
clung to the crusading ideal as his motivation and was deeply
shocked when he first saw pagan religions in Cozumel. It was
here in Tabasco where to war cries of St Jago and San Pedro
he won his first victory against a vastly larger army of Aztecs.

Afterwards, the Conquistadors allegedly said, 'Heaven must have fought on our side since our own strength could never have prevailed against such a multitude of enemies.' This battle shattered the confidence of the Aztecs and increased that of the Castilians, so it set in motion not just the conquest of Mexico for the Catholic faith but, as the process was repeated, it resulted in the whole of Central and South America being forcibly converted to Christianity. Camargo wrote in his *History of Tlaxcala*, 'The prowess of the Spaniards, the white gods (*Los Dioses blancos*) as they were often called made them to be thought invincible.' The apparently insignificant battle at Cozumel changed the whole balance of world religions for the next half a millennium. Up to that point Islam might have been regarded as the religion more likely to achieve world dominance and Protestantism might have been a greater empire builder than Catholicism. So Cozumel ranks perhaps just behind Saxa Rubra and Abu Badr in the list of battles with a long-term religious outcome.

The religion of the Aztecs that Cortes set out to destroy (whilst at the same time taking possession of their gold) was also their own main reason for making war. Perhaps due to the unstable nature of their earthquake-prone terrain and their bouts of freak weather, the Aztecs had become obsessed with punitive disasters sent from on high. Their response was to commit themselves to high numbers of human sacrifices. To meet their targets, often tens of thousands for a single new temple inauguration, they needed large numbers of prisoners of war. So even if they had no other reason for waging war against their neighbours, they did so – sometimes by mutual agreement – to top up the numbers required for immolation. Their neighbouring Nahua-speaking Toltecs were neither ethnically nor religiously very different from themselves but had been settled longer in the region and did not have quite such an aggressive or paranoid attitude to their state religion. 'A great object of their military expeditions was to gather hecatombs of prisoners for his (Moctezuma's) altars' (William H. Prescott). It was one of the most perverse examples of religious warfare in the whole of human history.

So not only was promoting their religion one of the overriding motivations for the military build-up of the Aztec state, but the massacre of prisoners to appease their blood-thirsty gods was an added incentive for making war. As Valliant puts it, 'Revenge, defence and economic motives were inextricably mixed with the need for the sacrificial victims requisite for the proper adoration of their gods ... battles were treated as an earthly re-enactment of the titanic struggles of gods.' Thus many of their wars became pre-organised rituals conducted in ceremonial dress and with the emphasis on self-sacrifice from both sides, not martial proficiency. Hence when there were no other motives for a war they staged the so-called War of Flowers. The losers in these battles were whenever possible kept as prisoners for sacrificial ceremonies, were treated with honour and guaranteed a good afterlife.

The Aztecs in their own rather peculiar way had been remarkably successful in creating a dynamic and sophisticated new state in unpromising conditions, driven to aggressive war by an obsessive devotion to their gods. Yet despite their prowess they fell remarkably easy victims to a tiny Spanish force whose superior weaponry cannot alone account for their victory. To some extent the Aztecs were victims of their own psychosis and the family squabbles of King Moctezuma II (1466–1520). At battles like Otumba in 1520 as many as 200,000 may have been slaughtered by very much smaller numbers of Spanish opponents and similar huge numbers were noted in the capture of their capital Tenochtitlan, later the site of Mexico City.

The reasons for the similar success of Francisco Pizarro (1478–1541) in defeating with his hugely outnumbered army the substantial Inca empire are equally hard to explain, though again family quarrels at the top played their part. For the Incas had huge momentum from the rapid conquest of numerous neighbouring states stretching right down the east coast of South America and into its mountainous hinterland. They had achieved this with a relatively small but elite army to which they then conscripted recruits from each new colony that they acquired ready for the next tranche of conquests. The level of religious motivation in this was considerable.

Inca religion had four vaguely interlocking strands. The official faith was sun worship, as in so many other states. The chief Inca at the time was Atahualpa (d. 1533), a direct descendant of the Sun God and infallible, rather like the emperors of Japan, so as in Japan emperor/sun worship was the main driving force of their empire-building. As each new colony was conquered new state temples were erected to create imperial conformity. Alongside this, to provide spiritual comfort for the Inca elite, was the domestic worship of the creation god Viracocha Kon Tiki. Beneath this level were the regional religions of each colony, which were allowed to continue but with the regional gods incorporated into the imperial sun-cult. Finally, the lowest tier consisted of the numerous localised cults, which were again incorporated without persecution under the umbrella of the state religion. Thus the Incas avoided trampling on the many mini-religions of their conquered subjects, and instead aimed not just to tolerate but embrace them, so that the new citizens were motivated to work and fight for their new masters. The system was extremely successful but, as with the Aztecs, the Spanish invasion of Peru coincided with family dysfunctionality at the top: Atahualpa had only recently snatched his brother's throne. Hence Pizarro's remarkable victories at Cajamarca in 1532 and again at Cuzco in 1537, the downfall of Atahualpa and 'bringing word of the true God'.

Thus a vast area of Central and South America was easily conquered by the Spanish and Portuguese Catholics. The Portuguese also drove out Christian colonists from Brazil, both Catholic French and Protestant Dutch, the French having been defeated by Mem de Sà who founded Rio de Janeiro in 1567. The ethnic religions rapidly collapsed as the populations were decimated by imported European diseases and by the ruthless, genocidal exploitation of the workforce by the new Spanish and Portuguese masters.

The Spanish conquistadors were undoubtedly mainly motivated by greed but probably also quite genuinely believed that they were doing God's work. In their wake came substantial numbers of priests who had every intention of making sure that the religious follow-up of the conquests was efficient and effective. It was claimed that up to eight million of the native Americans were converted. The task was made easier by the fact that the quarter of a million or so Spaniards and Portuguese who emigrated to the new colonies thrived and stayed Catholic, whilst the aboriginal inhabitants died in huge numbers from European diseases or overwork. It was also made easier by subtle appeals to the native Americans using images not too far away from their old gods, as for example when the

Virgin of Guadeloupe made her first appearance in 1531 and could be usefully identified with the Aztec goddess Tonatzin.

By comparison the efforts at Catholic missionary work in North America were much less obvious, though the activity of the French Jesuits under men like Jean de Brebeuf among the Huron confederacy of Canada did create violent outcomes, which, together with the arrival of European infectious diseases, took a serious toll on the indigenous population.

Equally the Pequot War in New England (1636–1638) was mainly fought because of pressures on the fur trade and food supplies but the Puritan colonists were undoubtedly guilty of massacring the Pequot Indians in considerable numbers and selling others into slavery. The genocidal behaviour of the Puritans was later justified by preachers such as Increase Mather and his son Cotton Mather (1663–1728), both of them also responsible for witch hunts.

'But kings and peoples must sometimes take up arms to execute such public vengeance. On this basis we may judge wars lawful.'

John Calvin, *Institutes* IV20

23

PORTUGUESE CATHOLICS AGAINST ISLAM AND SHINTO

'...for him, conversion and enslavement were
interchangeable terms.'
Peter Russell, *Prince Henry the Navigator*

If the Spaniards were partly inspired to conquer the Americas by
their experience of the Reconquista it is reasonable to suggest
that the Portuguese expansion in Africa and Asia had a similar
religious component. Its first great pioneer, Prince Henry the
Navigator (1394–1460), was a junior member of the Portuguese
royal dynasty and took part as a young man in the conquest of
the Moroccan city of Ceuta in 1415, the beginning of Portugal's
overseas expansion and seen at the time as a mini-crusade.
Subsequently Henry made it his life's work to explore the
African Atlantic coast, destroying Muslim pirate ships with the
justification of reclaiming Christian prisoners from the Muslims
and converting some of the crews.

Once Henry's caravels began to probe farther down the African
coast the opportunities for profits from the slave and commodity
trades led to the occupation of Madeira from 1419 and the Azores
from 1427. It was then a question of capturing the various Muslim
trading posts down the coast of Morocco and Mauretania, reaching
Senegal by 1441 and providing Portugal with the beginnings of a
highly profitable overseas empire where most of the groundwork
had been done by enterprising Muslim traders. This brutal empire-
building was justified as a back-up of the Portuguese crusade

against Islam nearer home and was characterised at times by gratuitous violence; Vasco da Gama once deliberately blew up a shipload of over 300 pilgrims heading for Mecca.

This process accelerated with the contributions of the aggressive Admiral Alfonso de Albuquerque (1453–1515) who followed up the exploratory voyages of Vasco da Gama by occupying ports on the Malabar coast in 1503 and capturing the Muslim port of Goa, with encouragement from the local Hindus. Preliminary settlements in Cochin and Colombo soon followed and by 1511 the Portuguese had taken Malacca.

Albuquerque's near contemporary, the similarly aggressive Francisco de Almeida (1460–1510) began mopping-up operations and plundered prosperous Muslim trading posts on the African east coast, where most of the traders were of Omani or Yemeni extraction. Having passed the Cape of Good Hope, he captured Kilwa and burned down the major Arab-held port of Mombassa, killing most of the inhabitants. Appointed governor of India with a mission to take over the spice trade, he pioneered bases in Bombay, Cochin, Calcutta and Jaffna, in each case aiming to supplant Muslim trading posts. This provoked retaliation by a Muslim coalition led by the Ottoman Turks with support from the Egyptian Mamluks and the Sultan of Gujarat, but he won a major victory over their combined fleets in the seas off the Indian port of Diu in Gujarat in 1509. This could be seen as the beginning of what is referred to as the Ottoman-Portuguese War and though it was really just a commercial struggle for control of the highly lucrative spice trade, it was marked by atrocities that left behind an accretion of anti-Christian feelings.

Whilst the majority of trading ports that formed this new maritime empire had been taken from Muslim settlers and caused particular resentment to the Ottomans as the main Muslim super-power, the Portuguese also grabbed toeholds in China-Macau and Japan. It was in Japan that the Portuguese Jesuits inadvertently caused their only major war of religion. It had been the scene of one of their most successful efforts to convert the local people, a mixture of Buddhists and Shinto, to Christianity, but at the same time they became involved in politics, supporting Christian Japanese daimyos against non-Christian rivals as a means of extending their mission. A group of Christian samurai helped in the defence of Osaka Castle in 1615. This military-political involvement became even more ambitious during the leadership of the Italian Jesuit Alessandro Valignano (1539–1606) who advocated the use of Christian Japanese soldiers armed with Portuguese weaponry to help conquer China for Christianity. It was he who fortified the city of Nagasaki as a militant Jesuit base after the region had been overrun by Omura Sumitala, a Japanese Christian whom the Jesuits had backed in his feud with the Ryuzoji clan in the 1580s. Such Japanese barons were able to coerce their peasant underlings into accepting Christianity, so by 1570 there were an estimated 130,000 converts. Another Jesuit, Francisco Cabral (1529–1609), was similarly aggressive. The Jesuits showed no tolerance for Christians of other denominations: they recommended that some Dutch Protestant merchants should be crucified as pirates, a suggestion the Japanese rejected.

The mission was too successful for the peace of mind of the Japanese authorities, including the regent Toyotomi Hideyoshi (1536–98). A number of powerful Zen Buddhists felt undermined and retaliated with a massacre of Christians followed later by the expulsion of all foreign traders except for a tiny Dutch enclave at Nagasaki. This period of violence in turn provoked a Christian rebellion engendered not just by religious persecution but also the current economic climate, so the Jesuits were not entirely to blame. The Shimabara rebellion in 1637 was led by fifteen-year-old Amakusa Shiro Tokisada (1621–38), referred to as 'heaven's messenger'. It ended in a crushing defeat in which 37,000 Christian Japanese were massacred.

The long-term effect of the Jesuit campaign was to cause a Shinto/Buddhist counter-offensive that led to the virtual elimination of Christianity in Japan. Perhaps even more importantly, the drastic clamp-down on foreigners entering the country isolated it from the rest of the world for more than 200 years from 1639 until 1853. When the 'Black ships' of the US Navy suddenly entered Edo Bay that year, they brought with them military technology of which the Japanese had been unaware, or at least had ignored. This display of nautical fire-power was a shock for the now outdated military class of samurai and the conservative shoguns. This led to the Meiji Revolution, the frenetic rearming of Japan and ninety years of Shinto-led empire-building to make up for lost time. So, while it may seem extreme to blame the Jesuit missionary campaign of the early seventeenth century for Pearl Harbor in 1941 or Hiroshima in 1945 there is a connecting thread.

Meanwhile back at home King Sebastian of Portugal began a somewhat ill-prepared crusade against the Muslims of Morocco where he was supposedly helping the deposed Sultan Abu Abdullah to regain his throne. It ended in disastrous defeat at Alcazarquivir in 1578, the Battle of the Three Kings, with 8000 killed including the childless King Sebastian. Portugal was almost bankrupt and soon as a result to lose its independence to the acquisitive Philip II of Spain.

Some ninety years later however, a revived Portugal was able to wage a successful war for mainly commercial reasons against the semi-Catholicised Congolese. The Battle of Ambuila (Mbwila) in 1665 demonstrated superior European firepower, causing around 5000 deaths and securing the new colony of Angola.

The Portuguese had also come up against the Protestant British and for the British East India Company based in London, both Catholics and Muslims were the opposition. Founded in 1601 as a monopoly trading company it had a largely Puritan board of directors and soon started recruiting chaplains who helped 'to guard the morals and morale of their operation' (Daniel O'Connor). Certainly, the religious legitimation of the Company's aggressive expansion did help motivate the private army which it used, and its representatives were soon identifying divine agency in their fighting off Portuguese rivals on the Indian coast. Captain John Weddell referring to the sinking of some Portuguese ships in 1630 commented 'thus it pleased God to curb their pride' and their ambassador in Delhi Sir Thomas Rowe wrote of 'the power of God against rebellious atheists'. The gradual conquest of the Indian sub-continent by the British East India Company and its profiteering from the opium trade were thus given some legitimacy by the patronage of the Anglican Church.

One of the other terrible aspects of Portuguese colonisation was the setting up in 1560 by Francis Xavier of the Goa Inquisition, which was to last more than 200 years. Its main role was to inflict severe punishment, sometimes burning at the stake, on all ex-Hindus whose conversion to Christianity was suspected of being superficial.

'The Portuguese justified their actions ... seizing ports like Zanzibar and Kilwa from the Muslims as part of a Christian crusade, acts that could be described as crimes against humanity.'
John Reader, *Africa*

Japanese 1942 war propaganda poster showing Buddhist support for Japanese 'Holy War' against the United States of America.

bruno. eodem die unipfo monaf, terio uibente papa tria untrib' pmuf cancellis facrarunt alta ria. Tunc papa uñ facñdo nuf fafq; agendo. p' alia falutis hc taïnta. corl epif g cardinalibuf multozq; pfonif. huiemodi .... habiur adpñin.

tutelamq; commendauit. nili deo et beato Petro eiufq; uica rus. romanif fcilicet pontificat' Auox numero uel ordini duuna me dignatio licet indignum af fociauit. me olim monachum priozenq; monafteru huuif. fub domno ac uenerabili hugone

Pope Urban II, who launched the Crusades at Clermont in 1095 with the slogan *Deus Vult*, 'God wills it'.

George W. Bush was portrayed as a crusader when he launched the invasion of Iraq and in turn Islamist groups condemned the Americans as 'evil crusaders'.

Vladimir Putin gave huge support to the Orthodox Church, which in return gave moral support to his war in the Ukraine. Pictured here is Patriarch Kirill greeting Putin.

A 1940 Wehrmacht uniform button still displays the Prussian war slogan of *Gott mit Uns*, God is with us, first used in 1701. (Courtesy of BrokenSphere under Creative Commons Share-Alike 3.0 Unported)

The same motto appears on this royal standard backing Bismark's war against France in 1870. (Courtesy of Trajan 117 under Creative Commons Share-Alike 3.0 Unported)

The hugely significant Battle of Milvian Bridge or Saxa Rubra in AD 312 was exploited retrospectively by the Emperor Constantine to justify his taking control of Christianity and making it part of the imperial infrastructure. (Courtesy of the Rijksmuseum)

The even more important Battle of Abu Badr or Uhud in 620, in which Mohammed's tiny army defeated the pagans of Mecca, thus ensuring the survival and expansion of Islam. (Courtesy of The David Collection)

The Battle of Karbala in 680 was the first great clash between what became the Sunni and Shiite factions of Islam. (Courtesy of the Brooklyn Museum)

The Siege of Acre during the Third Crusade was notable for what would now be termed war crimes. (Courtesy of the British Library)

Above: The Battle of Grunwald or Tannenberg in 1410 was part of an ongoing struggle between the Crusader Teutonic Knights and the Catholic kingdom of Poland.

Left: The Battle of Kosovo in 1388, a turning point in the conquest of the Christian Balkan states by the Muslim Ottoman Turks.

Left: The Battle of Mühlberg in 1547 was the first full-scale confrontation between the Catholics and Protestants. It was a Catholic victory but had no lasting effect. (Courtesy of the Rijksmuseum)

Below: After the Battle of White Mountain in 1620, fought between Bohemian Protestants and Austrian Catholics in the first major event of the Thirty Years War, twenty-seven leaders of the Bohemian Protestants were executed in what is known as the Old Town Square. Twenty-seven crosses mark the spot today. (Courtesy of Julie Otten)

A depiction in the *Theatrum Europaeum* of the Sack of Magdeburg, scene of some of the worst atrocities of the Thirty Years War.

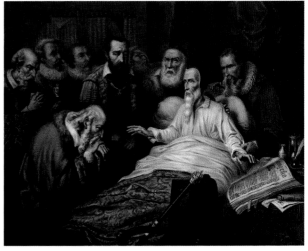

Above left: Martin Luther, the Protestant reformer who nailed his Ninety-Five Theses to the door of All Saints' Church in Wittenberg on 31 October 1517. (Courtesy of the Rijksmuseum)

Above right: John Calvin, the other key Protestant reformer. Having fled to Switzerland in the face of anti-Protestant violence in France, in 1536 he published his seminal *Institutes of the Christian Religion*. (Courtesy of the Wellcome Collection)

The Emperor Charles V, who waged war against the Lutherans in Germany. (Courtesy of the Metropolitan Museum of Art)

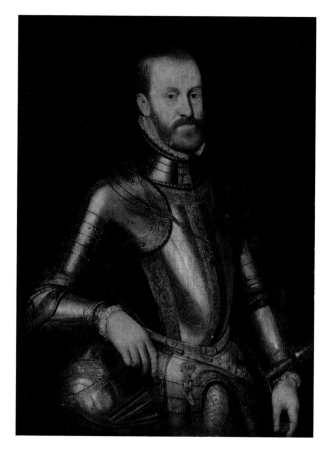

Charles V's son, King Philip II of Spain, who took the main lead in the Eighty Years War against the Calvinists in the Netherlands and with his Armada launched a 'Holy War' against Protestant England. (Courtesy of the Rijksmuseum)

The Emperor Ferdinand II, who wiped out the Protestants in Styria and then as Emperor presided over the worst excesses of the Thirty Years War. (Courtesy of the Metropolitan Museum of Art)

Shah Abbas, the Shiite Sultan of Persia who waged war against the Sunnis in India. (Courtesy of the Rijksmuseum)

Aurangzeb, the Mogul Emperor who persecuted Hindus, Shiite Muslims and Sikhs. (Courtesy of the Metropolitan Museum of Art)

Ayatollah Khomeini, the Shiite leader of Iran after the Iranian Revolution, who waged war against the Sunni dictatorship in Iraq.

Abu Bakr al-Baghdadi, self-styled caliph of the Islamic State.

A statue commemorating Hong Xiuquan, the self-styled brother of Jesus and leader of the Taiping Rebellion, the costliest religious war of all time. (Courtesy of Jakob Montrasio under Creative Commons 2.0)

Taiping Regaining the Provincial Capital of Ruizhou by Wu Youru.

Above: The raid on Harpers Ferry by the religious fanatic John Brown, an event which helped trigger the American Civil War. US Marines led by Robert E. Lee storm the engine house containinig Brown and his followers. (Courtesy of the Library of Congress)

Left: Guan Yu, a Chinese general who was deified after his death as a god of war. He is immortalised in the Chinese epic *Romance of the Three Kingdoms*. (Courtesy of the Wellcome Collection)

The warrior Sikh Guru
Gobind Singh. (Courtesy of the
Wellcome collection)

Buddhist monks undergo military
training in the Japanese army
in 1930.

The Buddhas of Bamyan, two sixth-century Buddhist sculptures, were carved into a cliffside in Afghanistan. They were dynamited by the Islamist Taliban government in 2001 for being idolatrous. (Left: Courtesy of UNESCO; right: courtesy of Carl Montgomery under Creative Commons 2.0)

US Army paratroopers secure an area in Ghazni, Afghanistan. Ghazni has been a base for Sunni Islamic militarism since Subuktigin in AD 977. Operation Enduring Freedom, the war in Afghanistan, began on 7 October 2001 and is now the longest war in United States history. (Courtesy of the United States Army)

24

OTTOMAN SUNNI MUSLIMS VERSUS CHRISTIANS AND SHIITES

'The Pope opened up a correspondence with him though he might have been surprised by Bayezid's ambition to make the high altar of St Peter's a manger for his horse.'

Jason Goodwin, *Lords of the Horizons*

The Ottoman dynasty was founded by Othman (d. 1326) the leader or bey of a small fanatical clan on the hilltop frontier of Turkey. He made it a convenient and profitable duty to wage holy war or *ghazwa* against the infidel Greeks of Constantinople. He and his men were thus ghazis and his son's capture of the great Greek city of Bursa a few miles from Constantinople was the beginning of a rapid expansion into Christian territories, which by 1526 had reached Budapest.

The Koran permits a commander to take one fifth of all the booty after any conquest and in 1365 Sultan Murad I Ghazi or the Victorious (1326–1389) contrived also to take one fifth of the captives, an innovation authorised by his court theologians. Thus according to some sources he founded the regiment of janissaries who were to form the backbone of the Ottoman army as it extended its conquests into Europe. A levy of boy children from all the conquered Christian territories in the Balkans and beyond provided the raw material for what became the most efficient troops of the era. These boys were converted to Islam. The janissary marching song includes the line: 'Overwhelm the enemies of the Motherland and thus shall those cursed ones suffer abjection.'

In 1389 Murad I won the first Battle of Kosovo, which marked the downfall of yet another Christian nation, Serbia, and left a lingering antipathy between Christians and Muslims in the Balkans. The fighting was so bitter that the two armies virtually destroyed each other, causing total losses of 50 to 60,000. Some Balkan Christians, particularly Bosnians and Albanians, not only converted in significant numbers to Islam but reached high positions in the Ottoman government.

Murad's son, Bayezit I Ilderim, the Thunderbolt, continued the aggressive jihad and according to Gibbon, after his victory over the Crusaders on the Danube at Nicopolis in 1396, would have overwhelmed the rest of the Balkans but for an attack of gout. The causes of this battle lay in a break during the Hundred Years War, which suggested to Pope Boniface IX that the now idle French army should form a crusade to support the Poles and seek revenge on Bayezit. The unstable French king Charles VI, known as the Mad, saw this as a chance to pose as 'the chief Christian king'. The casualties in the battle were extremely heavy. The crusaders massacred 1000 prisoners beforehand and the Turks the same number afterwards, while up to 12,000 of both armies were slaughtered. Not long afterwards, as we have seen, Bayezit was overwhelmed by an even more aggressive Muslim warmonger, Timur the Lame.

Bayezit's grandson Murad II (1404–1451) crushed an army of treaty-breaking Polish and Bulgarian crusaders at Varna in 1444, again with heavy casualties on both sides. This battle was also the outcome of a crusade conceived by Pope Eugenius IV to take advantage of the fact that Murad had agreed to a ten-year truce and abdicated in favour of his teenage son. This crisis led to him revoking his abdication and leading his troops to victory.

The Christians tried yet again to stop the Ottoman advance, this time under the Hungarian leader John Hunyadi (1406–1456) who had been declared 'Athleta Christi – Champion of Christ' by Pope Pius II. This ended with the disaster of the Second Battle of Kosovo in 1448, which finally gave the Ottomans total control of the Balkans and left Constantinople completely surrounded by Muslim territory. To add to the crusader misery their camps were stricken by plague, which killed Hunyadi among many others, in 1456.

It was Murad's son Mehmet II who finally extinguished the Orthodox Greek Empire when he captured Constantinople in 1453. Ottoman casualties were extremely heavy owing to the number of failed assaults on the huge walls before the Turks finally broke in. Then Mehmet gave his soldiers the Islamic allowance of three days looting, in which some 30,000 inhabitants were slaughtered or enslaved. The result of this was not just to give the Ottomans a new capital, but by ending the city's role as the centre of the Orthodox Church, to give Moscow the chance to assume that position as the Third Rome (v. Pt 2 Chapter 17).

Despite being tolerant of Jews, whom they welcomed as skilled entrepreneurs from areas like Spain where they were persecuted by the Inquisition, the Ottomans had a strong antipathy towards some of their fellow Muslims, particularly the Shiites. They regarded Shiites as politically disruptive since they favoured rule by divinely appointed imams rather than the autocratic non-priestly sultans, so they regularly expelled them from Constantinople (by this time Istanbul) and its environs to the outskirts of their empire.

Selim the Grim (1465–1520) took some pleasure in his holy war against Persia and the Syrian provinces of the Mamluks. In 1513, concerned that Shiism might spread across the border, he invaded Persia and won a victory at Chaldiran (near Khoy in north western Iran) after which he massacred some 80,000 Shiites in Tabriz, but then withdrew when his own troops began to mutiny. This war was both territorial and part of Sunni/Shiite antipathy and it inaugurated a forty-year period of strife during which the Shiites, despite many losses, continued to survive.

Similarly, having ethnically cleansed the Alevi/Alawi Shites in his own heartland, some 40,000 of them, Selim was alarmed at possible contagion from the Syrian Alawis, then ruled from Cairo by the Mamluks. (For the fate of the Alawi Shiite minority and their role in the Syrian civil war of this century v. Pt 4 Chapter 40). Despite the fact that the Egyptian Mamluks were fellow Sunnis their control of the Red Sea spice trade and their possession of the holy cities Jerusalem and Mecca meant more than their religious leanings to Sultan Selim. He conquered Egypt at the battle of Ridaniya in 1517, massacred another 40,000 Shiites in the Lebanon region and added Syria to his empire. As a bonus he persuaded the exiled Abbasid caliph to hand over his title to him, thus enhancing the legitimacy of his dynasty with the title, one that of course had particular religious connotations among Muslims across his now huge empire.

His successor Caliph Suleiman the Magnificent went back to the more customary invasions of Christian territory, famously capturing the island of Rhodes from the Knights Hospitaller in 1522. He then beat the Hungarians decisively at Mohács in 1526, a battle which Hungarians still regard as a shattering blow to their independence. Their King Louis II was killed, along with some 14,000–20,000 of his soldiers and the country was split between the Ottomans and the Hapsburgs. However, even Suleiman failed to capture Vienna. By this time the Ottoman Empire was approaching its peak and Islam threatened the heartland of Europe, as it had before the battle of Tours in 720. But the end of Suleiman's long career began to reveal chinks in Muslim invincibility: in 1565 he had to admit failure in his attempts to conquer Malta and as he lay dying at the siege of Szigetvár in Hungary a year later, the losses were so heavy on both sides in his final battle that it was clear that expansion was coming to a halt.

Not only had the Ottoman's highly efficient army dominated on land but it now had a navy which controlled much of the Mediterranean. However, in this area too they began to show vulnerability. The sea battle of Lepanto in 1571 was one of the most important battles between Christians and Muslims of the modern era. In it the fleet of the Holy League, mostly Spaniards and Austrians, defeated a large Ottoman navy, allegedly sinking 30 ships and killing 30,000 of 'the sempiternal enemy'. The victors gave the credit for the victory over the 'wretched infidels' to the Virgin Mary and their use of rosaries before the battle; hence the subsequent feast day of Our Lady of the Rosaries. Admiral Andrea Dorea had in his cabin an image of Our Lady of Guadeloupe.

The Turks soon recovered from Lepanto, however, at least physically if not psychologically, and in 1683 conducted their second siege of Vienna with a massive army of perhaps 250,000 inspired by the sacred standard of the Prophet. The Emperor Leopold I fled and the abandoned city was close to surrender when a Polish army under John Sobieski came to the rescue. The Poles made a sudden attack on the besieging force and routed it. It was the beginning of a long, slow retreat as Christian firepower gradually overtook the technologically static Ottomans (v. Pt 3 Chapter 28).

Meanwhile in West Africa there had been some new Islam-driven wars of expansion. According to legend, the Keita dynasty of Niani, now in Guinea on a tributary of the River Niger, was descended from Mohammed's personal muezzin Bilal, one of whose seven sons had settled in Manden. It was the tenth king of this dynasty, Sundiata Keita (*fl* 1215–55) who took the superior title of *mansa* (emperor) after conquering neighbouring states like Gao. After a pilgrimage to Mecca, his descendant, the remarkable Kankan Musa, started building new mosques in Timbuktu and this Mali empire survived into the fifteenth century until conquered by fellow Muslims the Songhai. Timbuktu was captured by the aggressive Songhai king Sunni Ali in 1468 after a long and brutal siege.

This Songhai Empire, the largest Islamic empire in African history, was in turn attacked in 1591 by a large Moroccan army under a new Berber dynasty from the Draa valley, east of Agadir. The dynasty's founder Abu Abdullah had a vision in which he discovered he was descended from Mohammed's daughter Fatima and her husband Ali, so he had a divine mission to wage jihad against the Portuguese infidels. He and his successors waged successful jihad to liberate the coastal towns like Agadir and took control of Morocco, angering the Ottomans who naturally perceived him as a quasi-Shiite. This dynasty not only drove the Sunni Ottomans out of Morocco but also the Christian Portuguese, whom they famously defeated at the Battle of the Three Kings in 1578 (see above), when King Sebastian of Portugal was killed with great numbers of his army. The supposed apogee of this dynasty came with the hugely ambitious Achmed al Mansur (1549–1603) who sent his artillery across the Sahara and despite losing half his 40,000 troops in the desert still had the firepower to crush the Songhai Empire, subsequently devastating Gao, Timbuktu and Djenne and bringing back hordes of slaves to grow sugar in the Sousse. By this time, it was hardly holy war.

'By this scimitar
That slew the Sophy and a Persian prince
That won three fields from Soltan Solyman...'
William Shakespeare, *The Merchant of Venice*

26

CIVIL WARS – PROTESTANTS AND CATHOLICS AGAINST EACH OTHER AND AMONG THEMSELVES

'Our danger has no end, for the Protestant Estates will without doubt be strengthened in their hatred by this.'
Johann Count of Tilly in a letter to the Emperor after the massacre at Magdeburg

The Thirty Years War in Germany (1618–48) was one of the most devastating wars in European history up to 1914 and though there were other factors it certainly began with religious differences. Veronica Wedgewood described the war as 'morally subversive, economically destructive, socially degrading, confused in its causes, devious in its course, futile in its result'. Yet as she points out, it seemed to be inevitable following the seventy years during which the different regions of Germany had pursued opposing versions of the Christian faith since the defeat of the Protestant Schmalkaldic League at Mühlberg by Charles V in 1547, and the subsequent unsatisfactory treaty of Augsburg by which the Holy Roman Empire had agreed that each principality of the empire could choose its own religion.

The war started with a rebellion by the Protestants in Bohemia against the Jesuit-influenced imperial government which had demolished a new Protestant church building. As Bireley puts it, the war 'seemed to flow spontaneously from an outraged Protestant assembly'. The protesters ejected three of the imperial representatives from the windows of the Prague palace, a severe provocation, the infamous defenestration of Prague. But for a pile of horse dung they would have been killed, so the Catholics claimed that 'God worked a miracle' by giving them a soft landing. Jesuit priests such as Wilhelm Lamormaini urged the emperor in Vienna to take strong military action, as did his colleague Adam Contzen in Munich, whilst the Capuchin monk St Lorenzo da Brindisi was sent to Prague to stiffen Catholic resistance there. The Bohemians, as we shall see, went on to choose a new Protestant king from the Rhineland but this was destined to escalate a minor provincial rebellion into a war that involved nearly the whole of Europe.

This war was one of the first in which printed propaganda played a major role. The mass publication and distribution of pamphlets with lurid illustrations facilitated venomous attacks from both sides emphasising the evils of opposed sects and nations: 'Croats eat children.' There was also glorification of heroes such as the Protestant leader Gustavus Adolphus, the Swedish king (Swede or Sued was turned backwards by the propagandists to show that he was Deus, or God).

At one point it appeared that perhaps around 70 per cent of Germans had abandoned the Catholic Church but by 1618 the balance was perhaps closer to 50/50. There were several reasons for this. After 1534 Pope Paul III had drastically reformed the church, eliminated many of the scandals which had led to the Reformation and endorsed the founding of the Jesuits four years later to lead the Counter-Reformation. There were now serious differences among the Protestants, between the more conservative Lutherans and the revolutionary Calvinists, who, as Veronica Wedgewood put it, 'exhorted all true believers to violence and took special delight in the more bloodthirsty psalms.' This and sporadic outbreaks of peasant violence and angry mobs meant that some of the Protestant princes began to have doubts as to whether it was really in their interest to split with the Catholic Church after all.

There were additional external pressures due to the renewal of the Eighty Years War in Holland; Spain was anxious to keep its supply lines along the Rhine to sustain its army there, while the Dutch and their Protestant allies such as the British and Swedes wanted to block the route and prevent reinforcements.

The small Czech kingdom of Bohemia, a semi-independent part of the Hapsburg empire with a long history of anti-Catholic activity since the pioneering days of Jan Hus (v. Pt 2 Chapter 19) became the focus for confrontation. By this time Bohemia was a volatile mix of Catholics, Lutherans, Calvinists, Utraquists and Anabaptists. The childless Emperor Matthias (1557–1519) was close to death and had led a largely bloodless revival of Catholicism, but he chose as his heir in Bohemia his aggressive nephew Ferdinand, a man likely to cause huge alarm for the majority of Bohemians. Ferdinand's record as a persecutor of Protestants in his dukedom of Styria was already notorious. An otherwise genial but not desperately intelligent man, he had been schooled by the Jesuits in Graz and regarded it as his divine mission to stamp out Protestantism. The response to his nomination as their king was for the Bohemian Protestants to sink their differences and stage a coup d'état symbolised by that defenestration of the three Catholics at the Prague city hall. They then declared independence.

The Hapsburgs under their new emperor-elect reacted by sending an army to recapture Bohemia but it was defeated by a mercenary force led by Count Mansfeld. The Bohemians meanwhile chose as their king a man just as unsuitable as Ferdinand; Frederick the Prince Palatine of the Rhine was not only a Calvinist but a mediocre leader and had none of the qualities needed to face a major onslaught. The fact that his wife Elizabeth was daughter of the British Protestant King James I was to be of no help to him. The Protestants were heavily defeated at the Battle of White Mountain and the royal couple were driven into exile.

A chain of events was set in motion whereby the German princes took sides either with the Empire or with its opponents, and not all of them chose the side appropriate to their religion. The same applied to the nations outside Germany who entered the war, most notably the French and the devious Cardinal Richelieu, who for political reasons chose the Protestant side. Even the Ottoman Muslims seized the chance to join in on the Protestant side, since they wanted to make inroads in Hungary and Vienna was one of their prime targets. Their plan to invade Poland in 1620 precipitated the Polish-Ottoman War, which, after a battle won by each side, ended in stalemate.

The overall casualties of the Thirty Years War have been estimated as between 3½ million (Geoffrey Parker) and 7–8 million (Norman Davies *et al*) but perhaps only around 10 per cent of these were battle casualties, most of the rest were massacred or died of disease or starvation. Of the 'outside' participants the Lutheran Danes suffered badly over four years (1625–29) though they captured Hamburg as a prize. The Swedes (1630–35) who regarded the Hapsburgs as a threat to their Protestant church were more successful under the brilliant Gustavus Adolphus and won Pomerania for themselves but destroyed some 18,000 villages and 1,500 towns, whilst the opportunistic French (1635–48) came off best with useful gains of territory to set against the loss of perhaps 10,000 men. The Hapsburg side gained nothing for around 20,000 direct casualties, many more if you counted their Catholic allies like the Bavarians.

The worst single atrocity was the massacre in 1631 of 20,000 Protestant inhabitants of Magdeburg by mercenary troops of the Catholic League, a new group founded in 1609 in imitation of the extreme French Catholic League. The massacre was described as divine punishment by one of their commanders, the dedicated Catholic warrior and dashing cavalry commander Heinrich Count Pappenheim (1594–1632), who had cut his teeth fighting for the Catholics in Poland. It was more likely a spontaneous reaction by frustrated imperial troops rather than an officially sanctioned bloodletting. Both typhus and bubonic plague wiped out substantial numbers. Some regions fared worse than others; Württemberg losing three quarters of its population, Brandenburg half, mostly in the wake of harvests gobbled up or destroyed by passing troops from both sides. Casualties in the large number of pitched battles varied: around 14,000 for each of the two battles of Breitenfeld, 8,000 at Lützen, Nordlingen and Rocroi around 10,000 each. The figures were higher than would be expected for clashes at that time because of the number of mercenaries involved and a general collapse in the norms of martial behaviour.

One of the grim by-products of the war was a renewed outbreak of witch-hunting. Another was the experience in modern warfare it provided for a number of Scots and Irish mercenaries who, as we shall see, provided the pool of trained manpower that made the Scottish First Bishops' War and English Civil War so easy to start.

Despite supporting the Protestant cause in Germany, France had resumed persecution of the Huguenots at home and this resulted in a rebellion centred round La Rochelle, which suffered a protracted siege with substantial casualties. The significant expansion of France at this time due to the Catholic Cardinal Richelieu casting aside his religious obligations and exploiting the German civil war to enhance France's frontiers along the Rhine was thus an indirect result of Ferdinand's attack on the Bohemian Protestants.

The English Civil War, or War of Three Kingdoms, was caused initially by a clash between Lutherans and Calvinists but soon developed into something much more complex. It cost over 850,000 lives and led to further clashes in Scotland and Ireland. Initially on the high Lutheran side were King Charles I (1600–1649), obsessed with his own divinely ordained right to rule, and Archbishop Laud, whose insistence on a new prayer book and liturgy including what the Scots called 'the idolatrous habit of kneeling' caused riots when it was first introduced in Edinburgh in 1637. A female market-stall owner hurled a stool at the head of the preacher in St Giles Cathedral; she had probably been put up to it by a group of strongly Calvinist church ministers such as Alexander Henderson of Leuchars, who became an able and effective propagandist for armed rebellion. In response to unwelcome pressure from the Lutheran regime in London and Canterbury he organised the passing in Scotland of the National Covenant, which abolished bishops along with Laud's other impositions of formal liturgy. Then with the help of John Leslie, Earl of Rothes, he encouraged a group of highly experienced Fife army mercenaries to return from Germany to raise an army to defend Scotland from invasion. This became the First Bishops' War or War of the Covenant (1639), which ended with the Scots able to demand what they wanted from a humiliated Charles I. There then came a successful Scottish invasion of England that created the financial crisis leading to the English Civil War.

For Charles I it was a severe humiliation, especially as he had no money to pay for his army and reluctantly had to summon an obstreperous parliament so that he could beg for permission to raise taxes. Also, partially as a consequence of the unrest in Scotland there was a rebellion of Catholics against Protestants in Ulster in 1641, which led to at least 4000 Protestant direct casualties.

It was provoked by the aggressive colonising policies of King James I who had been encouraging Scots Presbyterians and English Lutherans to move to Ireland and displace the existing Catholic peasantry. These plantations eventually provoked armed rebellion and local atrocities. The Scottish Covenanters force sent to exact revenge was later defeated by the Catholic Confederates led by O'Neill at Benburb in 1646, continuing what was virtually an Irish religious civil war that lasted on and off at least until the Battle of the Boyne in 1690.

The confrontation between king and parliament led inexorably to the English Civil War of 1642 where the causes were primarily political; but there was even in England a considerable dislike for Archbishop Laud, so we could perhaps allocate a 70 per cent politico-economic against 30 per cent sectarian causation for the war. Most sects were not exclusively on one side or the other, but most Calvinists or Puritans and most moderate Lutherans were on the parliamentary or Roundhead side, along with the extreme groups like the Diggers and Levellers, whereas most high Anglicans were Royalists, along with a few crypto-Catholics, though Prince Rupert, a senior Royalist commander, was a Calvinist from Germany.

Cromwell was a strict Lutheran with a Puritan and Independent streak. There was strong religious motivation in Cromwell's rapid rise to the top of the parliamentarian army and his ultimate success in winning the war. He referred to his 'divine mission... I had that strange sense of being led on by God.' His New Model Army was recruited from 'godly, precious men' and when it was successful he wrote 'God was with our new Model Army.' Initially the parliamentary side had been glad to receive support from the recently triumphant Scots, who certainly helped win the Battle of Marston Moor, but as the Scots demanded an abolition of bishops in England as well as in Scotland this was too much for the Anglicans and too much in a different way for Cromwell. He and the New Model Army regarded Presbyterian assemblies as just as unwelcome as the rule of bishops. In fact, there was now a deep split between the predominantly pro-Presbyterian English parliament and the anti-Presbyterian but pro-Independent army.

The Scots now naively believed first that Charles I, and later his son Charles II, were more likely to support Presbyterianism in England than was Cromwell, so having helped Cromwell win the

First Civil War they changed sides. For the sake of Presbyterianism they launched the Second and Third English Civil Wars, or Wars of Three Kingdoms, which lasted until their defeat at Worcester in 1651. Of Charles II's 16,000 troops on that day, the vast majority were Scotsmen.

There had also been a short civil war in Scotland between the now increasingly strident Calvinists under the church-dominated Scottish regime and a Royalist force led by a former Covenant supporter, the Marquis of Montrose, helped by a large Catholic contingent from Ireland. After a series of brilliant victories by Montrose his troops were routed at Philiphaugh in 1645. Promised quarter, some of them surrendered, but Calvinist ministers persuaded the Covenanter General David Leslie that clemency was foolish and some 300 were slaughtered after the battle, most of them women and children camp followers.

The religious motivation was perhaps stronger than the political during Cromwell's Irish campaign in 1649, which he referred to in terms of a holy war. The defeat of the Catholics and consequent massacre at Drogheda was not at the time regarded as a war crime but a righteous punishment of rebellious heretics, a judgment of God. The Catholic Church had played a part in encouraging Irish resistance and in the civil war that followed by sending Capuchin missionaries from a special college in Antwerp to encourage armed rebellion,

The suppression of Scottish Calvinism was revived by Charles II in 1662 when he once more imposed episcopacy and again evoked armed response. There was the Pentland Rising of 1666 but more significantly the bitter struggle of the Cameronians which climaxed in the battle of Bothwell Bridge in 1679. Walter Scott in his *Old Mortality* gives a brilliant description of the extreme sectarian hatred of the opposing forces, high Lutheran versus extreme Calvinism with phrases like 'the slaughter of the Amalekites' happily reclaimed to justify gratuitous violence during the so-called 'killing times'.

The next sectarian war in Britain was back to Catholic against Lutheran and was provoked by King James II (1633–1701) who from 1686 stubbornly tried to infiltrate Catholics into the British army and government as a prelude to some kind of localised counter-reformation and a return to royal authoritarianism.

The response in 1688 was the invitation sent by British Lutherans to the Dutch Calvinist William of Orange (1650–1702) to invade England as a potential replacement king. James II's army with its smattering of Irish Catholic recruits disintegrated in the crisis so the war did not really begin until James was in exile and had recovered his own health sufficiently to make a counter-attack with French help. This French support showed some initial signs of success and there were several bruising sea battles such as Beachy Head in 1691 and La Hogue a year later, but it had really ended in 1690 with what turned out to be the most famous British sectarian battle between Catholic and Protestant at the River Boyne, as well as the equally dramatic siege of Londonderry. William's continued wars against the French were probably partly motivated by his ongoing fear of Catholicism.

All the various attempts at a restoration of the Stuart dynasty to the British throne, particularly those of 1715 and 1745, had a religious element; obviously, both sides were aware that the replacement kings were Catholics. It would however be wrong to suggest that Jacobites were overwhelmingly Catholic, though many of the Scottish clansmen clung to the old faith. It does however help to explain why the majority of Scots were against both the Old and Young Pretenders, as they represented both royal authoritarianism and anti-Protestant tendencies.

Overall, sectarian differences were a significant cause of civil and sometimes international warfare in the British Isles 1588–1745, and perhaps cost at least 1½ million lives.

A third area where religious civil war resurrected itself was in France when Louis XIII and Cardinal Richelieu began suppressing the Huguenots and the casualties escalated with the siege of Montauban 1621–24 and of La Rochelles 1627–29. This provoked international interference with the British on one side and Spain on the other, resulting in some 30,000 fatalities. This civil war in France ended when Louis XIV (1638–1715) repealed the Edict of Nantes in 1686 and approximately two million Huguenots either had to accept Catholicism or emigrate. At least 10 per cent of them did so. While Louis, particularly later in his reign, was a dedicated Catholic and much influenced by the Jesuits, his many wars were entirely aimed at the glorification of his rule and dynasty. When it suited him he defied the papacy and allied himself with Protestants against his greatest rivals, the Hapsburgs in Vienna, who were Catholic. However, he regarded himself as a divinely ordained monarch – Dieudonné – who as well as persecuting the Huguenots also suppressed Jansenists and Quietists.

Even though he fought no wars for religious reasons he regarded himself as having divine sanction to increase the Bourbon empire. He also on occasion used religion as an excuse for war, as with his invasion of Holland in 1672. He had some difficulty in persuading his ministers to agree to the project, so to denounce the Dutch as heretics provided some additional motivation for waverers. In addition, large numbers of French Huguenots had already sought asylum in Holland and Prussia.

The Peace of Westphalia that ended the Thirty Years War in 1648 gave a substantial boost to the state of Brandenburg-Prussia. It gained East Pomerania and Magdeburg as well as sovereignty over East Prussia. It also encouraged the state's ambitious Hohenzollern rulers to regard themselves as Protestant champions. In consequence they were attracted to the ideas of the Pietist Philipp Jakob Spener (1635–1705). This people-friendly version of Lutheranism sponsored church support for the ambitions of the nation, preaching the concept of self-sacrifice and austerity for the sake of national growth. Halle University turned out teachers and preachers to educate young Prussians to dedicate themselves to service to the nation, the ethic which was to provide a framework for the wildly aggressive militarism of Frederick the Great. His conquest of largely catholic Silesia, adding 50 per cent to the land area of his kingdom, cost the lives of half a million of his own people. The Gott mit uns motto of the Prussian kingdom was to survive alongside the Pietist support for expansion until 1914 and beyond.

'In such a regiment the actual practice of religion was of the utmost importance and steps were taken to procure chaplains. These would sometimes combine the role with that of fighting men.'
Antonia Fraser, *Cromwell Our Chief of Men*

26

NEW WORLDS – CHRISTIANS AGAINST HEATHENS

'We had sufficient light from the Word of God for our proceedings ... fleeing inhabitants were received and entertained with the point of the sword.'

John Underhill, *Newes from America* 1637

The Christian subjugation of the New and Third Worlds had begun in brutal fashion with the conquests of Cortes and Pizarro in Central and South America and was to continue with varying degrees of violence until 1914.

In the case of North America the motives for ethnic cleansing of native Americans were far from purely religious; competition for fur trading and quarrels over agricultural land played a major part. The supposed heathenism of the Indians did, however, present a good excuse for disinheriting them from their lands. Captain John Underhill came from a fanatical puritan family exiled from England to Holland. John was hired in 1630 by the Massachusetts Bay Colony to organise its defence against the attacks of the Pequot tribes. As we have seen, this resulted in a war 1634–8 that featured the Mystic Massacre of 1637 and Underhill justifying slaughter from Biblical precedent, announcing that he was 'taking up the cross'.

In 1675 when the colonists responded to a series of attacks by a coalition of Wampanoags and other tribes under the leadership of Metacomet (1638–1678), otherwise known as King Philip, the hero of the war was the Puritan Major Benjamin Church with his

Puritan Rangers. At this time Christian converts among the native Americans were known as 'praying Indians'.

The connection between British empire-building and the missionary zeal of the Anglican church was endorsed by the foundation in 1701 of The Society for the Propagation of the Gospel in Foreign Parts and the poet/priest John Donne praised the Virginia Company for its missionary zeal. As Rowan Strong argues, it was thought that 'trade and colonisation would strengthen the position of Protestant monarchs against imperial Catholic Spain.' Of course the Catholic Portuguese and Spaniards had been much quicker off the mark, conquering South and Central America and successfully converting to Roman Catholic Christianity most of the ethnic populations that survived their barbarism. The French Catholics had also made significant inroads in North America.

In due course the feeling of moral superiority of the New World Anglicans and Puritans compared with their European counterparts turned the idea of ethnic cleansing into part of what they called 'the manifest destiny', a divine mission to cleanse the world of heretics, pagans and autocrats, which helped justify the Indian Wars of 1850–80 and the Mexican War of 1840. As many 30,000 Native Americans may have been killed.

Similar mini-genocides were evident as the Dutch, Spanish, French, Portuguese and Belgians expanded their empires. The Dutch East India Company (VOC) was at war almost constantly, most often against its European rivals, Spain, Portugal and Britain. The Amboyna massacre of 1623 was a typical flash-point for inter-Christian battles in Java. The VOC had its own army backed by chaplains supplied by the Dutch Reformed Church and while keen to convert Muslims and others to Christianity, their prime motivation was the profits from the spice trade; hence their war to reinstate the Muslim Sultans of Mataram, who provided a stable infrastructure for trading that suited the Dutch. They had a three- and sometimes four-sided conflict in what is now Indonesia owing to the various resentments of the indigenous people, the Muslim trading settlers, Chinese immigrant workers and their own Calvinist colonials. This resulted for example in the massacre of 10,000 Chinese in Batavia in 1740, followed by the Java War of 1741–3.

In Eastern Europe, Ivan the Terrible's successful siege of Kazan, capital of the Muslim Tartars in 1552 was the prelude to the relentless advance by Russian traders and the Orthodox Church into the pagan regions of the Urals and beyond. His army of 150,000 was preceded by banners of the warrior saints Demetrius and George and slogans proclaiming that this was a holy war. So far as Ivan was concerned all his enemies, Swedes, Poles and Livonians, were just as much heretics as the Tartars. Kazan was largely ethnically cleansed of Muslims and with a new cathedral became a forward base for Russian Orthodoxy into Asia, later joined in that role by Astrakhan. Soon the Muscovites were inviting the Catholic Hapsburgs to become their allies in the southward advance against the Turkish enemies 'in Christ's name'.

Ironically, many of the irregular troops used to manage the Russian drive into the Caucasus and eastwards into the Urals were neither strictly Russian nor Orthodox but often landless Lithuanians and Poles. These so-called Cossacks, a term sometimes also applied to Tartars or other ethnic minorities, were self-supporting pioneers who built up trade and spearheaded the drive towards Siberia where the thinly spread population was largely Muslim or pagan and their lands undeveloped. The brains behind this campaign were from 1558 the Stroganov family, which had already achieved commercial success in the salt trade and now proved brilliant in searching for minerals and furs. As the leader of the Ukrainian Cossacks, Yermak Timofeyevich (1532–1585) put it, the 'godless ones' serving 'the Sultan of Siberia' had attacked the region of Perm that belonged to 'the holy Prince of Muscovy'.

Once the Romanov dynasty took over in 1616, all wars were holy wars. Its first two tsars, Michael and Alexis, were both monk-like in their devotions and their antipathy to the Catholic Poles and the Muslim Persians remained strong. In 1653 the aggressive new Orthodox Patriarch of Moscow, Nikon, blessed the start of a new invasion of Poland, which resulted in Russia gaining substantial tracts of the Ukraine.

'If the secret should be discovered by my countrymen the Dutch they would cut my throat on the voyage.'
Jonathan Swift's Lemuel Gulliver pretending to be Dutch and having failed to perform the obligatory ceremony of trampling on the crucifix required before sailing from Japan.

27

THE MANDATE OF HEAVEN – CONFUCIANS AGAINST MUSLIMS IN CHINA

'After about a century of Ching rule the Celestial Empire
extended once more from the Pacific to the Pamirs, from Siberia
in the north to the offshore islands in the south.'

Hilda Hookham, *A Short History of China*

The Manchu/Ching/Qing dynasty which finally ousted the Ming
in 1644 had begun their invasion of China as an act of revenge
against Ming oppression. Their own religion was fairly primitive
shamanism practised in their Manchurian homelands, but once
past the Great Wall in Beijing it suited them to make use of the
Confucian infrastructure, and to take over the traditional role of
emperors as 'the mandate of Heaven'. Back in 221 BC the first
emperor of a united China had combined two previous titles,
Huang (God King) and *Di* (sage or semi-divine) into *Huangdi* to
which the Qing/Ching added the title *Shengzu* (Holy Lord). So the
strong tradition of god-like emperors was continued and it was
this divinely authorised imperialism that formed the background
to the expansionist wars of the Qing from the 1690s to the 1750s.

To justify the ousting of the Ming they adopted their victims'
Confucianism but blamed them for letting it become corrupted
and self-indulgent. They also soon adopted Tibetan Buddhism.
Eunuchs were banned, long hair and homosexuality were outlawed
and large numbers of Ming loyalists were massacred, as in
Yangzhou. The Qing passed laws to create a stricter moral code

but for their own ends exploited the Confucian sense of duty and obedience to reorganise their army and provide the framework for a massive expansion of the Chinese Empire to include Taiwan, Chinese Central Asia, Mongolia and Tibet, creating a multi-ethnic single state that survived their fall in 1911.

Eastern Mongolia and Korea (which was Confucian) were conquered in the 1630s, then Taiwan in 1683 by the aggressive fourth member of the dynasty, Emperor Kangxi (1654–1722) who like his father was a Tibetan Buddhist. He then took advantage of a civil war among rival rulers of Mongolia in 1696 where their ambitious Khan Galdan had been a Buddhist lama trained in Lhasa before seizing the throne from his brothers. Kangxi defeated his fellow Buddhist Galdan and took most of Mongolia into his steadily increasing empire. Buddhist Tibet itself was conquered by the Qing in 1720 and the Islamic cities of Xinjiang and Kashgar, home of the Uighurs, in 1759 by the Emperor Qianlong (1711–1799). Here there was a significant population of Chinese Muslims who became an oppressed minority that subsequently rebelled on several occasions, such as the Dungan revolt of 1862 and the rebellion by the Emir of Kashgar Yakub, put down in 1877, The area was still suffering a degree of ethnic cleansing in the twentieth and twenty-first centuries, first by Maoists who wanted rid of Islam, and then by the peoples republic, which wanted conformity.

By the end of the eighteenth century the new Chinese frontiers were beginning to encroach on similar expansion by the Russians and the two super-powers came to an understanding.

'The emperor (Kangxi) approved the dedication of the Great Mazu Temple honouring the goddess Mazu for her assistance during the Qing invasion (of Taiwan).'

K. Bergman, *Taiwan City Guide*

'Confucius had shaped a central perception of Chinese security strategy symbolised by the defensive, non-aggressive Great Wall.'

Yuan-kang Wang, *Harmony & War: Confucian Culture and Chinese Power Politics*

28

MORE HOLY LEAGUES – CHRISTIANS AGAINST MUSLIM TURKS AND ATHEISTS

'At a real crisis of the Catholic faith the Archduke of Austria in his capacity as Holy Roman Emperor could appeal to what remained of the crusading spirit in Europe and as the head of Latin Christendom might expect the support of the Vatican.'

H. A. L. Fisher, *A History of Europe*

Among a number of factors that led to a major confrontation between Christians and Muslims in eastern Europe in the 1680s were sectarian divisions among the Europeans. Whereas the Ottomans were solidly Sunni and had given up any efforts to convert their millions of Christian subjects to Islam, the dominant Catholics to the north of the Danube were much less tolerant. Thus the Orthodox Christian Cossacks of the Ukraine objected to Jesuit plans to make them become Catholic, whilst the Protestant minorities of Hungary and Transylvania objected to Catholic bullying by their rulers in Vienna.

After a succession of ineffectual sultans, the Ottoman Empire had been revived in 1656 by a series of able viziers of Albanian stock, the Kuprili, and they still had the best and largest standing army in Europe. Their main potential opponent, the Jesuit-trained Holy Roman Emperor Leopold I (1640–1711) had a much smaller army when he took over in 1658; his empire was a mixture of unruly German princes and rebellious Hungarians who preferred their Viennese overlords to be weak.

The new crisis had begun with a Cossack rebellion against the Catholic Poles in 1648 with asymmetric support from Russia (Orthodox) and the Crimean Tartars (Muslims). Unusually for them, the Poles in response chose a strong king, Jan/John III Sobieski (1624–1696) who spearheaded the attack on the rebels and then drove the Turks out of Podolia in 1675. Thus, Sobieski became a Catholic hero figure who now began talking in terms of a crusade to 'exterminate the barbarians'. Though he put Poland first and regularly switched alliances, sometimes even seeking Turkish help, he perceived the Ottoman revival as his most serious threat and joined forces with the Emperor Leopold in 1683 to help repel the expected Ottoman onslaught on Vienna.

In July 1683 the pious Sultan Mehmet IV (1643–1693), known as a holy warrior, officially declared jihad in Belgrade and sent an army of 100,000 men to besiege Vienna. The emperor had no army capable of withstanding such an attack, but Sobieski came to his aid three months later and won a major victory over the besieging army. Encouraged by this, Pope Innocent XI invited the three great Catholic monarchs to unite against the Turks, Leopold and John Sobieski, who accepted the challenge, and Louis XIV, who refused. However, a number of French nobles like the Condés and Prince Eugene of Savoy went to join the Christian army. The Holy League was assisted by the Venetians and later also by the Russians, so that in the Second Battle of Mohács (1687) in Hungary it reversed the result of the first, fought in 1526 (v. Pt 3, Chapter 24). The Turks suffered a further major loss as the Holy Roman Empire recovered most of Hungary.

In 1699 Prince Eugene achieved a victory at Zenta on the River Tisa in Serbia where the Ottomans lost 30,000 killed, a third of them drowned. They were forced to cede their half of Hungary and Transylvania to Leopold, then Podolia and the Ukraine to the Poles. The Venetians had briefly conquered Dalmatia and most of Greece, also with the encouragement of the pope.

It had not been a genuinely holy war on either side, more about empire building or empire protection, but it clearly was a major setback for the Islamic super-power. It also gave impetus to the drive of Russia towards the Black Sea coast and of Austria towards the mouth of the Danube and the Balkans, a rivalry that was to prove disastrous for world peace 215 years later in 1914.

Meanwhile Tsar Peter I the Great of Russia (1672–1725) had radically modernised both Russia and the Russian Orthodox Church, dispensing with patriarchs and taking it under government control with a Holy Synod. He then used the church as a fund-raising body to help fill his war chests and presented his prolonged war against the Lutheran Swedes as a holy war to save Mother Russia. He was thereby continuing the work of the first two Romanov tsars, who had made devotion to Orthodoxy the most important prop of the new dynasty's claims to autocratic rule. By creating a new capital city at St Petersburg, which was in territory previously held by the Swedes, he also shifted the emphasis of the Russian Church from its focus on Moscow to the new St Peter and Paul Cathedral in St Petersburg, which was effectively dedicated to the Romanovs and helped linked the tsar's name to the apostle.

The Empress Catherine (1729–1796) had been a Protestant German princess but converted to Orthodoxy as part of her route to power once she arrived in Russia and married Peter III. Her ambitions centred on the further expansion of Russia and religion played little part in her thinking, but one of her longer lasting favourites was the ex-soldier monk Grigori Potemkin (1739–1791) whom she picked out to be her man in the Holy Synod. He remained a devout follower of Orthodoxy and when he went back to soldiering religion was a major factor in his strategies. He was passionate about the idea of freeing the Orthodox populations of Georgia and Armenia from Persian control and this was achieved in part by diplomacy in 1783. The same applied to the Christians under Turkish Ottoman rule in Wallachia and Moldavia, which were brought into the Russian empire after his Turkish campaign (1768–74). He regarded his campaigns to annex the Crimea and Kuban as a holy war, though there was no real suggestion of converting conquered Tartars to Christianity. The Nogai people swore their oath of allegiance to Catherine over copies of the Koran and drank the toast in vodka, since wine was forbidden by their faith. After Potemkin's death she ordered a further attack on Persia in 1795 to prevent Georgia slipping back into Muslim hands.

One of Europe's most aggressive monarchs at this time, Frederick II the Great of Prussia (1712–1786) was single-minded in his ambition to expand his kingdom at all costs but was not one to ignore religious motivation if it would help his case, so he exploited the fact that Prussia was Protestant to encourage other Protestant states in Germany to support his war against Catholic Austria and the Hapsburgs.

The French Revolutionary Wars of 1792–1802 were without question primarily political but there were religious undercurrents. The French population resented the extravagances of the Bourbons but it was also becoming increasingly anti-clerical because the French church was seriously overmanned and overpaid. The antipathy towards the clergy resulted in many of them seeking asylum abroad, where they preached opposition to the new regime. As the distrust between the government and the clergy deepened the Constituent Assembly in 1790 took over all church property and closed all the monasteries. It also insisted that all priests swore an oath of loyalty to the state, a request which many refused. In response Pope Pius VI (1717–1799) condemned the Constituent Assembly and banned numerous texts, including *The Rights of Man*. The following year France declared war on Austria, the largest Catholic power in Europe.

Faced with the daunting prospect of invasion by a coalition of well-armed monarchies, the French became even more hostile to their own church, which was regarded as a hotbed of treachery against the Revolution. By 1794 the Reign of Terror had replaced the church with a new Cult of the Supreme Being followed by the Goddess of Reason. There was a range of de-Christianising measures; they banned all church services and the wearing of any form of clerical dress. Two hundred priests were murdered in an outbreak of anti-clerical rioting. The most significant church-backed resistance came in 1793 from the Vendée, where a new force called the Catholic & Royal Army, with the sacred heart as its emblem, fought a brutal regional war against the Committee of Public Safety, leading to some 160,000 deaths. The rebellion was put down and followed by an almost genocidal scorched earth period of revenge.

By this time the French war against the Hapsburgs in Italy had been raging for four years without much success. Then in 1796 the young Napoleon was given his first serious command and sent to take over. Having scored a series of unexpected victories against the Austrians he then attacked Tuscany and the Papal States, where he scored an easy victory over the papal army at Fort Urban. Pope Pius VI had no choice but to sue for peace. The France-Vatican relationship remained extremely strained and when some riots in Rome led to the murder of a French envoy Napoleon had the perfect excuse for a renewed attack on the Holy City. He captured Rome in 1798, arrested the pope and sent him to be imprisoned in the fortress of Valence, where he died soon afterwards. In many ways it was a reprise of the Investiture Wars of the three Ottos and of the Avignon papacy, as Napoleon wanted both an imperial crown and total control of the church. The new Pope Pius VII (1742–1823) signed a concordat with Napoleon and attended his coronation in Milan in 1804 but five years later excommunicated him. He was imprisoned until 1814.

In the south of Italy Cardinal Fabrizio Ruffo organised the peasants of Calabria to form the Army of Holy Faith in our Lord Jesus Christ and attacked the French-held city of Naples with 17,000 men, their objective to restore the Bourbon king and expel the atheist French. The *Sanfedisti* soldiers took an oath which ended with 'I swear ... to spill the blood of infamous liberals to the last drop' and promised to maintain 'implacable hatred against enemies of our Holy Roman Catholic religion'. They took Naples with help from Admiral Nelson and the Royal Navy. Jonathan North in *Nelson at Naples* makes a strong case that the seizure by Nelson of the Republicans who had surrendered on the understanding that they could leave for France was akin to a war crime.

The next significant use of the word 'holy' in European military parlance came in 1815 from Tsar Alexander I (1777–1825) who had been inspired by the mystic Madame Krüdener. His Holy Alliance was one mainly directed against republicanism and atheism after the defeat of Napoleon.

Ephraim Lipson considered that 'the Holy Alliance has been greatly misunderstood, partly because its purpose was misinterpreted but also its practical significance overrated.' Notably Tsar Alexander, self-proclaimed champion of the Orthodox Church, gave an initial hint of support for the Greek Independence campaign in 1821, but then joined with the Holy

League in condemning it as smacking of liberalism. Even the Patriarch in Istanbul did not want the status quo disturbed. However, anti-Ottoman feeling built up in many parts of Europe and intervention had some appeal as people could now envisage easy military victories over the Muslims.

In Greece itself the organisation named the Sacred Band, *Hieros Lokhos*, adopted the motto of the Roman Emperor Constantine (v. Pt 1 Chapter 4) 'In this sign conquer'. Founded by Alexander Ypsilandis on the model of the Sacred Band in Thebes (371 BC) it recruited exiled Greek students from Wallachia and Moldova, required an oath of loyalty to the Greek Orthodox Church and had the objective of fighting for Greek independence from the Ottomans. The Sacred Band concept was revived in the war for Cretan independence in 1866 and again in 1942 by Greek officers fighting Germany in North Africa.

Meanwhile three arms of the Orthodox Church – Greek, Serbian and Bulgarian – which had been under Ottoman control for at least four centuries began to flirt with the possibility of encouraging rebellion. Back in 1596 the Serb patriarch had instigated a holy war against the Ottomans in the name of St Sava, which had been brutally suppressed. There was a further Serb uprising in 1804 under Karadorde Petrovic (1768–1817) backed by the church and motivated by the tax policy of the Ottomans who taxed Christians far more heavily than Muslims. The Greek Orthodox Church also favoured the founding of *Filiki Eteria*, the Lucky Brotherhood, in 1821, for though it was influenced by Freemasonry its oath of allegiance was to the church and it boasted of 'the Authority of the Twelve Apostles'. It was this group which set in motion the eventually successful Greek War of Independence, which was viewed by many European regimes as a strike against Islam as well as against Ottoman autocracy.

Serbia and Montenegro followed the same route in 1870 and inspired a revival of the Bulgarian Orthodox Church, which in turn inspired the Bulgarian rebellion of 1876. This was again motivated by the Ottoman discriminatory tax policy. The atrocities committed by the Turks in retaliation so shocked Europe that the Russians intervened with an attack on the Turks. The Russo-Turkish War of 1877–8 ended when Russia accepted the truce offered by the Ottoman Empire under pressure from the British, who were alarmed at Russia's movement towards Constantinople. The Serbs and Montenegrins also rebelled and the Turks were forced to grant independence to Bulgaria, Serbia became an independent kingdom in 1882, and Bosnia and Herzegovina were handed over to Hapsburg protection.

Whilst the various Orthodox churches had good reason to support the drive for independence for the Balkan nations, it was a different situation for the Catholic Church in Italy, where the papacy had a vested interest in keeping Italy divided so that it could retain the Papal States and the city of Rome as a separate principality. Pope Pius VII, a conservative who revived the Inquisition, the Jesuits and the ghetto, condemned the pro-independence *Carbonari* in 1821. He also opposed Greek independence.

The at first liberal Pope Pius IX (1792–1878) made desperate efforts to maintain the status quo. The Austrians still held most of north east Italy and the Bourbons had the kingdom of Naples and Sicily, where the religiously motivated *Sanfedisti* helped stir up popular opposition to creating an independent Italy. The two main promoters of Italian reunification, Camillo Cavour and Guiseppe Garibaldi, were both anti-clerical and aimed to confiscate the property of the Catholic Church. With French help King Victor Emmanuel of Savoy drove out the Austrians and captured the Papal States despite resistance from Pius IX in 1860. In 1867 a largely volunteer Papal Army, including the battle-hardened Zouaves, defeated Garibaldi at the Battle of Mentan thus delaying the capture of Rome for another three years. Then in 1870, when the French garrison had to be withdrawn from Rome to defend Paris, Victor Emmanuel seized the chance and the Pope's tiny army had to hand over the city and it became the capital of a united Italy.

In post-Napoleonic France, where the church was enjoying a major revival, the deeply unpopular Charles X (1757–1836) saw helping the Greeks as a way of improving his standing. It was in the same vein as his later attack on Muslim Algeria in 1830 – 'skirmishing against the Dey' – which, though it was a military success against mediocre opposition, failed to save him from dethronement a few weeks later. What it did achieve was to provoke a new Islamic jihad in North Africa.

The other Catholic nation which became embroiled in a Muslim war was Spain, which had lost the last shreds of its American empire in 1898 and fancied replacing it with more territory in Morocco. It thus became involved in the expensive Rif Wars, which afforded the Spanish army and one of its generals, Franco Bahamonde, fighting experience that could be applied to the task of toppling the Spanish Republic in 1938 (v. Chap 36).

'The Zouaves were brave and honourable soldiers who fought and died for a sacred purpose.'
Catholic Herald, 2017

29

SUNNI MOGULS AGAINST HINDUS, SHIITES AND SIKHS

'...the hostilities between Muslims and Hindus which undeniably increased during his (Aurangzeb's) reign were precisely those which led two and a half centuries later to the partition of the sub-continent and the appalling communal massacres of 1947.'
Bamber Gascoigne, *The Great Moguls*

The Mogul dynasty came to power initially in India by conquering fellow Sunni Muslim sultans in Delhi, so their invasion was hardly a holy war, but later as they expanded their empire they resorted to the old formula, sometimes genuinely. Babur (1483–1530), their founder, was a descendant of the hyperactively aggressive Timur (v. Pt 2 Chapter 18) and born in what is now Uzbekistan. He was a landless prince looking for a kingdom and his first incursion into India was far from being a jihad, for he was invited by the local Hindus to come to their aid against their oppressive Muslim master, the Sultan Lodi. Babur, a so far fairly unsuccessful adventurer from the Samarkand region, responded with an amazing victory over the much larger Delhi army at Panipat in 1526. His skilled use of artillery against elephants proved successful. Yet his next major victory was against the Hindus at Khanwa in 1527, when he was faced by a large alliance of Rajput princes and some renegade Afghan Muslims who had survived Panipat. This was enough of a challenge to force him to call it a jihad and to promise Allah that he would give up wine if he won a victory. So far as the renegade Muslims were concerned, he damned them as kafirs or heathens for supporting the Hindu cause.

Similarly, Babur's grandson, the third Mogul emperor Akbar (1542–1605) declared jihad against the Hindus in 1556 and won the Second Battle of Panipat against another Hindu alliance. In 1567 he secured the Muslim hold on all northern India with his victory over the Rajputs at Chittor and over the Hindu kingdom of Mewar a year later. This included a siege that was followed by mass suicide among the surviving defenders and their wives (for the women this was the practice of *sati* that Akbar subsequently tried to abolish throughout his empire). In return for his victory Akbar had vowed to make a pilgrimage to the shrine of the Sufi mystic Moinuddin Chishti (1142–1236), so he was at least conscious of his need for Muslim credentials.

Akbar was however far from being a fanatical Muslim and it was he who sought to bridge the gap between Muslims and Hindus by encouraging the development of Sikhism, which he imagined could be a kind of blend of the two that might satisfy everyone. He had summoned a conference of rival religious groups to work out a common strategy and was impressed by the ideas of the first Sikh Guru Nanak (1469–1539), particularly the idea that all religions shared the same single god. As it turned out, his ideas soon proved to have a life of their own and the Sikhs would not be satisfied to be a compromise between the two old religions. As it was also to turn out, having had opposition to war as a major platform they were to change their minds once they faced persecution.

There was another Muslim jihad in southern India when in 1565 the five Deccan sultans, mainly Shiites, united to crush the Hindu Vijayanagara Empire based at what is now Hampi, a world heritage site, on the Deccan plateau in southern India. The five sultans including those of Bijapur and Golkonda heavily defeated the Vijayanagara in 1565 at Talikota fifty miles south of Bijapur. It marked the end of the last great Hindu monarchy in India. Allegedly around 100,000 Hindus were killed during or after the battle.

Meanwhile there was a revival in Shiite power in Persia by the energetic Shah Abbas I (1671–1629) a committed Shiite himself and in particular a devotee of the Imam Hussein. Though enthroned by a military coup led by an extreme militant

Shiite sect. the *Qizilbash*, or Red Heads, he quickly re-staffed his army and eliminated the Qizilbash to whom he owed his throne. Thereafter he began a concentrated effort to push back the Sunni Ottomans and rebellious Uzbeks who were his prime enemies and drove them out of Persian territory. He then persecuted the remaining Sunnis. For commercial reasons he tolerated Christians, including the Armenians, though he forced some 30,000 of them to relocate to shore up his frontier provinces. He largely retained friendly relations with the Sunni Moguls, as the Uzbeks were their common enemy. He only waged anti-Sunni wars when it suited him politically.

The sixth Mogul Emperor Aurangzeb (1618–1707) had seized power from his brother in 1658 and incarcerated his father Shah Jahan, builder of the Taj Mahal. He was a stubbornly fanatical Sunni Muslim who was a brilliant tactician but lacked the vision to see the disastrous long-term effects of his intolerant policies. His attitude rather resembled that of the Holy Roman Emperor Ferdinand II (v. Pt 3 Chapter 25) who was responsible for the horrors of the Thirty Years War in Europe, determined to create religious conformity in his empire whatever the cost. Aurangzeb's literal trust in the Koran was such that he wasted resources trying to grow crops like dates, which suited the lands of Mohammed but not India. Even his first act of usurpation against his elder brother Dara he justified as holy war because Dara was not a strict Muslim like himself. Once in power he issued a series of directives to enforce strict morality, banned music, dancing girls, eunuchs, drugs and exotic clothes, an approximation of Sharia puritanism. He taxed all Hindus and executed the sixth Sikh Guru Bahadur (1621–1675) when he refused to convert to Islam.

His dislike of Shiites was encouraged by the interference of the Persian Shah Abbas II (1632–1666) who captured Kandahar in 1648. In 1664 Abbas encouraged a revolt against Aurangzeb by the Shiite sultans of the Deccan. This and other factors in due course led to Aurangzeb sacking the city of Hyderabad and invading Bijapur and Golconda, whose Shiite sultans he deposed and whose Shiite inhabitants he massacred or persecuted. He was also responsible at least indirectly for a massacre of Shiites in Kashmir.

Aurangzeb's reign was marked by mutual temple/mosque destructions by Muslims and Hindus but his most damaging attack on Hinduism was his rash invasion of Rajasthan in 1679, an act with numerous unfortunate consequences. It called forth an iconic new Hindu resistance leader, Maharaja Shivaji of the Marathas (1630–1680), who organised a damaging guerrilla campaign and also encouraged a rebellion by Aurangzeb's favourite son, another Akbar, who allied himself with the Hindu rajas against his own father. Shivaji had heavily defeated the Bijapur sultans at Pratapagad in 1659, the start of wars that lasted for 27 years.

As we shall see in the next chapter, Aurangzeb's attacks on the previously peace-loving Sikhs provoked them to armed resistance. Overall the effect of Aurangzeb's long, fanatical reign was to overstretch what had previously been a fairly cost-effective Mogul empire and so weaken it that in due course India was easy prey for the French and British colonists. It also left a residue of deep religious antipathy between the two main faiths, which was to cause nearly a million deaths during the decolonisation and partition process begun by the British in 1947 (v. Chapter 28).

In 1739 came the devastating attack on the Moguls and the sack of Delhi by Nadir Shah 1688–1747), who had seized the throne of Persia in a coup. Despite the Shiite dominance of Persia and the fact that Nadir Shah had probably been brought up as a Shia, religion played relatively little part in his motivation. In fact, he seems later to have veered towards Sunni and was trying to bring in a kind of Sunni/Shiite composite called *Ja'fari* that would end the split. It would have helped his strategy, as his army was split almost equally between Sunni and Shiite and his main enemy the Ottomans were Sunni; he had no desire for sectarian differences to interfere with his overall policies. His victory over the Moguls at Karnal in 1739 in the Punjab involved large armies and losses exceeded 10,000. It was like the First Battle of Panipat in reverse, for this time the Moguls relied on elephants and Nadir Shah on artillery. Nadir Shah's main objective had been to capture rogue Afghan mercenaries who had sought asylum in Mogul territory.

Of the three Muslim superpowers of this age the Ottomans and Moguls were Sunni whilst the Persian Safavids were Shiite, The Moguls had a near majority of Hindu and Sikh subjects whilst both the Ottomans and Safavids had significant Christian enclaves. All three had at times fractious relationships with each other, which, together with their internal fault lines, led to them weakening. All three were in due course to suffer threats from Russia as the new Christian superpower of central Asia.

'When fortune favoured them the Hindus returned in almost equal measure the barbarism of the Muslims.'
History of Jihad Web Site

30

SIKHS AGAINST MUSLIMS AND CHRISTIANS AGAINST SIKHS

'True Sikhs must henceforth be inducted through a baptismal
ceremony to the *khalsa* (the pure) and they must leave their hair
uncut, carry arms and adopt the epithet singh (Lion).'

John Keay, *India: A History*

Sikhism as founded by the Guru Nanak around 1499 was
without question originally a peace-loving religion, intended
partially to bridge the gap between Hinduism and Islam.
However, after suffering prolonged persecution by their Mogul
overlords, who were Muslim, the Sikhs gradually became more
militant. The fifth Guru Arjan Dev (1563–1606) pronounced a
new definition of the just war, or *Dharam Yudh*, a last resort
after all attempts at negotiation had failed, adding the proviso
that there should be no use of mercenaries, no looting and no
threat to civilians. He supported an armed rebellion against
the new Mogul emperor Jahangir in 1573 and paid for it with
his life. The Tenth Guru Gobid Singh went a stage further in
1699 and in response to the attacks by the fanatical Emperor
Aurangzeb formed a new army known as the Khalsa. His troops
were defeated and massacred by the Mogul army at the battle
of Chamkaur in 1705.

This was not the end for the Khalsa. They were more successful
in battle in 1710 at Sirhind on the Lahore-Delhi road, when the
Sikhs were led by a monk turned general, Banda Singh Baradur.
He was later captured and tortured to death by the Moguls but the

battle marked the beginning of a period of Sikh independence in the Punjab, though they were still subject to attack by the Moguls and by Muslim invaders from Afghanistan. The new militant Sikh state in the Punjab was further built up by the Maharajah Ranjid Singh (1780–1839) who restored the Golden Temple of Amritsar. After his death there came a series of military coups and palace revolutions during which the army held most of the power.

There was some understandable intransigence about allowing movement of British troops through the Punjab en route to the Anglo-Afghan wars of 1838 onwards. This supplied the British with an excuse or reason to attack the Sikhs. Two Anglo-Sikh Wars followed, 1845-6 and 1848-9, which led to the annexation of the Punjab by the British East India Company. In the first battles at Aliwal and Sobaron some 10,000 Sikhs were killed and 2,400 British East India Company troops. Several other battles were noted for brutality by both sides; at Chillianwalla in 1849 the Sikhs took no prisoners and nor did the British at Gujarat. Ultimately it was a failed war of independence for the Sikh state, which had only developed as a religious enclave. There was subsequently something of a Sikh diaspora due to the demand for their business and other skills, but the vast majority of some 24 million are still in the Punjab region of India, very few in Pakistan, around a million in North America and around 420,000 in the UK.

There was a revival of Muslim militarism as a result of the Anglo-French rivalry in India. French soldiers in the 1770s trained the local levies in Muslim regions like Mysore and Hyderabad and helped them to acquire muskets so that they could attack the British forces on equal terms. Hyder Ali, the ruler of Mysore, began the first of four Anglo-Mysore Wars fought between 1767 and 1799 and his son Tipu Sultan (1750–1799) continued his jihad with attacks on the Hindu Marathas and the British until his defeat at Srirangapatna. This was paralleled by the three Anglo-Maratha Wars of 1775–1819. To some extent at least, the increased level of hostility between the British occupying forces and both Muslims and Hindus was due to the burgeoning influence of the Evangelical movement in the British parliament, which portrayed Hinduism in particular as utterly evil. In the words of William Wilberforce, 'Our religion is sublime, pure and beneficent, theirs is mean, licentious and cruel.' Missionaries from all the British church denominations were competing to achieve mass-conversion of Hindus, largely failing but causing huge alarm and resentment.

The British East India Company from 1805 onwards took over real control of India from the Moguls who represented the ruling Muslim minority. The company developed a tacit alliance with the Muslims as they faced the task of controlling the vast population of Hindus. It suited the Muslims to take over managerial jobs and accept British style education so that they would maintain their post-Mogul status as they joined forces with the British to maintain dual control over the Hindus, who wanted rid of both the Muslim and Christian ruling classes.

Similarly, as Russia emerged as the greatest Christian threat to British control of India it suited the British to cultivate the Muslim Turks who needed help withstanding the erosion of their empire by the Orthodox Russians. That common interest of Protestant Britain and Muslim Turkey survived until after the Crimean War. William Gladstone pilloried Disraeli for favouring Muslims over Orthodox Christians when the Turks were proved guilty of atrocities against the Christians of Bulgaria. From that period in the 1880s onwards Anglo-Islamic alliances became less popular.

'The Turks are the one great anti-human species of humanity.'
William Gladstone's Midlothian campaign

'Unable to agree about steeples and much else the various denominations were united in their abhorrence of Hinduism.'
Lawrence James, *Raj – the Making and Unmaking of British India*

31

ONWARD CHRISTIAN SOLDIERS

'I believe in our active employment in a future life
and like the thought.'

General Charles Gordon

By a strange coincidence General Charles Gordon (1833-85) and his final enemy Muhammad Ahmad the Mahdi (1845-85) both believed in a form of reincarnation; Gordon perhaps a noble afterlife in another Christian army and the Mahdi considered himself an already reincarnated Messiah. Gordon was an ardent evangelist who had some unusual beliefs including one that God's throne was situated above Jerusalem, whilst the Devil's was above Pitcairn Island in the Pacific. Before his venture to Khartoum he had made a reputation for himself with his command of the 'Ever Victorious Army' fighting the supposedly Christian Taiping rebels in China on behalf of the Qing imperial government, which was in theory Confucian (v. Chapter 27). The Mahdi had been encouraged in his self-proclamation by the extreme dislike among the Sudanese tribesmen of the rule imposed on them by the Ottoman/Sunni Muslim Egyptian authorities, so his holy war had ulterior motives.

After the self-inflicted martyrdom of Gordon at Khartoum the destruction of the Mahdi's army by Kitchener also had ulterior motives because of Anglo-French rivalries in the Sahara, but this vicious confrontation between the machine guns of the British and the primitive army of the Mahdi became symbolic of the triumph of western Christian technology over the militarily backward Muslims. At Omdurman in 1898 11,000 of the enemy insultingly referred to as dervishes were killed by automatic fire compared with less than fifty of Kitchener's men.

The final expulsion of the last Mogul emperor by the British in 1857 after a war – the Indian Mutiny, or Rebellion – attributed to the British ignoring the Islamic laws against tasting pork and the Hindu ones against tasting beef, marked the end of one of the greatest Islamic empires.

We are entering the period which in Britain was characterised by what Thomas Hughes referred to as 'muscular Christianity'. His *Tom Brown's Schooldays*, published the same year as the Indian Mutiny, affirmed 'the least of the muscular Christians has hold of the old Christian belief that a man's body is given to him to be trained ... and used for the protection of the weak, the advancement of righteous causes and the subduing of the earth which God has given to the children of men.' It was a licence to conquer the pagan world for Christianity: 'The Englishman goes through the world with a rifle in one hand and a Bible in the other.' It was the done thing to volunteer to fight in 1914, and the government knew they could rely on that happening. Religious backing for this need to motivate volunteers was shown in new Christian organisations that had quasi-military structures, like the Salvation Army, the Boys Brigade and even the Boy Scouts.

In southern Africa there was a strong religious component in the start of the Boer War (1899–1902). The Afrikaaners being of Dutch descent were strongly Calvinistic and objected to Anglican influences on their traditional way of life. This was particularly true of the extreme wing of the Dutch Reformed Church, the puritanical Doppers, who dominated the Transvaal and included its president, Paul Kruger (1825–1904). One of the Vortrekkers, Anna Stenkamp, said that they were forced to trek by 'the shameful and unjust proceedings with reference to our (newly freed) slaves being placed on an equal footing with Christians contrary to the laws of God'. Thus the slightly more advanced humanitarianism of the Lutheran British led to a confrontation with the conservative Boers and 29,000 deaths in the concentration camps alone.

Dutch Calvinists still had their problems sustaining their fragile empire in Indonesia and became involved in a murderous war to subdue the Sultanate of Aceh, an area under the official protection of the Ottomans, because of its dominance in the pepper trade. In this protracted war the Aceh clergy or *ulema*, Sunni Muslims, notably Tengku Chik di Tiro or Mohammed Sanam (1836-1911) called for a holy war against the infidel Dutch invaders. He had undertaken the hajj to Mecca and mixed with Muslim scholars from other areas of what is now Indonesia who wanted to fight against the Dutch. The Aceh War or War on Infidels lasted from 1873 to 1904, cost 30,000 Dutch lives, 60,000 Indonesian lives and nearly bankrupted the Dutch government.

Other examples of apparently well-meaning Protestantism meddling in Africa with disastrous results included Buganda and Kenya. In Buganda a drive in 1885 by missionaries to reform the homosexual activities of the Bugandan royal court led to savage reprisals against the young male prostitutes. In Kenya an attack by Scottish missionaries on what was referred to as female circumcision (genital mutilation) in the 1920s contributed to the anti-British anger of the Kikuyu people, which eventually resolved itself into the Mau Mau rebellion of 1950. It cost 10,000 deaths and 80,000 imprisonments in appalling camps, leaving toxic tribal fault-lines for independent Kenya.

The Americas during the nineteenth century provide many examples of the ambivalence of Christianity towards slaves even after the abolition of the slave trade. The Bible was used to persuade slaves to accept their status with proper humility and by their owners to justify their own position of superiority. However, there were examples of Christian slave leaders encouraging violence to achieve freedom. The staunchly Catholic Toussaint Louverture (1742–1803), known as the Black Napoleon, led the initially successful armed revolt in Haiti in 1799, though this was largely inspired by the French Revolution. The French army sent out to suppress his revolution lost 60 per cent of its men to yellow fever.

Denmark Vesey (1767–1822), a black preacher in South Carolina founded the African American Methodist Church (AME) and planned an armed coup in 1822 that cost him his life. In Virginia a black slave and Baptist preacher Nat Turner (1800–1831) known by his followers as The Prophet, claimed to have visions which inspired his revolt in 1831, which in turn inspired the abolitionist John Brown (1800–1859) two decades later at Harpers Ferry (see next Chapter). In Jamaica 60,000 black Baptist slaves staged a revolt in 1831 that became known as the Baptist War, or the Great Jamaican Slave Revolt, led by Samuel Sharpe (d. 1832), a Baptist deacon. It was easily put down by the authorities and was followed by the killing of around 500 slaves by the enraged plantation owners. Three years later came the best-known revolt of Muslim African slaves in the Salvador da Bahia region of Brazil in 1835. Also known as the Male Revolt, it was inspired by a group of Arabic-speaking Yoruba preachers.

The nineteenth and early twentieth centuries had seen a massive expansion in several Christian empires, mainly at the expense of Muslims. In addition to the British absorption of Egypt as well as India, the UK established various protectorates over former Turkish provinces in the Middle East after the defeat of the Ottomans in 1918. Former Ottoman provinces with both ethnic and sectarian fractures were forced into existence as fragile new states such as Jordan, Palestine and Iraq: 'lines drawn in the sand' made more complex by the ill-judged Balfour Declaration of 1917 that promised the revival of the promised land concept as defined in the Old Testament.

Similarly, the French had been conquering Muslim territory in North Africa such as Algeria and Tunisia and into the Sahara, later sharing Morocco with the Spaniards. French anti-Muslim aggression left them later with a toxic legacy in Algeria (v. Chapter 28).

The Germans having come late into the scramble for Africa were guilty of genocidal war against the Herero as they created their new colony of German South West Africa. Kaiser Wilhelm II himself had his own mystical take on Lutheranism with a strong strain of anti-Semitism and a belief that the Huns were the chosen people. Meanwhile the Italians grabbed Libya and Somalia, later attacking the Christian empire of Abyssinia in one of the incidents that preceded the Second World War.

On an even grander scale the still Orthodox Christian Russians had conquered huge Muslim areas of central Asia, Uzbekistan, Kazakhstan, Turkmenistan and the edges of Afghanistan, where they were suspected by the British of threatening India. This phobia particularly applied in the area round the Black Sea where the Russians had been thrusting back the Ottomans ever since Potemkin's holy war in the Crimea. The fear that Russia would take Instanbul and push its way into the Mediterranean became a major issue in 1855, when a squabble between Orthodox and Catholic priests over the holy sites in Jerusalem provided the flashpoint for the Crimean War. In this situation three Christian nations, Britain, France and Piedmont/Sardinia came to the aid of Muslim Turkey to stop the expected Russian advance. It caused around 480,000 deaths of which about 180,000 were attributable to disease. Tsar Nicholas I (1795–1855) regarded it as a holy war and was distraught that his armies failed to win it. Remarkable as it sounds, he seems to have deliberately caught pneumonia to avoid the shame, or at least refused treatment for it, and so died.

The Russians' next effort at holy war had a better excuse and a better outcome, though the other powers would still not let them take Istanbul. The excuse was the massacre by ill-disciplined Turkish soldiers of around 30,000 Bulgarian Christians who had been inspired to rebel against Ottoman rule by the newly re-established Bulgarian Orthodox Church. As we have seen this provided Russia with the excuse to lead an Orthodox coalition and fight the Russo-Turkish War of 1877-8, which cost around 335,000 lives. It led to the independence of Bulgaria, Romania, Montenegro and Serbia, all Orthodox regions, from Ottoman rule, and a few extra bits of territory for Russia, but the other European nations would not let Russia capture Istanbul. The most potentially dangerous consequence was the revival of Serbia, which soon revealed ambitions to become Greater Serbia.

In the former Ottoman territories that had originally been Christian the mosques soon disappeared with the exceptions of Bosnia and Albania. In regions which had previously been Muslim but were now ruled by Christians the conquerors made little real effort to convert Muslims and it is highly doubtful that they could have succeeded if they had tried. In almost every case their motives were political and economic, but their state churches undoubtedly welcomed the opportunity to extend their own empires. If the Russian Orthodox made little effort in Asia they had certainly tried hard to convert Catholics and Protestants in the Baltic States and Poland, and even in the east a Russian Orthodox priest holding up a cross led the troops in the storming of Tashkent in 1870.

In some areas, Christian rebellions against Muslim rule still failed, such as the Greek effort to free Crete in 1866–9 and the revolt of the Maronite Christian peasants in Lebanon in 1858, which turned into a civil war against the Druze. The worst example of this was the rebellion of the Christian Armenians who had for centuries been treated as inferior infidels by the Turkish authorities. The Turks condoned looting and maltreatment of Armenians by their Muslim Kurdish neighbours. The Armenian revolt of 1895 was put down by the brutal Sultan Abdul Hamid with around 200,000 deaths. When he was deposed in 1908 the new regime of Young Turks regarded Armenia as a soft and popular target to let them show their muscle. The genocide that followed cost around another million lives and innumerable deportations. In our context it has to be noted that the Young Turks policy was dictated by nationalism, not Islam, since to some extent they were wanting to reduce Islam's influence on the state, but by 1916 their main reason for ethnically cleansing the Armenians was the suspicion that they were in a secret alliance with their fellow Christians in Russia, so there was a religious component.

Islam had come to Indonesia by sea and been spread by Sufi monks and merchants but was then conquered by the Dutch to become the largest concentration of Muslims in one subject state. To compensate for Calvinist control of Indonesia, there was the Anglican foundation of Singapore alongside Anglican control in Malaysia and Burma and the French Catholics in Indo-China/Viet Nam.

Sub-Saharan Africa was split among French, Belgian and Portuguese Catholics, Lutheran Germans, and Anglican British, with the surviving Dutch Calvinists at the Cape, but whilst there were Muslim subjects, the majority populations had their local ethnic religions so succumbed more easily to Christian missionaries.

Thanks to the fluke that it was a Genoese Christian sailor working for the Spaniards rather than, as nearly happened, a Muslim sailor from Spain who first crossed the Atlantic, it was Catholic monks rather than Sufi Muslims who set about converting those of the ethnic populations of Central and South America who survived the diseases and ill-treatment brought by their conquerors. So after about 1600 the Christians overtook the Muslims not only in overall numbers but also in technology and industrialisation. The general subjugation by Christian powers of nearly every Muslim state in the world had created the potential for future asymmetric conflicts.

The same could be said about three or four other faiths, certainly Hinduism, which had exchanged Muslim masters for Christians, the Buddhists and the Sikhs. In the case of the half-Confucian Chinese Empire it had not been conquered, but it had been humiliated and infiltrated. The only non-Christian faith that had struck back by 1918 was Shinto in Japan. (v. Pt 3 Chapter 34)

'Would you be such a coward as not to defend yourself
with a pocket knife?'
President Paul Kruger of Transvaal, a member
of the minority Dopper sect.

32

MINE EYES HAVE SEEN THE GLORY – THE AMERICAN CIVIL WAR

'Intelligence, patriotism, Christianity, and a firm reliance on him who has never yet forsaken this favored land, are still competent to adjust in the best way all our present difficulty.'
Abraham Lincoln Inaugural Address

The origins of the American Civil War are very complex but it is clear that while it was not a religious war in any conventional sense there were significant religious undertones and very deep quasi-religious obsessions. The sectarian differences between the more episcopalian and fundamentalist South compared with the less established but more liberal and millennialist North were relatively minor, but there were serious variations in the interpretation of a few key biblical texts, in particular the words of St Paul suggesting (Ephesians 7. 5) that 'slavery was ordained by God.' By contrast the fire-brand William Lloyd Garrison proclaimed in New England that slavery was incompatible with the brotherhood of man. Garrison in turn had absorbed the ideas of John Rankin (1793–1886) a Calvinist Presbyterian minister who wrote *Letters on Slavery*. He was himself part of the so-called Second Great Awakening. This began among Baptists and Methodists in the Appalachians and peaked in the 1840s evincing a passionate commitment to banishing 'the evils of society' in preparation for the Second Coming. Rankin was also was a pioneer 'Conductor' on the Underground Railroad, the escape route for runaway slaves organised from the southern states. This deeply felt and widespread feeling that it was a new millennial age pervaded the North in particular, and supported the nascent Republican Party founded by anti-slavery activists in 1854.

To appreciate the other religious undercurrents of the period, however, it is necessary to look further back. The founding fathers of New England had been Puritans and men like John Winthrop in 1630 had preached about the 'special destiny ... a special and unique Providential Mission ... a Covenant with God' aimed at producing an ideal Utopian nation, or what Ernest Tuveson referred to as 'the redeemer nation'. The churches organised fast days to emphasise the self-sacrificial aspects of an 'ennobling war'.

Until the big influx of Catholic immigrants from Ireland and Germany in the 1840s the country had been Protestant, but the incomers upset the balance and provoked a severe anti-Catholic bias. Preachers like Lyman Beecher (father of Harriet, the author of *Uncle Tom's Cabin*) not only coined the new slogan 'Manifest Destiny' but referred to 'the demonic enemy ... a Roman Catholic conspiracy to spread Romanism across the American West'. In this atmosphere a convent was burned down in Charlestown and there were anti-Catholic riots in Philadelphia. This tied in with the urge to expand the United Sates, in particular in 1845 to take over Texas, which was then governed by Catholic Mexicans. This led to the Mexican Wars of 1846, which were described in some quarters as a 'Protestant Crusade' and which, though they were very popular in the Protestant north, were condemned as aggressive imperialism by others such as Ulysses S. Grant. Grant even suggested later that the US Civil War was punishment for the attack on Mexico.

There were therefore already signs that religious feelings contributed to the popularity of war in the United States; and the first half of the nineteenth century had seen further application of force as part of the manifest destiny of the United States. The Mexican War of 1846 and the Indian Wars of the 1850s which cost some 30,000 lives, mainly Native Americans, had followed the pattern of eliminating both Native American and Hispanic problem areas on the new frontiers. In these wars God had been 'on the side of the Americans', but by the late 1850s God was split between two sides, despite the fact that destiny was supposed to favour unity. And where there was argument there was swift resort to the gun; when the prominent Massachusetts abolitionist preacher Henry Ward Beecher, son of Lyman, addressed those emigrating westwards he said they should all be equipped with rifles, which were thus nicknamed 'Beecher's Bibles'.

A typical example of religious near-hysteria providing a potential flash-point for war was the incident at Harpers Ferry. John Brown (1800–59) came from Puritan stock and was much influenced by the preaching of Charles Finney of Oberlin College, who presaged the Second Great Awakening of Christian perfectionism. In this heady atmosphere Brown came to believe he was 'the instrument of God'. His first escapade, the murder of five slavery supporters at Ossawatomie, made him an instant hero in New England and his subsequent raid on Harpers Ferry in 1859 made him a post-mortal legend.

Certainly, the abolition of slavery was the issue that divided opinion between the northern and southern states, but it need not have started a war if the two sides had agreed to split the nation between them and go their separate ways. The actual cause of the war was the determination of Abraham Lincoln not to allow that to happen.

Despite being brought up by two fervent Hardshell Baptist parents, Lincoln had no great admiration for organised religion, nor did he have strong views on the abolition of slavery, but he was a strong believer in 'the doctrine of necessity' and the Union. His use in an 1858 election speech of the phrase 'a house divided cannot stand' was borrowed from Jesus as quoted by both Mark and Matthew, while in his inaugural he justified the possibility of war as 'a firm reliance on Him who has never yet forsaken this favoured land'.

Even if Lincoln himself was motivated more by political than religious or moral sentiments his Republican Party was overwhelmingly abolitionist and the notional Third Great Awakening of the late 1850s had strengthened feeling even more. However, the Confederacy also had a 'godly covenant', regarded Washington as 'a godless government' and chose as its motto 'Deo vindice' (With God our protector). Both Confederate generals Robert E. Lee and Stonewall Jackson had strong religious principles and a belief in a God-given right to victory. The Confederate president Jefferson Davis was a recent convert to episcopalianism but along with them encouraged a hugely successful missionary effort begun in Richmond, Virginia, in 1861 that led to the conversion of some 150,000 Confederate troops, among whom it was noted 'there was a great religious spirit.' So both armies were well supplied with chaplains, both sides had national fast days and their own jeremiads, both believed fervently that God was on their side and both fought with considerable ruthlessness.

'Obstacles may retard, but they cannot long prevent the progress of a movement sanctioned by its justice and sustained by a virtuous people.'

Jefferson Davis

33

THE CHINESE MESSIAH

'Hong Xiuquan's career as a religious leader began with visions
in which a golden-bearded old man ... told him
to annihilate demons.'
Patricia Buckley Ebrey, *Cambridge
Illustrated History of China*

It is not surprising that the vast area controlled by the Manchu
dynasty of China should in due course be plagued with rebellions,
nor that religion should play a significant part in promoting them.
We have already seen how the White Lotus Society, a millenarian
sect that believed in the imminent return to earth of the Buddha, had
raised an army to topple the alien Yuan dynasty in 1352. (v. Pt 2
Chapter 12) By the late eighteenth century the Manchus were
similarly unpopular, corrupt and blamed for excessive taxation.
From 1774 to 1877 there was a succession of civil wars involving
derivative forms of three religions, Buddhism, Christianity and
Islam, all of them causing considerable numbers of casualties.

The first of these incipient civil wars was the Eight Trigrams
Rebellion of 1774 in Shandong. The sect was a breakaway group
from the White Lotus with similar millennarian expectations.
After capturing three cities it was violently suppressed. Twenty
years later came the main White Lotus Rebellion of 1794–1804, a
larger affair covering the impoverished mountain areas of Sichuan,
Hube and Shaanxi. This was suppressed with an estimated
100,000 deaths, but the figures are unreliable. Nine years on

came another Eight Trigrams Rebellion by the Tianli Sect, which actually stormed the Forbidden City before being overcome with around 20,000 deaths.

In many respects the Taiping Rebellion of 1850–64 was a typical anti-imperial rebellion of discontented peasants, rather like those of the Red Turbans and White Lotus, but whereas these two had both been inspired by Buddhist monks, the Taiping rising was Christian.

Hong Xiuquan (1814–64) belonged to the minority ethnic group the Hakka and came from poor farming stock in the area of what is now Guangzhou. He showed early ability but became bitter after several times failing the imperial civil service exams, not surprising since the pass rate was low and subject to bribery. At some point he started having visions and became a pupil of an American Southern Baptist missionary who converted him to Christianity. His visions and his study of the Bible convinced him that he was the younger brother of Jesus destined to destroy demons and drive Confucianism and Buddhism out of China.

His stance appealed to his down-trodden fellow Hakkas and by 1850 he had some 20,000 followers. His new militia defeated a small force sent by the Manchu court to destroy him. Thus inspired, he gathered more supporters and founded the Heavenly Kingdom of Transcendant Peace or Taiping in 1851. Two years later he captured the major city of Nanjing and made it his capital, passing new laws to outlaw opium, introduce sexual equality and a variety of other popular reforms, defying the conservative and autocratic Manchu regime in Beijing.

The Manchu army was so incompetent that the Taiping government was able to defy it for eight years and it was only the recruitment of western officers like General Gordon (v. Chapter 31) that eventually helped the Manchu to make real headway. The failure of the Taiping to capture Shanghai in 1861 was the turning point and three years later Hong Xiuquan died, perhaps after poisoning himself with what he thought was manna. It was significant that one of the men most responsible for recruiting a more effective Chinese militia to combat the Taiping was a Confucian scholar, Zeng Guofan, concerned that his own native faith was being overrun by a foreign one.

The Third battle of Nanjing alone cost around 100,000 lives and estimates generally of total casualties including non-combatants are over 20 million, most of them from collateral plagues and starvation. So it was by far the costliest holy war since the reign of Timur and perhaps the costliest in casualty terms of all time, unless we accept the Pacific War in that category, including as it does something like 18 million Chinese civilian deaths.

The evident incompetence of the Manchu armies in suppressing the Taiping surely gave some encouragement to a series of Muslim uprisings in China from 1862 to 1877. The other source of inspiration came from the fact that a number of Sufi scholars had gone to study in Mecca and the Yemen, then returned with radical ideas. The largest of the risings, known as the Dungan or Hui/Uighur rebellion, with as its extension the Panthay Rebellion in Yunan, took many years to suppress.

In addition to religious differences there were of course also ethnic pressures and economic exploitation to fuel the fire. To make matters worse there was civil war between rival Muslim groups. Yaqub Beg, a Tajik Muslim from Kokand (now Uzbekistan) who had seized control of Kashgar, declared jihad against the Muslim Hui in 1870 and assumed the title of Atalik Ghazi. By the time of his death and the collapse of his kingdom casualties were considerable, with the suggestion that up to 4 millon died in Shaanxi alone and perhaps the total may have reached 8 million, but the figures are unreliable. Significantly again, one of the government's more successful generals was the Confucian scholar Zeng Guofan who had helped suppress the Taiping.

'The White Lotus doctrines, particularly the incense burning ceremony that in the popular mind came to typify them, produced a coherent ideology among rebel groups, supplying the discipline to recruit armies.'

Frederick Moke, *Imperial China 900–1890*

34

SHINTO GOES IMPERIALIST

'The (semi-magical) aspects of the imperial institution were
modernised in the official cult of State Shinto ... the idea that the
emperor was an exceptional semi-divine being.'

Mason and Caiger, *History of Japan*

As we have seen (Chapter 23) the deliberate isolationism of Japan
after its suppression of Christianity meant that it had lost touch with
other nations' advances in war technology. So the notorious intrusion
of the uninvited American 'Black Ships' in Japanese waters in 1853
delivered a huge shock to the samurai warriors, who had never seen
floating artillery of this kind before. They suddenly became aware
of the inadequacy of their long-cherished but now outdated skills in
warfare. This triggered the so-called Meiji revolution of 1868 aimed
at fast-track modernisation and rearmament of the Japanese state.

The leaders of the Satsuma region samurai took the initiative in
planning a drive towards industrialisation and the building of a new
iron-clad navy plus acquiring an assortment of imported armaments.
However, their great contribution was to reinvent their own class
and stimulate a radical realignment of their rulers by forcing the
abdication of the last shogun. Whilst Buddhism and Shinto had
coexisted in Japan for over a thousand years and both had been
appropriately belligerent when required, the leaders now chose to
sideline Buddhism and adapt Shinto to provide the motivation for
their ultra-fast conversion of Japan into a modern economy with a
military capable of equalling the forces of the west.

The focus of the new state-sponsored Shinto was to be the Emperor Meiji who had just assumed the Chrysanthemum Throne in 1867 at the age of sixteen. For centuries the emperors of the Yamato dynasty had been powerless figureheads but they still retained their aura as direct descendants of the Sun God, Amaterasu. The new ideology accepted that Japan must learn from 'the detested civilization of the barbarians'. The kimono, the hair-knot and teeth blackening were abolished as 'absurd practices of the past'. In 1869 the young emperor, 'the exalted one who lives above the clouds', was transferred in a gold-lacquered sedan three hundred miles from the old capital at Kyoto to Edo, which had its name changed to Tokyo in its role as the new capital. The Yasukini Shrine was built to honour the dead of the Boshin War that had helped the overthrow of the old regime of the Tokugawa shoguns.

The stage was now set for the full indoctrination of the Japanese people as the instruments for fulfilling the imperial destiny embodied in Meiji, the earthly representative of a god that had existed for thousands of years and would continue forever into the future. His semi-divine status was crucial to the new Shinto, which was in turn crucial to the plans for providing Japan with a large new empire. The age-old Samurai ethic of bushido was adapted to a spirit of mass devotion to the state and self-sacrifice to complete the 'holy task' of turning Japan into a world power, the idea of *Hakko ichiu*, the four corners of the earth under one roof and an emperor with the divine right to rule the whole world. Shinto scholars like Shoin Yoshida trained the new breed of nationalist politicians like prime minister Prince Ito Hirobumi (1841–1904) who presided over the first Sino-Japanese War.

The period from 1892 to 1933 saw the plan put in to action. At each stage there had to be what was called an Incident (*jihen*), usually some form of contrived injury allegedly inflicted on the Japanese by the intended victim. Thus, the murder of some Japanese diplomats in Korea, probably at the hands of the Japanese secret service, was blamed on the Chinese. For each war that it waged Japan always sought to put the blame on the victim – including the first incursion into Korea.

Then another 'incident', the death of a few fishermen on the disputed Pescadores Islands, was the excuse for sinking most of the Chinese navy and annexing Taiwan (briefly the Republic of Formosa) in 1895, winning both the territory and its highly profitable trade in opium. In the process some 14,000 Taiwanese were killed and though few Japanese soldiers died in the fighting there were huge losses due to cholera and malaria in the aftermath.

In 1904 came the war with Russia that enabled Japan to acquire territory round Port Arthur on the Chinese mainland, followed by the annexation of Korea in 1910. Significantly, a number of Zen Buddhist monks fought in the Japanese army against the Russians. By this time the Buddhist priests, especially the Zen, had reacted to the state's favouritism towards Shinto by adopting a strongly imperialist posture of their own, competing head-on with Shinto for political approval. In 1896 the Buddhist scholar D. T. Suzuki had written in his *Treatise on Religion* that the attack on the Chinese had been 'a just war because the Chinese were violent, unruly heathens'. The Buddhists specifically encouraged wars against those whom they called 'heathens', like the Russians. In 1906 the Buddhist monk Inoue Enryon commented 'if the Russian army is the army of Christ, our army is the army of Buddha.' So Shinto and Buddhism came together to support the continued wars of conquest. The Honganji sect of Buddhists provided monks who would act as spies or agents provocateurs in helping Japan to find excuses (incidents) for attacking its neighbours.

Xenophobia and envy thus combined with emperor-worshipping Shinto drove the Japanese onwards, with further encouragement from fanatically nationalist Buddhists. In 1914, having chosen the winning side in the Great War, they annexed the German colonial islands in the Pacific and in 1928 resumed the battle with China after the so-called Jinan Incident. Then in 1931 following a further series of incidents including the blowing up of a train at Mukden by rogue Japanese agents, they invaded Manchuria. As we shall see (Pt 3 Chapter 37) the Rape of Nanjing and the raid on Pearl Harbor followed as the new empire had to sustain itself by conquering more and more territory to get rubber, oil, food and steel to compensate for its own lack of raw materials. At each stage the imperial Shinto was used to legitimise what others regarded as inhumane behaviour: slave labour in Korea and Taiwan, exploiting the opium trade in Manchuria, providing Korean 'comfort women' for the troops, ill-treatment of prisoners, germ warfare experiments and suicide pilots. Loyalty to the semi-divine emperor was driving them to paranoid self-destruction.

It could be argued that the wars started by the Japanese from 1895 to 1945 provide one of the most damaging examples of the exploitation of a religion in the whole of human history, with overall casualties, though no reliable figures exist, perhaps in the order of at least 30 million. It was a classic example of the deliberate exploitation of a religion by an aggressive elite desperate to build an empire for themselves at all costs.

'[The purpose of the Directive is] to prevent the recurrence of the perversion of Shinto and its beliefs into militaristic and ultra-nationalist propaganda designed to delude the Japanese people and lead them into wars of aggression.'
Directive for Disestablishment of State Shinto 1945

35

ARMAGEDDON – GOD IS WITH US

'This truly is a war of ideals; Odin is ranged against Christ and
Berlin is seeking to prove its superiority to Bethlehem. Every shot
that is fired is for His Name's sake.'

Rev Basil Boucher, 1914

'Religion was corrupted by secular nationalism to the point
where most of Europe's clergy saw nothing but merit in killing
fellow Christians of a different nation.'

George Weigel, *Against the Grain*

On 29 July 1914 the elderly and ailing Pope Pius X or his
secretariat allegedly made it clear to Count Maurice Palffy, the
Austrian Chargé d'Affaires at the Vatican, that Kaiser Franz Josef
should be encouraged to 'chastise the Serbs' for their part in the
murder of Archduke Ferdinand at Sarajevo. In hindsight it is easy
to condemn this approval of harsh measures against the Serbs. It
probably had only minimal effect on the decision-making of Franz
Josef, but it does reflect the fact that established religions do tend
to back wars waged by those they deem politically favourable to
the faith, promote the belief that God is on their side and that the
enemy are wicked and requiring punishment. In this case Pius was
alleged to wish secretly for the collapse of tsarist Russia so that the
Catholic Church could expand eastwards, but this is at odds with
his demonstrable desire not to encourage a major war. He died
three weeks later.

In the case of Pius it is also important to remember that the Orthodox Serbs were close neighbours of the Catholics in Croatia, who naturally were more favoured by the pope. It was also the case that the Germans, particularly during Bismarck's period in power, had been suppressing the Catholic Church in Germany since 1871 – the *Kulturkampf* – a stance later commended by Hitler, whilst the German evangelical churches obligingly pronounced that God was preparing a special destiny for the German nation. In fact it suited all the main religious groups to believe in the ordained pre-eminence of the Fatherland and by this time the Catholic Zentrum was strongly in favour of the war preparations.

Whilst there is no suggestion that the First World War can in any major way be blamed on religion there were a number of undercurrents that helped stir the toxic mix of political posturings of 1914. The tensions of the Balkans were exacerbated by the hatred felt for the Greek Orthodox clergy and Greeks generally by the poorer, more downtrodden Orthodox believers of Serbia and Bulgaria. In addition, there were age-old tensions between the Catholics in Croatia and Slovenia and both the Orthodox Serbs and the Muslims in Bosnia, Kosovo and Albania. Their religious differences underpinned their ethnic ones and it was the Balkan problem which was most responsible for starting the war. The Croatian historian Vjekoslav Perica considered that 'religion in this case has been instrumental as a factor in galvanising conflict.' In particular, the Russian habit of supporting the Orthodox Church in Serbia was extremely dangerous for peace.

In addition, once the Turks had begun to recover from the pre-1914 assaults on their territory they reorganised themselves under the leadership of the Young Turks, aiming to salvage what was left of the old Ottoman Empire. Once they decided to join the Austrian-German side they reverted to type by declaring jihad on Russia and the other allies. Kemal Ataturk wanted to wean the Turks away from adherence to what he regarded as the old-fashioned, debilitating restraints imposed on progress by Islam, but he did not hesitate to fire up his troops to jihad when faced with invasion at Gallipoli. There was also the internal jihad which the Young Turks instigated from 1915 onwards against the Armenian Christians, later also the Assyrians and Greeks. Whilst this genocidal policy was mainly aimed at protecting the Turkic ethnic majority, it was also specifically Pro-Muslim and anti-Christian.

Essentially the decision to start the war, having begun with the murder of an Austrian Catholic by a Serbian Orthodox terrorist, was made by four equally pious leaders: the Russian Orthodox Nicholas II, the Catholic Franz Joseph, the Lutheran Kaiser Wilhelm II and the Anglican ministers of the Anglican George V. As Jonathan Ebel put it, 'Christianity was by then masculinised by the characterisation of Christ as an active, often militant man and Protestant leaders encouraged men to live lives of Christian action by becoming warriors against evil', whatever that evil was supposed to be. The Bishop of London, Arthur Winnington Ingram (1858–1946) shocked many by preaching the idea of 'a great crusade' in the summer of 1914. Archbishop William Temple with some hesitation justified the bombing of German cities. Canadian Protestants overwhelmingly backed Britain's actions in 1914. In his sermon at the Reichstag on 2 August 1914 the Lutheran pastor of Berlin Cathedral, Bruno Doehring, said 'God's presence encompasses our flags and leads our Kaiser to take up his sword and call for a crusade and a holy war.'

Once the war was imminent it was inevitably the job of established churches to back the political leaders rather than hold out for peace. They felt obliged to go with the flow and prayed to their god for victory, giving the lay regimes confidence that God was on their side. They also had the advantage of prescribing a good afterlife for their followers and this promise was usefully extended to dead soldiers. During the war they earned their keep by burying the dead, consoling the bereaved and promising eventual victory. Religious and ethnic identities were merged.

The concept of God being on the winning side was conveniently modernised by the philosopher Hegel, who argued that it was the divine will that the strong should overcome the weak, a kind of Darwinian solution echoing the übermensch concept of Nietzsche, which appealed to Wagner and Hitler.

It is a truism that the various men prominent in leading their nations into this war were nearly all devout Christians, except for the Young Turks who were for the time being slightly anti-clerical Muslims. Tsar Nicholas II (1868–1918) was devoted to the Orthodox Church, which was vitally important for the survival of his brand of autocracy. In addition, along with his wife he was in thrall to the extraordinary holy man, Grigori Rasputin, for his help in caring for their son Alexei. He later exploited the relationship to interfere with the war effort, specifically in the disastrous sacking of the commander-in-chief, Prince Nikolai.

Helmuth von Moltke (1848–1916) who had masterminded the initial assault on the Western Front that devastated Belgium and brought Britain into the war was an ardent admirer of the spiritualist cult of Rudolf Steiner, who claimed to 'reach him on the other side' after his death in 1916. Generals Hindenburg and Ludendorf were both solid Lutherans who accepted the duty of mass sacrifice for the sake of the Fatherland. Field Marshal Douglas Haig was a committed Christian who referred to being 'helped by a power that is not my own', a tendency which Denis Winter described as 'an unhealthy development in his already existing trend towards delusions of infallibility' that led to him sending hundreds of thousands to their deaths.

Von Moltke was also a great supporter of Kaiser Wilhelm's project to mobilise anti-British, Russian and French feelings in their Muslim colonies. The idea had been first suggested by the oriental scholar Max von Oppenheim, to destabilise key areas like the Caucasus and India by encouraging jihad against the allies, a low-cost means of increasing Germany's war effort. Thus likely areas were bombarded by jihadist propaganda, aided by a fatwah and declaration of jihad from Germany's ally, the Sultan of Turkey. In the end little was achieved except to provoke retaliation in the form of T. E. Lawrence organising an anti-Turkish jihad in Arabia. Both were classic examples of religion being exploited for military benefit.

One of the unexpected areas where religion was used to motivate participation in the First World War was in the United States. The President, Woodrow Wilson (1856–1924), had been strongly against entering the war, but once he understood the pressure of public opinion after the sinking of the *Lusitania*, he began to use biblical language to justify the dispatch of troops. This was backed up by many American church leaders, who had also previously been against the war, but now in Richard Gamble's words 'transformed from principled pacifists to crusading internationalists'. Terms like holy war, crusade, apocalypse and Armageddon became commonplace in political rhetoric.

The war was notable for the proliferation of memorials, stained glass windows and other iconography glorifying the dead, to the point where David Canadine has suggested there was 'a calculated union between church and nation to transcend the horrors of war ... to present the public with a more sanitised and justifiable version of the conflict.' Although religion played only a peripheral part in starting the Great War the established churches in every participating nation played a significant role in supporting their governments and encouraging their armies. Christians slaughtered 20 million of their own faith.

After the Armistice the German high command began to look for whom to blame for their defeat and along with the already fiercely anti-Semitic ex-Kaiser Wilhelm II (and young ex-corporal Hitler) they fastened on the Jews as the chief culprits.

For Russia the war ended just after the Bolshevik coup in 1917 but it was far from the end of fighting, for the subsequent Civil War between the White and Red Russians went on until 1922. Was there a religious component in this war, which caused around 2,700,000 deaths? The first problem is whether communism, the ideology being fought for by the Red Army, should in any way be classified as a religion. The response to that could be that communism did not require the existence of any god and in 1843 Marx had famously described religion as 'the opium of the people', but on the other hand communism did engender some of the obsessive attitudes that characterise religious warfare. The second question is the extent to which the Russian Orthodox Church supported the White Army in this extremely bitter war. In fact, the church was officially prohibited by the new government from backing the rebels, but it had a considerable vested interest in their possible victory. Most of the White officers were conservative supporters of the church, violently anti-semitic and wanted a return to tsarist autocracy and their traditional religion.

In the end the tsarist Whites lost the war. Lenin persuaded many of the Muslim minorities to support the Reds on the basis, false as it turned out, that the Bolsheviks would grant independence to Muslim regions, a policy which the Whites strongly opposed. It should also be remembered that large numbers of tsarist officers fought on in the Red Army as if their careers had never been interrupted. The conclusion perhaps should be that religion did play a part in this war but a very small one.

One smaller scale war which emerged from the First World War that had a religious dimension was the Easter Rising in Ireland in 1916. Whilst its main motivation was the desire for home rule and a republic, the fact that it was also essentially between a majority Catholic population and a Protestant government meant that the ethnic and religious fault lines were very similar and anti-Catholic feeling among the Protestant minority was a significant provocation to violence, a problem which lingered on for most of the century.

> 'There are no atheists in foxholes.'
> Attributed to William Thomas Cummings
> at Bataan, 1942

> '...later generations found the passionate religious
> commitment deeply troubling.'
> Barry Hankins, *American Evangelicals*

36

GUERNICA – CATHOLIC
AGAINST REPUBLICAN

'The burning of all the convents in Spain was not worth
the life of a single Republican.'
Prime Minister Manuel Azana

It would be very unfair to blame the Spanish Civil War on the
Catholic Church and it was far from being just a religious war,
but certainly religious sentiment provided the flash-point for
a particularly brutal war that cost as many as half a million
lives. It was also significant that the bulk of the winning army
had come from Morocco, where fighting Muslims had become
a mini-crusade since the Hispano-Moroccan War of 1859, so
the mindset of conscripts was that communists were enemies
of religion.

It often happens that when a state transforms suddenly from
an authoritarian monarchy to a fairly liberal democracy, the
shock is too severe and the transition clashes with too many
vested interests. This was especially true of the foundation of the
Second Spanish Republic in 1931, which saw the departure of a
discredited dynasty, the Bourbons, and the withdrawal of political
support from the Catholic Church that had for so long maintained
a vice-like grip over Spanish life. The removal of the king was
followed by an understandable outbreak of anti-clerical feeling, a
release of pent-up hatred against a wealthy organisation that had,
according to the new Prime Minister, Manuel Azana, held back the
progress of Spain for centuries.

Perhaps the fact that almost all of Spain had been conquered by the Muslims back in the eighth century and the Reconquista had taken so long resulted in the Catholic Church in Spain developing a paranoid level of self-protection. It had encouraged the expulsion of all Jews and Muslims or their compulsory conversion to Christianity. It had discouraged the spread of basic education in case Spaniards learned to read and question the Bible. It had grown wealthy and overmanned, had constantly supported reactionary regimes and the military. Even women's suffrage was something the church condemned. Hence the high level of anti-clericalism among urban Spaniards.

The new republican government felt free to embark on a major attack on the church and this was perhaps too swift, too radical and too upsetting for many of the population. To the horror of the clergy their role in education was savagely reduced, with secular education now the norm, then monks and nuns were banned from becoming teachers in state schools. Divorce and civil marriage were introduced, religious processions were banned and most church properties were confiscated. There were widespread outbreaks of church burnings and attacks on the clergy.

Pope Pius XI responded in 1933 by condemning the policies of the Spanish republican government in the strongest terms. Clerics like Archbishop Pedro Segura of Toledo, a professed admirer of the Inquisition who condemned cinema-going and dances, attacked all the government's proposals before resigning his post, proclaiming that no state should tolerate any religion except the Catholic Church. The pendulum had swung too far, and a number of organisations began to spring to the church's defence, albeit most of them also objected to the republic on political grounds. These included the monarchists and Carlists, joined in 1933 by the Falange, recently founded by Primo de Rivera and CEDA, the Confederation of the Autonomous Right. The Jesuits who had already been expelled from Spain several times made their usual comeback and contributed with extreme right wing positions.

Meanwhile the republicans were self-destructing, coping badly with strikes, economic downturn and party in-fighting. Anti-clericalism persisted and several thousand priests and nuns murdered. Then General Franco Bahamonde (1892–1975) who had gained a reputation by his suppression of rebellions in

Morocco and controlled an army there of 30,000 men, decided to support the Falange. He staged a military coup with two other generals, both of whom were to be conveniently killed in plane crashes, leaving Francisco Bahamonde to become the new *caudillo*.

The Civil War of 1936–9 began with Franco going to the aid of a little nationalist garrison in Toledo that was being pounded by Republican guns. His relief of the Toledo garrison confirmed his claims to be leader of the right and he was acclaimed Generalissimo. The troops he had saved from the siege promptly set about massacring the several hundred wounded soldiers left behind by the Republicans, an early example of the viciousness which was to typify this war. In the few months after the Nationalist victory at Badajoz, around 4000 soldiers and civilians were slaughtered, but this was small compared with the siege of Madrid in November 1936 when 47,000 Republicans were killed, the majority civilians, compared with the Nationalist losses of 5000.

Although the Spanish Civil war was more about politics than religion it had a strong religious element due to the pent-up antagonism towards the Catholic Church built up over several centuries, coupled with the fact that it suited Franco, like all right-wing army officers, to cultivate the church as a boost to his credibility. 'The Spanish Church heated up the atmosphere before the war and added fuel to the flames afterwards' (Hilari Raguer).

The Spanish Civil War provided a proving ground for German and Italian fascism and a test-bed for Soviet militarism. The Condor Legion from Germany, the bombing of civilian targets in Guernica, and the *Truppe Volontarie* from Italy and the International Brigades supporting the republic all contributed to the build-up of international tension before the Second World War. It was a proxy war between quasi Christian fascism and atheist Russian communism.

"Its (the Catholic Church's) hierarchy rallied to the cause and prominent churchmen were seen giving the fascist salute.'
Anthony Beevor, *The Spanish Civil War*

37

THE HOLOCAUST

'The opportunistic character of Stalin's religious policy was
evident in the revival of Orthodoxy in 1941 as a contribution to
the patriotic war effort and a means to seduce Soviet allies.'
Richard Overy, *The Dictators: Hitler's Germany
and Stalin's Russia*

'I had an excellent opportunity to intoxicate myself with the
solemn splendours of the brilliant church festivals.'
Adolf Hitler, *Mein Kampf*

It would be ridiculous to suggest that religion played any major
role in starting the Second World War, except from the Japanese
standpoint since they had been pre-conditioned to fight to the death
for a semi-divine emperor descended from the Sun. In Germany it
was much more about ambition, revenge, racism, empire-building,
recovery from economic collapse and the conflict between left
and right-wing politics. However, underneath it all there were a
number of significant religious undercurrents.

Hitler had spent his youth in Austria and attended Catholic
schools where as an altar boy he seems to have been deeply
impressed by an abbot whom he later described as his 'highest and
most durable idol'. He was confirmed in Linz Cathedral in 1904
and though he soon stopped believing in the message he retained
huge respect for the way that the Catholic Church refused to alter
its creed and for the authoritarian way that it imposed its will.

'He was deeply influenced by the Roman Catholic Church ... its skill in dealing with human nature and the unalterable character of its creed' (Alan Bullock). He also remained impressed by the church's mastery of spectacle, which he later imitated. Similarly. he drew on the same qualities that he had observed in the political processions organised in Vienna by Karl Lueger, founder of the Christian Social Party, which viewed Catholicism as a means of halting the drift to the left. When Hitler moved to Bavaria he was therefore intellectually well-equipped to win over the Bavarian People's Party, which was overwhelmingly Catholic and though he later abandoned it, he used it as an essential stepping stone as he attempted to gather support for his own ideas.

Hitler had on the other hand extreme contempt for the German Protestants, referring later to their priests as 'submissive as dogs', but realised the need to keep in with them in the early stages of his rise to power. Both Ludendorff and Hindenburg, whose support he needed, were northern Protestants and Hitler to some extent exploited the basic distrust that existed between the mainly Protestant north and the strongly Catholic Bavaria (the German population balance in 1933 was around 70 per cent Protestant to 30 per cent Catholic). He also made use of the rival Catholic political groups like Klausner's Catholic Action Group until he was strong enough to do without them. Klausner was shot in 1933 and the Catholic Centre Party was outlawed on the pretext that it had been concocting a conspiracy with the Austrian Christian Socialists, though Hitler had needed their help to win the presidency of the Reichstag for his ally Herman Goering.

Despite his dislike of the Protestant majority Hitler carefully cultivated its members. His propagandists promoted him as the new Luther and he was imitating exactly Luther's policy towards the Jews in blaming Jewry for the 1918 defeat. Nazi supporters in the Lutheran and other Protestant Churches founded the German Christian Faith Movement under Ludwig Mueller, who was made a Reich Bishop in the forcibly united Reich Church. The church endorsed Hitler's ideas about the master race and the elimination of Jews in 1933. It banned reading of the Old Testament as a book written by Jews. The more Hitler grew in confidence, the more he despised the Protestant church and the more the Protestant hierarchy tried desperately to win his approval, as described by Steigmann-Gall in *The Holy Reich*. Their chief theologians such as Walter Grundman exploited the anti-Semitic strain of Lutheranism to 'redefine Jesus as an Aryan and Christianity as at war with Judaism'. The teachings of St Paul were dismissed because he was a Jew, the Old Testament was kept out of the way and 'Christianity purged of Jewishness'. The German Protestants appeared to back both the holocaust and the military struggle that would turn the *Volk* into a master race. Bishop Martin Staase was a prominent Nazi and Pastor Paul Schwadke served as an officer in the *Sturm Abteilung*.

Hitler's authoritarian stance appealed to the Vatican. Pope Pius XII indicated approval of the National Socialist Party when it signed its concordat with the Catholic Church in 1933. His rejection of much of Nazi dogma notwithstanding, Cardinal Faulhaber, who was a key figure in negotiations between the Nazi regime and the Catholic Church, described Hitler's success as an 'immeasurable blessing'. In addition, the Protestant churches had ascribed defeat in 1918 to God's punishment for the Germans' neglect of the church, so they were not averse to a strong nationalist leader, particularly one who was opposed to atheistic communism.

The national church, which had despaired of the Weimar republic, now supported National Socialism and most Nazi members seem to have been Christians. Under Hitler's minister for church affairs, Hans Kerri, there was encouragement of the Positive Christianity movement, with its 'Aryan' God who was believed to express himself through race and blood. It was announced that Jesus had not been a Jew and that Hitler was 'the herald of a new revelation'. When it suited him Hitler could pose as 'a soldier of Christ'. Even his rabid anti-Semitism had a morbidly apocalyptic style that recalled the hysteria of medieval Germany when the Jews could be blamed for the execution of Jesus as well as for everything else. His war against the Jews therefore had many of the characteristics of a religious war and his hypnotic radicalisation of the German population owed much to the techniques of Christianity. 'The National Socialist movement in Germany is a prime example of how religion and nationalism reinforce and aid each other in a common struggle for power' (Gary Lease).

Hitler was well aware of the usefulness of the church, for example even his annexation of Protestant Bohemia involved hints of release from a half-Catholic state. After his conquest of Poland in 1939 he pronounced that it was 'the task of priests to keep the Poles content, stupid and dull-witted' so that they would provide a cheap labour force for the Reich. He appreciated that educational suppression had been a key feature of Catholicism for several centuries and was mildly disturbed when the pope condemned his invasion of Poland and later his genocide of the Jews. This among other reasons was why he considered taking over the Vatican after the deposition of Mussolini in 1943.

Similarly, Stalin had been brought up in the Russian Orthodox faith, attended a seminary and had at one point been a trainee priest. Once in power he had followed Lenin's precepts in clamping down on the church and between 1936 and 1939 purged priests and closed churches. However, he was realist enough to know that the infrastucture of Orthodoxy could be exploited to help prop up his regime and this was particularly true in wartime when the Orthodox priests were happy to console war widows, to condemn National Socialism as the enemy of religion and even to claim occasionally that Stalin was 'God's chosen one' to save Russia. For them it meant fewer church closures and for Stalin it meant a useful morale boost when he was suffering regular defeats. Like so many Russian leaders before him, he fell back on the old theme of saving Holy Mother Russia from its enemies. The song *Sacred War*, which he commissioned proved very popular: 'This is the peoples' war/A sacred war'. All bishops were now allegedly vetted by the KGB as a prelude to aiding them in some of their activities. Thus, the two least obvious candidates for becoming religious heroes during 1939–45, Hitler and Stalin, did to some extent achieve that status.

Mussolini's alliance with the Catholic Church was much more predictable, as he could appreciate the strength of the Vatican outside as well as inside Italy, he needed its support and despite his jealousy of its power bent over backwards to appease it. He had his own children baptised and remarried his wife in a church before finalising his Concordat with Pope Pius XI in 1929.

Similarly, in 1941 the new fascist dictator of independent Croatia (Nezavisna Država Hrvatska, NDH), the Ustasha leader Ante Pavelic (1889–1959), proclaimed his Catholic credentials and was initially welcomed by the clergy. He encouraged ethnic cleansing of Orthodox Serbs, Jews, Roma and Muslims. When asked for approval Pius hesitated. Croatia had long been a bastion of Catholicism in the Balkans and he sent an apostolic visitor.

Elsewhere in Europe it was business as usual. National churches came into their own to console the bereaved, give courage to the warriors and bolster the morale of their respective states with optimism based on the assumption that God was on their side and would ensure victory in the end.

The fourth unlikely religious hero of the Second World War was the uninspiring and visibly non-military Emperor Hirohito of Japan, but as we have seen (v. Pt 3 Chapter 34) Japan had begun its holy war of empire-building back in 1895, so for them the attack on the US fleet at Pearl Harbor was just an extension of a prolonged campaign in which Hirohito was caught up whether he liked it or not. The alternative for him would probably have been deposition, as had been the fate of his father Taisho, accused of mental instability. Having acquired Taiwan and Korea before the First World War, then added all the German colonial islands without any effort in 1914, Japan had recommenced activities with the invasion of Manchuria in 1933.

By this time the mass brain-washing of the Japanese people begun in 1870 after the Meiji Restoration was well-advanced under the banner of National Spiritual Mobilisation, the concept of absolute obedience to the state, and the new version of bushido with its theme of 'no surrender'. The term *kokutai* referred to Japan as the only nation in the world with a divine leader and it demanded the worship of dead war heroes at the Yasukuni Shrine. Children were indoctrinated at school with the duty of self-sacrifice to help complete the 'holy task'.

Not only did State Shinto provide the legitimacy for aggressive war supported by the entire population, but it permitted what other nations would regard as war crimes, such as the Nanjing mass rape and massacre and the maltreatment of prisoners of war. As Walter Skia puts it, for the Shinto propagandists 'the divine oneness of the Japanese was an attribute not shared by any other people', so it justified the wave of terrorism and political assassinations 1921–36 and the sacred war of 1931–45.

As we have seen Japanese Buddhism had by this time caught up with Shinto in its enthusiasm to support aggressive policies.

This was particularly true of the Zen Pure Land sect. The Zen monk Harada Daium Sogaku (1871–1961) wrote: 'The unity of Zen and war of which I speak extends to the furthest reaches of the holy war now under way.' The Rinzai priest Ichikawa Hakugen was a strong advocate of war and another described the attack on Pearl Harbor as 'a holy day on which Shakyamuni (Buddha) realised the way.' Colonel Sugimoto promised that all Buddhist soldiers killed in the war would live on as Buddhas. One of the leaders most responsible for the Pacific War, Prime Minister Hideki Tojo (1884–1948) was a practising Buddhist whose grandfather had been a Buddhist priest. His predecessor as prime minister during the Manchuria campaign was another Buddhist, Fumimaro Konoe, who later committed suicide after urging the emperor to surrender in 1945.

The Buddhist General Iwane Matsui, in charge at the time of the Nanjing massacre, denied responsibility but was convicted of war crimes and executed in 1948. He was a member of the ultra-nationalistic Nichiren sect of Buddhism, which dated back to the thirteenth century and predicted a future golden age that would follow after a world war. Other members included Kanji Ishiwara, the man who had plotted the Mukden Incident, a railway sabotage designed to propel Japan into war with China. Yet another was the self-appointed Buddhist priest Nissho Inoue, who helped plot the attempt to mass-murder Japanese politicians in 1932.

The Chinese attack on the Japanese settlement in Shanghai in August 1937 is sometimes regarded as the first battle of the Second World War, two years ahead of any real fighting in Europe. It was instigated by the Nationalist regime of Chiang Kai-Shek (1887–1975) who wanted to take on the Japanese in a more favourable environment than Manchuria. Despite vastly superior numbers he failed to expel the Japanese and it cost some 200,000 Chinese lives, four times the number of Japanese.

So for Japan the War in the Pacific was a warped form of religious warfare. For example, it could be said that the Battle of Okinawa in June 1945 had an underlying religious momentum evidenced by the suicidal defiance of the Japanese garrison, of whom around 120,000 died along with nearly as many civilians, and the hundreds of kamikaze pilots who accounted for most of the US casualties.

Whilst the official motivation of the people for war came from State Shinto it is surprising to find that Buddhism, despite being rejected by the Meiji revolution, at times competed with Shinto in advocating aggressive war. Most of the Buddhist monasteries and temples seem to have followed the government line in preaching the uniqueness of Japan in the world and the fact that it deserved world domination. Overall the followers of the two religions bore massive responsibility not just for starting the Pacific War but also for the bloodthirsty way in which it was waged. Not surprisingly, State Shinto was banned by the American occupying force in 1945. Two religions, State Shinto and Zen Buddhism, played a major part in providing the motivation for a conflict that caused over 30 million deaths, often competing with each other as to which would be the most nationalistic. In fact religion was such an important factor in radicalising the population that it is hard to see how quite such an extreme war could have been conducted without it.

Just as the First World War was followed by a major civil war spearheaded by communists, so was the second. Two lapsed Buddhists, Mao Tse Tung (1893–1976) and Chiang Kai-Shek (1887–1975) led opposing Chinese armies in 1946–7 with the loss of some 6 million lives. We are again faced with the question of whether or not there was any serious religious involvement in this war. Mao had thrown off his Buddhism at an early age, despite remaining very fond of his mother who had first taught it to him. Chiang on the other hand had only ceased being a Buddhist because that was a condition for marrying his glamorous wife, Song Meyling, to please whom he became a Methodist Christian.

In middle age both men were utterly ruthless and both fighting for their individual right to be sole autocrats of China, only divided by the fact that Mao had a leftist ideology modelled on Soviet Russia whilst Chiang had been an admirer of Nazi Germany. Mao was already guilty of numerous purges, as was Chiang, who had organised the White Terror in Shanghai. Both had already fought on opposite sides during the pre-1937 civil war, both had then been temporary allies to fight the Japanese invasion, then reverted in 1946 to fighting for control of China.

By this time religion was almost irrelevant, for they had their own confirmed ideologies. Yet Mao's came closer to being what Patricia Buckley Ebrey calls 'almost a sacred mission' and his indoctrination procedures, such as confessions and public humiliations, had features reminiscent of conventional religions. However, he condemned Confucianism as a feudal relic, regarded Buddhism as outdated and had no time for the Muslim minorities in China who had separatist tendencies. Chiang at least encouraged the support of the Muslim leaders, some of whom he described as blood brothers, and had already shown this by aiding the Muslim Hui war-lord Ma Zhongying in his jihad against Xinjiang in 1931. The Chinese Muslims thus supported the anti-communist side, and the Russian Muslims supported the communists, but both for the same reason, the (false) promise of independence.

Chiang as a newly converted Christian also incorporated some Methodist values and some Confucian elements in his so-called New Life Movement, an attempt to create a new ideology of self-sacrifice for the nation to combat Marxism. For some years he was supported by another Methodist general, the war-lord Feng Yuxiang, who according to rumour had baptised his troops with a hose pipe, but Feng disagreed with many of Chiang's policies and they fell out in 1933. Overall, this was a war between two rival factions desperate for power that exhibited undertones of religious influence but no more than that – except in so far as the apocalyptic vision of communism so much resembled the millennial visions of the old religions.

Christianity did react to this during the period known as the Cold War. In 1947 President Harry S. Truman concocted a new version of the Holy Alliance with the support of Pope Pius XII, with his own country Italy in danger of succumbing to communism. Everywhere the capitalist west was urged to assert its divinely ordained morality and resist what was later termed 'the evil empire' of communism. NATO was founded in some people's minds as a 'spiritual counterforce' to block the spread of atheism. The first actual war of the Cold War was in Korea where Russia supported the drive by the ex-Protestant Kim Il Sung (1912–1994) to conquer South Korea, a region which had suffered much under the Buddhist/Shinto regime from Japan and was now the scene of a strong Catholic resurgence. 'The Cold War was one of history's greatest religious wars, a global conflict between the god-fearing and the godless' (Dianne Kirby).

The nuclear deterrent justified its title and apart from Korea the only other serious fighting was in Vietnam, where the Americans attempted to exploit religious prejudices to little avail. Archbishop Fulton Sheen (1895–1979) like Ronald Reagan, portrayed it as a spiritual battle between the forces of good and evil, adding the idea that it was leading to a national revival in religion.

'The religious dimension of the Cold War was of particular significance in the United States, a nation whose people and leaders stressed their religiosity and considered their country to be a special moral force in the world.'
Dianne Kirby, *Religion and the Cold War*

'The Second World War [was] when the Russian Orthodox Church underwent the greatest revival it was to experience in seven decades of Soviet rule.'
Steven Miner, *Stalin's Holy War*

38

ISLAM REARMS – MUJAHIDEEN AND TALIBAN

'The fighters went into battle not under the colours of some new territorial identity but under the green banner of the Prophet.'

G. H. Jansen, *Militant Islam*

It is not easy to pick the moment when Islam began to recover from the shock of continual defeat at the hands of the technologically superior Christians, but two events stand out towards the end of the eighteenth century.

The first was the campaign mounted in 1744 in Turkish-occupied Arabia by Muhammad ibn Abdel Wahhab (1703-87) to return Islam to its roots and establish a state with unadulterated Sharia law and a determination to assert its independence. His alliance with the Saud family enabled the foundation of a near independent state with only nominal inclusion in the Turkish empire. Thus, Wahhabism gradually spread throughout the Muslim world and was to be the cornerstone of many Muslim national rebellions for the next two centuries.

The second was a tiny instance of jihad when Elisha Mansour/ Mansur Ushurma, a Sufi Sheikh based in Chechnya led a forlorn rebellion in 1785 against Russian rule in the Naqshbandi area of the Caucasus. He survived for six years before being captured and in that time ran a strict Sharia-based community, which re-emerged in 1917 as the Caucasus Imamate under the jihadist Najmuddin Hotso.

A few years after the Chechen rebellion, in 1804 Uthman dan Fodio launched a holy war against neighbouring pagans around Sokoto in sub-Saharan Africa and created an independent Islamic empire, the Sultanate of Sokoto, which survived until conquered by the British as part of their Nigerian colony. This example inspired another new Islamic state in Africa, Masina, near Timbuktu, founded with a jihad against his pagan neighbours in 1810 by Shehu Ahmadu.

None of these events marked the end of Christian military dominance. But though the Ottoman Empire was beginning to weaken it did not fall until 1918 and though the Moguls had become little more than British puppets they clung to some vestiges of their power till 1857. However, from about 1790 there were many hundreds of jihads against Christian domination right across the Muslim world and many of them developed into prolonged holy wars.

In 1803, a group of Indonesian Muslims who had been on pilgrimage to Mecca and absorbed the ideas there of Wahhabism launched a jihad against their Dutch masters in Sumatra that lasted for over three decades. This was extended by the Padri War of 1821–38, an aptly named jihad that reflected Muslim antipathy to the ministers of the Dutch Reformed Church as well as their lay rulers. In nearby Java in 1825 came another anti-Dutch jihad led by the Javanese Prince Diponegoro (1785–1855). Various other Indonesian jihads continued, including the Aceh jihad (1873–1912) in the north, up to the Japanese conquest and the final decolonisation by the Dutch after the Second World War.

In China too, as we have seen (Chapter 27) there were several jihads, rebellions against the Manchu dynasty, one by Khoja sheiks in the Kashgar area in 1820 that was repeated several times until 1863, another in Kansu/Shaanxi from 1862 to 1877.

On the Indian sub-continent there were also sporadic jihads. Another pilgrim to Mecca who came back fired with Wahhabist fervour was Hajji Shariatullah (1781–1840) who launched an anti-British movement in 1821 that eventually became militant. Similarly, Sayyid Ahmad after returning from Mecca in 1823 led his Mujahideen to found a small new fundamentalist Muslim state on the North West Frontier at Peshawar, from which he waged holy war not just against the British but also the Sikhs. He was eventually killed by Sikh troops in 1831.

Then in the far south of India came a series of Mapilla Muslim jihads directed against the Hindus from 1836. This was followed by the First Afghan jihad, or Auckland's Folly, of 1839–42, which was anti-British, responding to British paranoia about Russian encroachments in the area and led by Emir Akbar Khan (1816–48) leader of the nationalist party in Kabul. He had already defeated the Sikhs at Jamrud near Peshawar in 1836. His destruction of a British army under Lord Elphinstone in the Gandamat Pass with 16,000 casualties caused waves of alarm in Britain.

All the regional jihads were put into perspective by the Indian Mutiny or Rebellion of 1857, when both Muslim and Hindu soldiers serving in the army of the British East India Company reacted violently to the belief that the cartridges for their new Enfield rifles required them to put either pork fat or beef fat in their mouths. It was therefore a kind of religious war and the suppression by the British led to the final removal of the Mogul dynasty, so to that extent it was a major setback for independent Islam. What British rule did for the next ninety years was to suppress most overt expressions of inter-faith hatred between Muslims, Sikhs and Hindus until it eventually exploded with disastrous results in 1947.

Statistics on casualties remain unreliable, as does information on the perpetrators of the violence, but it is at least clear that mob violence spread from Calcutta in late 1946, that Hindus, Muslims and Sikhs attacked each other with encouragement from their various leaders, that criminal elements and mercenaries were involved and that it was one of the worst religious civil wars in history, with a death toll of around half a million people. In Hyderabad Muslim militias, the Razakars, committed atrocities against Hindus, which were avenged by Indian Army and police personnel. In the Punjab Mujahideen from the Muslim League were organised by men like Syed Akbar Khan.

Meanwhile in North Africa there had been a predictable Muslim backlash against the French who had invaded Algeria in 1830. Abd al Qadir Emir of Mascara (1808–1883), a Sufi scholar and fanatical marabout who claimed descent from the Prophet Mohammed, led a jihad against them between 1832 and 1847 until captured and exiled to Damascus. He became the hero of the Algerian independence movement.

In 1881 came the holy war of the Mahdi in the Sudan against Anglo-Egyptian forces, leaving a new Mahdist state that survived until it was brutally crushed by the British general Herbert Kitchener, who was known in the area as *Dajjal* (Satan). Among a number of other Madhis waging holy war was Muhammad abd Ullah Hassan who had also picked up Wahhabist ideas while on pilgrimage to Mecca and launched his war in 1895 against the British, Ethiopian Christians and any local Muslims who did not come up to his exacting standards.

The Russian invasion of Chechnya and Dagestan, the Murid War of 1829–1859, had been prompted by their annexation of Georgia in 1804 and the need to protect communications between it and Moscow. The local Muslims responded with a revival of strict Sharia law and the message that Islam would be at risk unless all Russians were expelled.

The Caucasus jihad was resumed by Imam Shamil (1797–1871) from Dagestan and Ghazi Molla (who could recite 400 hadith by heart). They founded a fundamentalist, Sharia-based Caucasian Imamate that lasted from 1834 to 1859. The anti-Russian jihads were to persist on a small scale in numerous Muslim enclaves such as Chechnya.

Despite the signs of incipient Islamic resistance the advance of Christian imperialism continued at the expense of Muslims. Morocco succumbed to France and Spain, and even after the defeat of the Ottoman Empire in 1918, its subject regions were only allowed haphazard semi-independence, such as the artificially created Iraq and Jordan, the British Protectorate of Palestine, the French of Syria. Though by this time many Muslim countries had found a new source of wealth in oil, it was Christian capitalism that had the technology to exploit it – and a new motivation for delaying Muslim autonomy.

Two key events restored the momentum. The first was the ill-thought-out Balfour Declaration in 1917 which promised a homeland for the Jews without calculating the inevitable consequence of displacing Palestinian Muslims from some of their own territory. This was to create tensions and was to be a rallying point for all disaffected Muslims for the next century, and provide the inspiration for al-Qaeda, Hezbollah and numerous other terrorist organisations, all of which were to wage holy wars of their own.

The second event was the arguably inevitable disintegration of the main Christian empires – Britain, France, Holland, Belgium and Italy – exhausted after the Second World War. They had only been saved from total destruction by the Americans, who disapproved of empires, and by the huge sacrifice made by the Soviet Union. A wave of decolonisation saw numerous Muslim states achieve independence, usually after an armed rebellion: Syria in 1946, Pakistan in 1947, Indonesia, the largest, in 1949, Libya in 1951, Morocco in 1955, Tunisia and Sudan in 1956, Somalia, Senegal, Mali, Chad, Niger and Mauretania in 1960, Algeria after a long war with France in 1962, Malaysia in 1963, South Yemen in 1967.

The most complex and dangerous of the decolonisation processes was the partition of India and the creation of Pakistan. Since the three main religions, Islam, Hinduism and Sikhism, overlapped each other territorially there was massive disruption in attempting to define new borders and when the plan was implemented there was an undeclared war in which between 500,000 and 1,000,000 people were killed. Since then there have been four significant wars between Hindu India and Muslim Pakistan, three of them over Kashmir, where the Hindu/Muslim overlap had been dangerously blurred.

The region of Jamma and Kashmir at the time of independence had 22 small states, of which 16 were Hindu and 6 Muslim. In 1947 Pakistan began the First Kashmir War and successfully took over a third of the region with combined casualties of around 7,000. The Second Kashmir War of 1965 was provoked by Pakistan infiltrating the region in order to stir up further rebellion. Then came a surprise attack by India in which outdated American tanks of the Indian army faced slightly more modern Russian ones from Pakistan at the Battle of Chawinda. The Indians failed to make progress, some 13,000 men died and little was achieved. A similar pattern was evident in the Third Kashmir, or Kargil, War of 1999, with deaths under 2,000. Kashmir remains a problem area; of the population of around 15 million, nearly 70 per cent are Muslim and they are well over 60 per cent even in the areas administered by India.

The Indo-Pakistani war of 1971 was less obviously concerned with ethnic/religious overlaps but more so with the aspirations of

Bengal or East Pakistan to win independence from the government in Islamabad a thousand miles away. However, there was a religious element; the West Pakistanis looked down on the Bengali Muslims as being much less strict and generally as an inferior race, so they had been imposing resented regulations on them for some time. The belligerent Pakistan president, Yahya Khan (1917–1980) sent in his troops, which led to considerable loss of life, though accurate statistics are not available. For political reasons the Indian Hindu government sided with the rebel Muslims of East Pakistan in 1965 against the dictatorial government of Islamabad to help the creation of a new Islamic state, Bangladesh, thus reducing Pakistani encirclement.

There was one new factor that affected the rate of western withdrawal from Muslim states, yet at the same time made them more sustainable and more confident: oil. The western powers might remove the political shackles but at least in the short term western technological prowess was needed to maximise oil income and the West was so obsessed with oil requirements that it was prepared to interfere politically. A classic example of this was the consequent nationalisation of western oil companies by the Iranian president Muhammad Mussadiq in 1951. His overthrow was engineered two years later by an Anglo-American undercover operation.

Some would argue that the later invasions of Iraq, where British oil interests had been evicted in 1958, had some of the same motivations. Both Iran and Iraq nursed resentment against foreign interference and complicated matters by dwelling on their own mutual antipathy according to their Sunni/Shiite heritages.

The Pahlavi royal dynasty in Iran survived the Mussadiq episode in 1951 but its efforts to modernise the state from the top down irritated rather than satisfied the conservative Shiite underclass, who were slow to reap any benefits. Still more it irritated their radical clergy, who felt undermined by the introduction of western ideas and comforts. The last Shah was forced out in 1975 and the Ayatollah Khomeini (1902–1980) was able to set up what was at the time the only theocracy in the world and the only Shiite-dominated nation apart from Syria. Hence it was a perceived threat to Middle East stability generally and to the Sunni minority dictatorship next door in Iraq particularly.

The other consequence of oil was of course to increase the wealth of several Muslim nations and since this coincided with their fear of interventions and their almost invariable detestation of the state of Israel, it made possible massive rearmament. By this means Iran and Iraq were able to wage a hugely expensive holy war against each other that cost around a million lives, half of them civilians caught in the crossfire. It was started in 1980 by Saddam Hussein, the Sunni dictator of Iraq, which had a Shiite majority, hence his worry that the new regime in Iran would encourage his own Shiite subjects to rebel. Believing that the Iranian army had been seriously weakened by the Ayatollah's culling of western trained officers he launched a pre-emptive strike, which led to the capture of the oil-exporting city of Khorramshahr in May 1982.

Saddam's success was short-lived and the war descended into stalemate with both sides entrenched in defensive positions, only occasionally managing 'human wave attacks' that achieved no real advantage but cost many lives. The People's Mujahadin of Iran supported Iraq and the Kurdish Sunnis supported Iran. Saddam used chemical weapons such as mustard gas against the Kurds and others, which in part generated the long-running phobia of so-called 'weapons of mass destruction' through which the USA and UK governments convinced themselves that they should invade Iraq in 2003 (v. Pt 4 Chapter 40).

Neither Iraq nor Iran scored a real victory and their mutual hatred continued to escalate and fuel their ambition to have nuclear weapons. The United States was exercised by such ambitions and intervened, leading to the disastrous Second Gulf War, which was followed by an internal war within Iraq between its Sunni minority and Shiite majority. Vis a vis Iran it led to threats, sanctions and continued hostile relations. It also gave Iran further reason to subsidise disruption by Shiite groups like Hezbollah in the Lebanon.

Meanwhile one of the longest lasting and most bitter religion-inspired civil wars in history had begun in 1978 when the secular-minded modernising dictator of Afghanistan, Mohammed Daoud Khan (1909–78) was assassinated. The country was riddled with ethnic and sectarian fault-lines and sandwiched uneasily between the communist USSR and belligerently

Islamic Pakistan. A theology professor from Kabul, Burhannadin Rabbani (1940–2011), formed a militant party, Jamiat-e Islami, mainly appealing to the Tajik ethnic group and devout Sunni Muslims. This took the lead in the rebellion against a strongly secular communist regime backed by the USSR. Other Mujahideen groups joined, notably the Hezb-e Islami Khalis. Then because of Russian involvement Pakistan and the US took the side of the rebels, helped train and arm the Mujahideen. Their ideology was strengthened with indoctrination periods at Pakistani madrassas. This civil war lasted over nine years until the Russians withdrew in 1989. It cost well over half a million lives and led to the dispersal of radicalised asylum-seekers across the globe. The civil war continued between rival ethnic groups of Mujahideen, who also had divergent versions of Sunni/Shia Islam, after which the Taliban gave shelter to Osama bin Laden, providing an impetus for American invasion.

The Lebanon suffered a highly complex civil war 1975–1989. The original problem stemmed from the political power exercised over a Muslim majority by a Christian minority, the Maronites (21 per cent of population) a regional sect compatible with Catholicism, which had been helped to maintain power by their French overlords during the colonial period and whose westernising policies offended the poorer, conservative Muslims. Muslim opposition was hampered by its own sectarian divisions, with a mix of Sunni (27 per cent) on the coast, Shiite (also around 27 per cent) in the south and Druze (6 per cent). Even as far back as the 1860s the Maronites had a civil war with the Druze, who were an offshoot of the Ismaili Shia, casualties around 10,000 (v. Pt 3 Chapter 31). The whole balance was badly disturbed when Palestinian refugees began to pour in and this turned to a flood when the PLO (Palestine Liberation Army) was ejected from Jordan in 1970. The resultant civil war produced a volatile range of hostile militias: the Maronites, the Sunnis including the PLO, the Shiites including the group that later developed into the hard-line Hezbollah, the Kurds and the Druze, descendants of the Ismaili sect of Shia. It was a messy war that saw popularisation of the car bomb, the AK47 and rocket-propelled grenades. Up to 150,000 were killed and nearly a million displaced.

The PLO was founded around 1964 and graduated from terrorism via guerrilla warfare to diplomatic respectability in 1991. Hamas was a Sunni militant offshoot of the Palestinian Muslim Brotherhood that was founded in 1987 after the first unarmed *Intifada* insurrection led to the death of several teenagers (v. Pt 4 Chapter 40).

The slowest group of new or revived Islamic states to emerge from Christian empires were those which had been part of the Soviet bloc. Most dramatically and with the longest-term consequences was the Soviet withdrawal from their client state of Afghanistan in 1988, following prolonged attacks from the Mujahideen, whose jihad was backed by the staunchly Muslim President of Pakistan, Zia al Haq, and by the US as part of the Cold War. Within three years the Soviet Union had imploded and among new Muslim states that emerged with little effort in 1991 were Turkmenistan, Uzbekistan, Kazakhstan and Kyrghyzstan.

The jihad in Afghanistan that had precipitated Russian decolonisation became self-perpetuating and this area became the nursery for a new breed of jihadists. A civil war between rival Mujahideen was brought to an end when Mullah Omar (*c.*1960–2013), an ex-Mujahideen himself, returned from exile with a new breed of fighters, the Taliban, formed in 1995. They successfully took control of Afghanistan, imposing strict Sharia law. He was given, or gave himself, the traditional title Amir al-Mu'minin, Commander of the Faithful or Leader of the Believers, and gave shelter to the fugitive Osama Bin Laden (1957–2011) whose destruction of the Twin Towers in 2001 brought the wrath of the US on both their heads. Driven from power and forced into exile again, he still managed to defy the world's greatest military power for a dozen years.

In Bosnia Mujahideen veterans of the Afghan and other jihads fought a bloody war against the Serbs on behalf of the Bosnian Muslims 1992–5. The religiously Orthodox ethnic Serbs in eastern Bosnia had been planning to carve up Bosnia between themselves and the Croats, so began a savage attack on the Bosnians, a race that was probably descended from the original inhabitants of Illyria, before the Slav influx, and who had converted to Islam in the sixteenth century. Some 8000 of them were massacred by a Serb force under Ratko Mladic in 1995. He was more of a die-hard communist than a devotee of the struggling Serb Orthodox Church. The Bosnians were also guilty of atrocities and their leader, the commander Amir Kubara, was condemned for war crimes, as was Mladic.

The Bosnian War was followed by the Kosovo War in which the previously oppressed Albanians in the area, mainly Sunni Muslims, retaliated against the Serbs. Albania itself had 60 per cent Sunni Muslim, 17 per cent Catholics.

Other derivative Mujahideen groups elsewhere in the Muslim world included the Hizbul of Kashmir under Sayeed Salahudeen, the Mujahideen in Chechnya, the Boko Haram, active in Nigeria, Chad, Niger and northern Cameroon, Hezbollah, the Shiite group founded in 1982 after the Israeli attack on the Lebanon, and al Shabaab in Somalia under a US college drop-out Omar Sharif Hammami, later affiliated to al-Qaeda.

As we have seen there were from 1945 onwards two overriding provocations for Muslims to make jihad. One was the Balfour Declaration with the subsequent transfer of Palestinian lands to the Zionists. The other was resentment of the colonial or ex-colonial powers, their materialism and technological bullying, their general assumption of a God-given right to interfere whenever their business interests were threatened. In a way these two strands of provocation merged, for the Jews since the diaspora were no longer like a Middle Eastern people but had been westernised. They were seen as the brains and the money behind western advances, so they were identified as part of the overall anti-Muslim conspiracy. To compound all this, they were the only power in the Middle East to have the bomb.

The Arab-Israeli War of 1947–9 was a re-enactment of Joshua's invasion of Canaan as described in the Old Testament, except that this time the land was promised by Balfour as well as God. At each stage of the Suez Crisis of 1956, the Six Day War of 1967, the War of Attrition 1967–70, the Yom Kippur War of 1972, the Lebanon Wars of 1982 and 2006, the response to the First and Second Palestinian Intifadas of 1987–93 and 2000–5, and the Gaza War of 2008, Israel had either gained territory or exacted revenge with Biblical self-justification. It had also regularly demonstrated its superior firepower, thus causing further rage among Muslim victims; as did the overt favouritism of the US, prompted in part by the fact that there were 6 million potential Jewish voters for any US president. Extreme Zionism played a part in Israeli decision-making, particularly in the gradual erosion of Palestinian territory on the Left Bank.

'I was born in Gaza, my family live there, but I am not allowed to visit them, yet any American or Siberian Jew is allowed to take our land.'

Ramadan Shalah interviewed in 2009

PART FOUR

THE LATE TWENTIETH AND TWENTY-FIRST CENTURIES

'A century after the Great War religion seems in many places to have retained its power to exacerbate strife but lost its capacity to calm and pacify.'

The Economist, 6 May 2014

'The conflict is no longer just about man-made ideology or temporal politics or an autocratic dynasty. It's also about interpreting God's will.'

Robin Wight *Time 24/6/2013*

'To the extent that nationalism can be defanged and modernised like religion where individual nationalisms accept a separate but equal status with their fellows, the nationalist basis for imperialism and war will weaken.'

Francis Fukuyama, *The End of History and the Last Man*

39

BUDDHISM REARMS

'Now is the time to rise up, to make your blood boil.'
Wirathu, the Buddhist monk known as 'the Burmese Bin Laden'.

When Francis Fukuyama wrote in 1992 that religion had been 'defanged' and was no longer likely to start wars he little guessed that in under a decade he would be proved seriously wrong. As we have seen, despite its original tradition of pacifism Buddhism has at times produced a number of militant groups that have used violence to achieve political ends, (Pokhran Buddha or Smiling Buddha was the code-name for India's first nuclear bomb test.) Numerous revolutions in China had been an alliance between Buddhist monks and disaffected peasants, whilst in Japan, Buddhism, despite being ignored by the new regime, still allied itself with Shinto to encourage nationalist aggression after the Meiji Revolution in 1867.

In more recent times the Sri Lankan Civil War of 1983–2009 was sponsored by a Buddhist elite. At least 90,000 Tamils were killed, many of them in a massacre during the last stages of the war. The war was not purely religious for there were deep ethnic differences between the mainly Hindu Tamils and the mainly Buddhist Sinhalese, but a Buddhist-dominated government was determined to prevent the Tamils gaining independence and thus dividing the island between two ethnic groups and two religions. To complicate matters, the Tamils, perhaps for the usual reason of economic envy, had a special dislike for the Muslim minority on the coast, an attitude later taken up by the Buddhists.

The revival of Sinhala Buddhism during the struggle for independence from Britain has been a major factor in fostering prejudice against the other two religions. Equally, the Shaiva sect of Hinduism to which around 80 per cent of 3 million Tamils belonged, added to their sense of ethnic independence. Radical Buddhist monks, the Buddhist Brigade or *Bodu Bala Sena*, founded in 2012, have also encouraged violence against the Muslim minority concentrated in Sri Lanka's ports like Aluthgama, where they had settled centuries earlier. Among apparently trivial anti-Muslim obsessions was the dislike of the halal method of slaughtering animals for food.

Further examples of Buddhist aggression are found in two other states where the religion is dominant but where there are also significant Muslim minorities: Thailand and Myanmar. Burma/ Myanmar with around 38 million Buddhists has a Muslim minority of Rohingya people mainly in the western regions of Rakhine and Meiktila. In that area anti-Muslim violence was preached by fanatically nationalist Buddhist monks like Ashin Wirathu (b. 1968) of the 969 Movement, who styled himself the Burmese Bin laden. This xenophobic tradition went back to the YMBA or Young Men's Buddhist Association, vaguely based on the British YMCA but in fact an effort to recruit Buddhist monks in particular to back the anti-British resistance. It was also a factor that Myanmar's half a million or so Buddhist monks were mainly disposed of as children in monasteries by poverty-stricken parents and retained a residual anger.

Whilst the main anti-dictatorship leader Aung San Suu Kyi (1945–) is a Buddhist, it should be remembered that her much revered father was a general and the prolonged and brutal military dictatorship of Burma was dominated by Buddhists. More recently, despite the stepping down of the military dictatorship, the government continued to condone the Buddhist persecution of Muslims. Some 500,000 Rohingya Muslims evicted from their homes were enclosed in vile refugee camps established on salt flats on the Bay of Bengal.

In Thailand 64 million Buddhists make up 94 per cent of the population and there were outbreaks of anti-Muslim violence encouraged by radicalised Buddhist monks and the Thaksin regime. The prejudice was partly ethnic in so far as the Muslim-dominated area of south Thailand was Malay rather than Thai and had independence aspirations. Basically, Sunni Muslims from the area once dominated by Arab traders represented just over 4 per cent of the population but remained an irritant to the 270,000 Theravada monks, who had their own internal problems. Militant monks like Lucan Pu Buddha Issara were involved in both the Saffron Revolution of 2009 and the Red shirt protest of 2010, reminiscent of the Buddhist White Lotus in China. It did not amount to civil war but it did involve severe localised violence.

It would be most unfair to blame on Buddhism the atrocities committed by the Khmer Rouge in 1975, but its leader Pol Pot (1925–1998) had been brought up as a Theravada Buddhist and even briefly served as a trainee monk in Pnom Penh. He had also become familiar with Christianity while studying at an elite French-run Catholic school before travelling to Paris, where he was converted to Marxism. In 1968 he joined in the Cambodian revolution and by 1975 was its leader, with a policy of establishing an agrarian utopia. In the next four years he presided over the massacre of over 1½ million people who stood in the way of his plans. This particularly applied to Buddhists and Catholics as they were regarded as too conservative for his new state.

One of the most peculiar Buddhist derivatives was in Japan, where in 1984 Shoko Asahara (1955–2018), born Chizuo Matsumoto founded the cult Aum Shinri kyo. He referred to himself as Jesus Christ and 'the Lamb of God'. With an admixture of Hinduism, apocalyptic Christianity and a touch of Nostradamus, he prophesied the end of the world in a nuclear Third World War. The cult was responsible for the Sarin gas attack on the Tokyo subway in 1995 that killed at least a dozen.

'Buddha preaches love and compassion. If Buddha is there
(in Myanmar and Sri Lanka) he will protect the Muslims
whom the Buddhists are attacking.'
Dalai Lama birthday speech, 2014

40

ARAB SPRINGS – SUNNI VERSUS SHIITE

'We will march on Rome in our quest to establish an Islamic state from the Middle East across Europe … and we will conquer both Rome and Spain in this endeavour.'
Abu Bakr al-Baghdadi, Caliph Ibrahim, July 2014

It was no coincidence that the vast majority of worldwide trouble spots during the first dozen years of the twenty-first century were in Muslim nations, and the common factor was the confrontation between the nominally Christian superpowers of the west and emergent Muslim states in the Middle East and Africa. The clash of cultures and races was intensified by religious fanaticism on the Islamic side, and complicated by the age-old division of Sunni and Shiite. It had been given huge momentum by the successful jihad against the communist Soviet Union in Afghanistan, which had trained an elite of dedicated mobile jihadists willing to fight or terrorise wherever there were Muslims looking for help.

Symbolically, the al-Qaeda attack in New York in September 2001 revealed just how deep was the bitterness created by four centuries in which Christians had used superior weapons technology to conquer or otherwise humiliate every Muslim state throughout the world. Not since the Assassins of Alamut had there been quite such an extreme concept of jihad nor such hatred of things western. The outrage caused by the Crusades 900 years earlier was reworked. The bitterness over the superior firepower of the European empires from the seventeenth century onwards was not forgotten, nor the transformations of the nineteenth century when all the fruits of the earth seemed to be first in Europe, then North America, and not in the frequently arid lands occupied by Muslims.

Then it was the westerners who knew how to exploit black gold. The humiliating collapse of the last two great Muslim superpowers, the Moguls and the Ottomans and the centuries when the Muslims were treated as heathens and barbarians drove scholars like the Palestinian Abdullah Yusuf Azam (1941–89), known as 'The Father of Global Jihad', to self-radicalise and search for recruits like the young Osama bin Laden.

Osama stood in the tradition of sheiks who were great motivators, fanatical students of the Koran who knew how to exploit the communication techniques and military novelties of their own era. Just as Sufi monks had reacted by exhibiting extreme austerity against the wealth and materialism of the caliphs, so Osama reacted against the huge wealth of his own family. His father had begun his career as a poor immigrant worker from the Yemen who built up a small construction company in the 1930s and started winning major contracts from the Saudi government. Thanks to his friendship with King Faisal and the new oil revenues he became a millionaire, with vast construction projects right across the Muslim world. He also became a serial polygamist with at various times twenty-two wives, never more than four at one time, and fathered at least fifty-five children, one of whom was Osama. His mother was discarded just a year after the boy's birth.

With so many senior siblings there were bound to be rivalries and attention-seeking, and there was no expectation that Osama would succeed his father as head of the business empire. However, he was sent to an elite school in Jeddah before going to the city's university. He was meant to read Business Studies but spent a lot of his time on theology and poetry, coming under the influence of Abdullah Azzam, himself an ex-student in the Cairo Al Azhar University where he had encountered the Muslim Brotherhood. Osama's views crystallised: he became anti-communist, anti-gambling, anti-capitalist, anti-Semitic, homophobic, disapproving of music, casual sex and chilled water. Shortly after his first marriage when still in his teens Osama answered a summons from Abdullah

Azzam to join him in Peshawar in northern Pakistan, where since 1979 Azzam had been helping to recruit and train Mujahideen or holy warriors to fight the Russian occupying force in Afghanistan.

Together bin Laden and Azzam created Maktab al-Khadamat, an organisation for raising money in Saudi to fund the new training camps. Here bin Laden deployed his undoubted business skills, his contacts and his inherited knowledge of civil engineering to help build access roads and underground bunkers for the fighters. For the next ten years Osama was involved in the war against the Russians until they withdrew from Afghanistan in 1989. After a brief return to Jeddah to bask in the glory of the Mujahideen victory Osama fell out with M. A. K. and his old mentor Abdullah Azzam, who was murdered soon afterwards in Peshawar.

When Saddam Hussein invaded Kuwait in 1990 Osama's offer of help to King Fahd of Saudi was unexpectedly rejected in favour of the Americans, a huge blow to his self-esteem. He headed off in 1991 to the Sudan where he created a new headquarters for himself near Khartoum, his base for the next five years during which he built up a new network for international terrorism known as The Base – al-Qaeda.

At the same time he built up his own successful civil engineering company, which provided day-jobs for his followers and profits to finance his other projects. From here he not only helped the local Sudanese government but organised a number of attacks in other parts of the world; the Aden bombing of 1992, the World Trade Center in 1993, the Khobar Towers in Riyad, USS *Cole* and the US embassies in East Africa. He also inspired related groups of terrorists in vulnerable regions like Algeria, Chechnya and Bosnia. In 1994 he was finally disowned by his family and it was his failed attempt to murder President Mubarak of Egypt that marked the end of his being allowed to operate from the Sudan.

Luckily for Osama his expulsion from the Sudan coincided with the victory of his former comrades in arms, now known as the Taliban, in Afghanistan, so he was able to move his base to Khost, from which he masterminded his most infamous attack, on the Twin Towers on 11 September 2001.

This led within weeks to Operation Enduring Freedom, at the outset the US's attempt in a NATO military alliance with the UK and Afghanistan to destroy al-Qaeda and the Taliban in that country. It later came to refer to counterterrorism operations in other locations such as the Philippines. It succeeded in driving the Taliban out of Kabul and helped to create the new Islamic Republic of Afghanistan under an elected president, Mohammed Kharzai, but motivated a Taliban resurgence under the elusive Mullah Omar loosely allied with two affiliates of al-Qaeda: the Haqqani Network and HIG (Hezb-e Islami Gulbuddin) a conservative group first founded back in 1977. Despite being sponsored by NATO and involving 43 countries this asymmetric war remained unwinnable with deaths among the anti-Taliban forces of around 14,000 and the jihadists up to around 30,000, including collateral damage. After thirteen years of the overall so-called War on Terror the organisation Physicians for Social Responsibility US estimated that total direct and indirect casualties amounted to 1 million in Iraq, 220,000 in Afghanistan and 8,000 in Pakistan.

In his final years Osama found sanctuary in Pakistan, which remained plagued by sectarian issues and divided loyalties. Of its roughly 190 million population, 97 per cent were Muslim, of whom about 20 per cent were Shiite, the largest concentrations of Shiites outside Iran, and the country also contained some 3 million Hindus. Its long confrontational relationship with India, which had 130 million Muslims, not far below the number in Pakistan itself, its obsession with Kashmir (v. Pt 3 Chapter 38) and its permeable frontier with Afghanistan made it a volatile area and perhaps the most dangerous of the nuclear powers. In addition, the oil-rich region of Balochistan, Pakistan's largest province bordering Iran to the west, had an awkward mix of Sunni and Shiite, which led to two decades of violence up to 2007.

The various manifestations of the Arab Spring across the north coast of Africa were almost entirely politically motivated, a struggle against oppressive dictatorships and economic discrimination, but inevitably religion did play a part in much of the civil unrest and civil warfare that followed.

In Tunisia where it was inspired by the self-immolation of the street vendor Mohammed Bouazizi in January 2011, the overthrow of the old regime of Ben Ali was accomplished with minimal force, and revolution was followed up without a civil war. However, the attempt by Islamists to dominate the new government did create unrest and this had to be resolved.

In Libya Colonel Gaddafi (1942–2011) put up much more of a fight until his death in October 2011. He had always proclaimed himself a devout Sunni Muslim who advocated Sharia law, the destruction of Israel and the formation of a new Islamic empire based on driving the Christians out of east Africa. It took a violent civil war to achieve his overthrow. In this process a number of Islamic militias took part and some of them continued the war after his death, including Ansar al Sharia, which retained a fanatical version of his own ideologies and was responsible for anti-western violence including the murders at the US embassy in Benghazi. As allies it had the AQM (al-Qaeda in Magreb) or Martyrs Brigade and these and other militias remained a threat to the stability of Libya.

In Egypt there was not civil war in the conventional sense since throughout its version of the Arab Spring the Egyptian armed forces could at any point have easily overwhelmed any opposition. In the early stages they responded to street violence by allowing the removal of Hosni Mubarak from power in February 2011, but then when the subsequent elections allowed the Islamist Brotherhood to form a government under Mohammed Morsi they began to regret their earlier actions. Mubarak had in the Nasser tradition led a secular Muslim state with a strong military, whilst Morsi was a somewhat impractical fundamentalist who soon became associated almost unintentionally with careless economics, anti-Semitism, support for the Syrian Sunni rebels and a dictatorial attitude which offended the secular-minded majority of Egypt's citizens. Encouraged by a new wave of civil protest the army stepped in to depose him in July 2013, effectively returning Egypt to military dictatorship under Abdel Fattah el-Sisi. The deep divide between a fundamentalist and a secular approach to government was for the time being not a primary issue, but extremists linked to ISIS in Sinai remained defiant and persecution of the Coptic Christians persisted.

In Yemen the ousting of the old dictator Ali Abdullah Saleh was accomplished with some difficulty; the country had been the scene of violence for some years. Around 65 per cent Sunni and 35 per cent Shia, both sects in the region were bedevilled by internal splits to make matters more complex. The result was that al-Qaeda, which already had a presence there, gained enhanced status as AQAP, a leading force for al-Qaeda once Osama began to lose effective contact. In 2015 a Sunni coalition led by Saudi Arabia launched a war against the Shiite Houthi rebels in East Yemen, who were then defended in a proxy war by Shiite Iran, which caused major civilian casualties, starvation, cholera and over a million displaced from their homes.

Other variants of Islamic ideology included the Salafi version of Wahhabism, which had significant numbers of followers in Saudi, the Emirates, Kuwait and Qatar, and was a source for jihadists. Sufism, with both Sunni and Shiite variations, was strong in Iran and Africa.

The worst war arising from the Arab Spring period was undoubtedly in Syria, which, like Iraq and Lebanon, had a volatile mix of sects and races. With over 70 per cent Sunni Muslim, the majority (60 per cent) were Arabs, but 9 per cent and 3 per cent of them respectively were Kurds and Turks. The 13 per cent Shia included a mix of the long-persecuted Alawites and 12'ers. The remaining 13 per cent were a mix of various branches of Christianity and Druze. Since 1970 when an army coup brought Hafez al Assad (1930–2000) and his minority Alawites to power it had been a dictatorial secular state in which the demoted Sunni majority would simmer with discontent. Thus, when the Arab Spring began, Hafez's reluctant heir Bashir Assad had strong military backing but was faced by a number of factions ranging from secular republicans to extreme Sharia-minded Sunni militias.

The Western powers would have been delighted to see the fall of Assad were it not for the fact that they dreaded he might be replaced by a fundamentalist. Syria saw mass killing and mass migration, chaotic bombing campaigns with more collateral damage than military results. Iran as the chief centre of Shiism supported Assad and his Shiite minority elite, and was backed by its ally Russia, which entered the war on the pretext of helping Orthodox Christians in Syria. The results were around 3 million refugees and half a million deaths.

From this mess emerged Abu Bakr al-Baghdadi (1971–) an Iraqi jihadist with a doctorate in Islamic studies, a ruthless Wahhabist with a driving hatred of Shiites and Christians. Claiming descent from Mohammed he preached the imminent arrival of a new Mahdi, promised to repeat the sixteenth-century victory over 'the army of Rome' at Dabiq near Aleppo, and that there would be four more legitimate caliphs before the apocalypse. Taking strength from the militant Sunni groups of Iraq under the umbrella of the Mujahideen Shura Council and also from al-Qaeda, he set about recruiting jihadists from all over the world to help him fight Assad. Having achieved some success there he became more ambitious and formed ISIS (Islamic State of Iraq and Syria) with the objective of creating a new empire taking in initially both Iraq and Syria. On the strength of this he conducted a lightning invasion of northern Iraq with considerable success, exploiting the fact that the Shia-dominated government in Baghdad had made itself deeply unpopular with the Sunnis of the north. To legitimise his rule he added al Husseini to his name, thus claiming descent from the Prophet's son Hussein, then adopted the ancient and prestigious title of Caliph Ibrahim. He espoused such violent and over-ambitious tactics that even al-Qaeda disowned him in 2014.

On 21 April 2019, Easter Sunday, three Christian churches and three luxury hotels in Colombo, the commercial capital of Sri Lanka, were attacked in a series of coordinated suicide bombings. Several other locations outside Colombo also suffered attacks on a smaller scale. At the time of writing, 258 people are known to have been killed, excluding seven suicide bombers. On 23 April, ISIS claimed responsibility and released a video purporting to show the suicide bombers swearing allegiance to al-Baghdadi. The bombers were members of National Thowheeth Jama'ath (NTJ), a previously obscure Sri Lankan jihadist group with a history of vandalism of Buddhist statues.

Iraq itself, with a population of around 32 million, 97 per cent Muslim with a ratio of 65 per cent Shia to 35 per cent Sunni, the former mainly in the south, the latter in the north, had ethnic and linguistic differences to add to its toxic mix. Saddam Hussein's Baath Party had ruthlessly stamped out all opposition, but as a Sunni from the north himself he had particularly suppressed the Shias and Kurds, so there was a tendency after his downfall for the Shia-dominated parliament to take revenge on the Sunnis. The withdrawal of foreign troops left a Shiite government struggling to keep control against Sunni rebels, yet apparently reluctant to reach the kind of compromises that would result in sound administration.

In the early twenty-first century the problem initiated by Moses around 3000 years earlier had still not been resolved. The Palestinians of Hamas were the Philistines, still resenting being pushed from their land, the Israelis were still defiantly using their military superiority to prevent the Philistines getting anything back. The neighbouring Muslim states were all united in refusing to acknowledge Israel's existence. Hamas was still receiving expensive missiles from its Muslim allies, and Israel was still being subsidised by the Jews of the diaspora. It was no longer a religious war in the technical sense, since it was all about territory, but the refusal of two groups of people to share their lands was due to religious more than ethnic incompatibility and the texts justifying their positions were still the Old Testament and the Koran.

'Its subject is not any more the elusive weapons of mass destruction of Saddam Hussein but the new generation of jihadists brought into being by the West's assault on what was until then one of the more secular countries of the Middle East.'
John le Carré, *A Delicate Truth*

'The latest sad news is that the Christian Crusaders (Americans) have burned a copy of the Holy Quran in Wardak (central Afghanistan) ... a heinous crime in a province that has been known for long as home of the holy warriors (Mujahedeen).'
Shahamat 2010 (Taliban magazine)

41

MILITANT CHRISTIANS AND MUSLIMS IN MODERN AFRICA

'It is somewhat problematic whether Idi Amin's religious
fervour is truly deeply ingrained or whether he uses religious
"inspiration" as a means of legitimisation.'
Samuel Decalo, *Coups and Army Rule in Africa*

As we have seen the penetration of Muslim traders and
sometimes armies down both the western and eastern coasts of
Africa had left residual minorities of Muslims scattered over
the sub-Saharan belt and the coast of the Indian Ocean as far
south as Zanzibar. The problems created by this irredentist
religious pattern were compounded by the artificial frontiers
drawn by the nineteenth-century colonial powers as they
divided Africa among themselves and introduced Christianity.
With the jihads originating earlier in the Atlas Mountains and
the desert, the whole area was so distant from the main sources
of Islamic learning that it produced unorthodox sects which
regarded themselves as infallible. There have been numerous
conflicts not just between Islam and Christianity, which often
coincide with ethnic differences, but also between rival versions
of Islam in majority Muslim areas such as Mali, Somalia and
Northern Nigeria.

The fanatical Nigerian preacher Maitatsine Marwa (d. 1980)
proclaimed himself a prophet and insisted on an ultra-conservative
adherence to his interpretation of Sharia Law. Preaching in Kano
in Northern Nigeria, which had been made part of the Islamic

Sokoto Caliphate in 1808 before its time as part of the Nigerian colony, Maitatsine was an ardent admirer of its jihad-waging founder Usman dan Fodio (v. Pt 3 Chapter 38). He therefore encouraged rebellion against the Nigerian government and was the inspiration behind the new group, Boko Haram (education is a sin) or Congregation of the People of the Tradition, advocates of war to create a pure Islamic state in the north-eastern Bornu region. Its trademark tactic was mass kidnapping of Christian schoolgirls as an emblematic attack on the principle of female education, abhorrent to strict Sharia principles.

Loosely connected were other groups vaguely affiliated to al-Qaeda such as Al Mourabitoun, or MUJWA (Movement for Unity of Jihad in West Africa) founded in 2011 and operating from Mali. The National Movement for Liberation of Azawad also started a jihad in Mali and in 2012 captured the three cities of Timbuktu, Gao and Kidal, destroying the Islamic monuments of Timbuktu. A fourth variant AQ in Mali was Ansar Dine. These groups competed with each other as well as attacking the common foe. All were connected with the Algerian terrorist group AQIM (al-Qaeda in Islamic Maghreb) and al Shabbab, first heard of around 2006 as the youth division of the Islamic Courts Movement in Somalia.

Sudan had a 90 per cent Muslim majority, mostly Sunni, but it had its history of Shiite Mahdism, and the grandson of Mohammed Ahmad, the victorious Mahdi of 1895, Sadiq al Mahdi, was still active. In addition, there were small Salafist or Wahhabist groups desperate to bring in Sharia law. The problems were compounded by racism as the mainly non-Arab peoples of southern Sudan and Darfur (once an independent Islamic sultanate) accused the racially Arabic regime in Khartoum of discrimination. The non-Arab response was the formation of the SLMA (Sudan Liberation Muslim Army), which in 2003 began a civil war. Khartoum responded with ethnic cleansing in Darfur; over 200,000 were killed and over 2 million displaced. The Sudanese leader Omar al Bashir was subsequently accused of war crimes. The Darfur crisis was compounded by the jihad of the Zaghawa, over 3 million of them straddling both Chad and Darfur, plus the feud between the more nomadic and violence-prone government-armed Janjaweed militias and the more settled Darfur peasantry. Darfur was also involved in the plans of Muammar Gaddafi to create for himself the Greater Islamic State of Sahel, adding Chad and Darfur to Libya, a project for which he had founded the Islamic Legion with recruits from across the Muslim world.

Of wars caused by Christian militias in Africa one of the most extraordinary was that fought in 1986 by Alice Auma or Lakwena of the Holy Spirit Movement, a Catholic who had visions telling her to lead the Acholi people in a war against the Kampala government of Uganda. After some initial success her army was heavily defeated outside Kampala.

This was soon followed by the Lord's Resistance Army led by Joseph Kony (b. 1961) who, in 1987, after being visited by thirteen spirits, announced that he was the spokesman of God. His rebellion against the Uganda government of Yoweri Museveni, an Anglican Christian turned communist, was also ethnically and economically motivated, for Kony, like Alice Auma, championed the Acholi people, a minority of just over a million living in northern Uganda. They had been treated as both a cheap labour force and a source of expendable soldiery for the previous regimes. Uganda had recently expelled most of its wealthy Muslim minority, but then had to replace them with immigrant Muslims to run its infrastructure; illogically, Kony's aim was to turn it into a Christian theocracy. His forcible recruitment of child soldiers ruined such credibility as he might have had and his attacks led to some 66,000 deaths and more than a million refugees, before his war effort spilled over ineffectually into the Central African Republic and the Democratic Republic of Congo.

Vincent Otti (1946–2007) from the Gulu district of Uganda, probably for a while the LRA leader in the Congo, was guilty of massacres there in 2007–8 and the displacement of some 300,000 refugees. He had pronounced that 'God is the one helping us in the bush ... we are fighting for the Ten Commandments of God.'

The Central African Republic has a dangerous patchwork of religions as well as tribes: of its 4½ million population, 51 per cent were Protestant Christian, 29 per cent Catholic, 15 per cent Muslim and 35 per cent native African. Having until 1979 been ruled by military dictator turned self-appointed emperor, Bokhasa I (1921–1996), a Catholic except for six months in 1976 when he became a Muslim, it continued having problems long after his deposition. Heavy fighting began in 2012 between the Seleka coalition of Muslim militias led by Michel Djotodia (1949–) and newly formed Christian militias alarmed at his success.

Nearby Chad was classified as a 'failed state' and had similar religious diversity: 55 per cent Muslim but a mixture of Sunni, Sufi, Shiite and other minorities, 20 per cent Catholic Christian, 14 per cent Protestant and around 10 per cent traditional local religions. It was basically also divided between the disparate and economically underdeveloped Arab Muslim region in the north and the sub-Saharan Christians in the south; hence civil warfare in which Chad's neighbour Islamic Libya under Gaddafi came to the Muslims' aid, whilst its old colonial ruler France attempted to mediate.

Tribal divisions and economic inequality have been the main causes of civil wars on the west African coast, but religion has also been a significant factor. Bjorn Maler in his *Religious Conflict in Africa* points out that 'the many varieties of traditional religion, Islam and Christianity have been used and abused for both oppression and liberation and all three have been accomplices in both armed conflict and extreme violence.' Charles Taylor (1948–) from the Arthington district of Liberia, later condemned for war crimes, was a graduate from a Massachusetts university, supposedly a Christian converted to Judaism but was trained as a guerrilla fighter and sponsored in Libya by Gaddafi, who funded his National Patriotic Front of Liberia and his coup d'état in 1989. Liberia had an 85 per cent Christian, 12 per cent Islamic profile and the civil war lasted from 1989 to 1996.

Neighbouring Sierra Leone had a roughly 70/30 per cent Sunni Islam to Protestant Christian mix, but sixteen different ethnic groups. It was Taylor's brutal intervention in the Sierra Leone Civil War of 1991-2002 that led to his condemnation for war crimes. Taylor was convicted in 2012 by the SCSL (Special Court for Sierra Leone) on eleven counts, five of them Crimes against Humanity: murder, rape, 'sexual slavery and any other form of sexual violence', enslavement and 'other inhumane acts'.

The Ivory Coast was roughly 35 per cent each for Muslims in the north and Christians in the south, the balance traditional tribal religions. The civil war of 2002 was mainly provoked by large scale Muslim immigration from across its borders; the Muslim area to the north was the main centre for rebellion, leading to several massacres. The president Laurent Gbagbo (1945–) was a Catholic history professor who was indicted for war crimes.

Burkina Faso, a land-locked state, formerly known as Upper Volta in the sub-Saharan area that was trawled by Muslim slave traders had around an 80/20 Sunni Muslim to Catholic Christian population, but the Sunni included a number of sub-sects and the area was threatened by extreme jihadist groups including Boko Haram and al-Qaeda in the Magreb (AQIM).

'The Central African Republic (CAR) is in the grips of its own disaster, the catalyst seen as religious intolerance where confrontations between the Muslim group Seleka and the mainly Christian and animist group anti-Balaka is committing serious human rights violations.'

Toby Cadman, *Al Jazeera*, 1 July 2015

42

NUCLEAR PROLIFERATION
AND FAITH

'I too have a nuclear button, but it is much bigger and
more powerful than his.'
Donald J. Trump on Kim Jong Un

The world map of religions and nuclear proliferation displays
the usual fault lines of world history. Israel has never admitted
developing its own nuclear capability but is generally understood
to have it and of course it was Jewish scientists who played a
major part in inventing the weapons in the first place. The high
quality of Israel's defence capacity, its Iron Dome, largely funded
by the United States, partly motivated by the voting capacity of the
Jewish diaspora across the Atlantic, means that one of the world's
smallest religions in one of the world's smallest nations, which
for historical reasons is one of the least popular owing to historic
prejudice and extraordinary favouritism shown it by the West, as
perceived by all its Muslim neighbours, is arguably one of the most
dangerous. Yet its population includes 17 per cent Muslims.

The potential acquisition of nuclear weapons by neighbouring
Muslim nations was therefore a cause for panic, as happened when
the Sunni Muslim regime of Saddam Hussein was believed to be on
the verge of building its own weapons of mass destruction (or the
world was led to believe it was). The American defeat of Saddam
and the fall of his Sunni regime meant that Iraq's Shiite majority
would take over and further complicate the situation. Of the three

major powers in the Middle East, Turkey is provided with nuclear cover by the United States, Saudi Arabia has the cash to purchase as much highly sophisticated defence equipment, including perhaps nuclear, as it wants, while Iran has been forced to delay its status as a nuclear power by severe sanctions imposed by most of the rest of the world.

Thus, the Judaism-Islam nuclear fault line is crossed by the probable Sunni-Shiite nuclear fault line. Iran under a belligerently Shiite regime and on the verge of full nuclear competence was theologically motivated to support fellow Shiites regimes in Iraq and Syria, plus numerous Shiite minorities elsewhere. Saudi Arabia, with an aggressive and very conservative approach to making all Muslims become Sunni Muslims, has followed a risky path by supporting proxy wars to achieve its Wahabbist agenda. Turkey too has advanced weaponry, alongside US nuclear support. In a region where monarchies have largely been abolished – Iraq, Egypt and Iran have all got rid of them – the Saudi dynasty has to justify its powers, its vast wealth, even its continued existence by demonstrating visible commitment to conservative Sharia-based Islam.

Beyond this there are other Islamic states, particularly former members of the Soviet Union, that might have the capacity to buy nuclear weapons on the black market. These independent post-Soviet republics include Kazakhstan (18 million population, 98 per cent Muslim), Uzbekistan (33 million, 79 per cent Muslim), Tajikistan (8 million, 98 per cent Muslim), Turkmenistan (6 million, 89 per cent Muslim) and Kyrgyzstan (6 million, 80 per cent Muslim). All have sectarian minorities and internal fault lines, both ethnic and religious. Of the mainly Christian ex-Soviet republics Ukraine has 42 million, 65 per cent Orthodox, Belarus 10 million, 82 per cent Orthodox and Moldova 3 million, 93 per cent Orthodox.

Of the five official nuclear powers which backed the Nuclear Non-proliferation Treaty of 1970, the United States and the Russian Republic have seen some revival in their Christian profiles, the US moving towards increased fundamentalism and Russia for its own reasons reverting from 1930s Leninist atheism to a sentimental attachment to the resuscitated Russian Orthodox Church. China too has backtracked somewhat from Maoist atheism, showing a revived respect for Confucian values. France and the United Kingdom have on the other hand seen a rapid and serious decline in the public and perhaps private importance of their main denominations of the Christian church. Officially atheist North Korea's obsession with developing its nuclear capability caused even more international concern than that of the Shiite government of Iran.

In addition to the static potential lines of religious and ethnic friction, there are also the mobile fault lines created by barely detectable submarines carrying nuclear ballistic missiles, with over forty being operated by the official nuclear powers, the US, Russia, China, United Kingdom and France and another forty or so were under construction. There were also single submarines already joining the pattern of threat from two of the non-official nuclear powers, India and Pakistan, which as we have seen have a volatile history. Making these fault lines even more dangerous is the reliance of the launch process on computerised communication, which is potentially open both to human error and to deliberate hacking organised by either official or rogue operators willing to risk nuclear war.

'Today it (nuclear confrontation) is focussed on quality and involves several nations not just two. The risk for nuclear conflict is higher than it was during the Cold War.'
William Perry, former US Defence Secretary,
Time, January 2018

43

THE STRANGE DEMISE OF SECULARISM

'In each of these countries, India, Israel and Algeria, secular elites failed to reckon with the religiosity of their own people and found themselves on the back foot among a rising tide of religious nationalism.'

Michael Warzer, *Times of India*

Of the rare occasions when a dead religion suddenly comes alive again perhaps the most remarkable was Russia, where the Orthodox Church had been driven underground for eighty years until it suited Vladimir Putin, an adult convert apparently, to resurrect it as a prop for his semi-perpetual presidency. He also showed considerable acuity in recognising that a long downtrodden religion would be much more popular than one which had held on to all its riches and pomp. Kirill, the Patriarch of Moscow (1946–) has proven an important ally for Putin's conservative domestic policies of opposing same-sex marriage, homosexuality generally, but particularly among Muslims as in Chechnya, and abortion. He has also blessed Putin's annexation of the Crimea in 2014 and through Father Vitalii of Slavkinov given some support to the pro-Russian fighters in the Ukraine. Igor Hirkin 'Strelkov', leader of the Donbas terrorists, had used as his cover a visit to the monasteries of Athos to procure holy relics to bring to the Crimea.

The church backed Putin's policy of supporting the Assad regime in Syria with the excuse that his use of air power would help save Syrian Christians, a move welcomed by the Syrian Archbishop Jean-Clement Jeanbart. Similarly, the highly influential priest, the celibate Vsevolod Chaplin, had preached 'the holy war against terrorism' and the special duty to protect Christian people living in Muslim countries, thus harking back to Tsar Nicholas I and his interventions to help Christians in the Ottoman Empire, which ended in his holy war in the Crimea. Russia's incorporation of Muslim enclaves into its territory, particularly the North Caucasus, later led to the migration of impoverished Muslim peasants into the West Siberian oilfields to find work, thus creating a rootless group of migrant workers highly susceptible to radicalisation and a recruiting ground for Islamic State, hence Putin's vested interest in suppressing it. Dokka Umarov (1964–2013) the traditionalist Muslim leader of Chechnya, made himself the First Emir of the Caucasus Emirate. He was declared dead in 2014 by an Islamic source. It was reported he was killed by poison the previous year.

The same pattern of politically useful revivals of religion has also been true of other ex-communist regions. The Serbian Orthodox Church sprang back into action to support Slobodan Milosevic in 1992 and blessed the shelling of Sarajevo, just as the local bishops backed Radovan Karadzic in Bosnia. One of the Serbian saints was after all Prince Lazar, defeated hero of the battle of Kosovo.

The former Socialist Republic of Uzbekistan developed its own militant Islamic force, the Hizb ut Tahrir, which has aimed to help the Muslim diaspora which straddles the Chinese border and encouraged the Uighur Muslims of Xinjiang in their efforts to survive oppression by the Chinese government. The Shaoguan Incident of 2009, a civil disturbance following the rumoured sexual assault of a Han Chinese woman, was followed by the Urumqi riots and a further clamp-down by the Chinese.

Another surprise was the reversal of secularisation in Turkey, where Islam had been kept out of politics since the days of Kemal Ataturk. Under Recep Erdogan Turkey turned away from Europe and Kemalist secularism towards a strong Islamist strategy, which included war against the Kurds. Since the late 1960s Turkey supported a significant right-wing paramilitary group, the Grey Wolves, responsible in recent times for the Bangkok bombing of 2015 and for an attempted coup d'état in Azerbaijan.

Even in that apparently most materialist of superpowers, the United States, there has been significantly increased support for fundamentalist versions of Christianity. Ronald Reagan pioneered the right-wing alliance with the church against 'the forces of evil' and was allegedly the first president to say 'God Bless America' at his inauguration. Islamophobic and belligerent presidents such as the two Bushes showed their Christian credentials. It is significant that a Gallup poll in 2000 showed that members of Protestant churches were much more supportive of the Iraq war than Catholics, Protestants were more likely to be Republicans.

With the further shift to the right in 2016 came the calls of Donald Trump's on-and-off strategist Steve Bannon (1953–) for a Christian Militia to take on 'the global war against Islamic fascism'. Bannon, from an Irish Catholic family, was too conservative for Pope Francis but had dabbled in Zen Buddhism whilst serving in the Navy and acquired an apocalyptic view of the moral decline of the world. Donald Trump, brought up as a Presbyterian, made a point of attending National Prayer Breakfasts and identified with the religious as well as political conservative right, feeding off its hatred for liberal championing of same-sex marriage and abortion. He also very firmly backed the far-right Israeli government of Netanyahu and added to tensions in the Middle East by recognising Jerusalem as the capital of Israel. His pro-Jewish stance was echoed by his Vice President Mike Peece, a former Catholic turned born-again evangelical. It is difficult to know how much of this posturing is genuinely based on moral or religious conviction. Just as Putin's stance has been described by some commentators as nothing more complex than a vague Russian patriotism, so Trump's conservative attacks on liberal mores and his casual racism were perhaps nothing more than the exploitation of 'identity politics' to provoke a defensive reaction in his supporters, as Bannon himself pointed out.

Similarly, in Western Europe resentment against the new liberal morality has linked up with religious nationalism and anti-immigration feelings to engender popular support for new right-wing parties. Geesty Wilders in Holland headed the Dutch party for Independence, which is anti-Islamic. The French National Front, the Hungarian Jobbik party, and the pro-Catholic CitizenGo organisation in Spain have all followed this pattern.

South and Central America have also seen significant religious convulsions owing to disillusionment with the Catholic Church that has dominated the area for 500 years, but is now seeing a serious drift away to Pentecostalism, particularly among indigenous peoples, with an average swing of around 12 per cent. One of the regions where the swing was greatest was Guatemala, where it reached 40 per cent. A Guatemalan general, Rios Montt (1926–2018) joined the California- based Church of the Word and became one of its teachers before launching a coup against the government in 1982 using apocalyptic language from the Book of Revelations, attacking both Catholicism and communism, the second target garnering him support from Ronald Reagan. To enforce his new regime he ordered the destruction of 600 villages. As many as 10,000 peasants were murdered and he was accused of war crimes. On a smaller scale, Pentecostalists came to dominate the Chiapas region of Mexico, partly due to resentment about taxation, and were involved in violence both against the Catholic Church and the government.

Among Muslim nations Iran was perhaps the first to enforce a strict de-secularisation, when under Ayatollah Khomeini it won significant support for holy war against Sunni Islamic neighbours. Having been ahead of the curve, however, Iranians eventually began to tire of Sharia austerity. Nevertheless, it preserved an unhealthy alliance with Russia and the Assad regime in Syria and pursued its proxy war against Saudi Arabia in the bloodbath of Yemen. The Saudi Arabian regime had made strict Wahhabism a justification for keeping its oppressive monarchy and parading its cash and credentials in armed support for all its Sunni allies, and its proxy war against Iran in the Yemen plus numerous other rebel Islamic groups in Africa and Asia.

Two other Islamic nations have shown a drift away from secularism, Bangladesh and Indonesia. There has been Islamic violence against Chinese elites, particularly in the contest for the governorship of Jakarta. Pakistan too, since the secular period of the Bhuttos, has clung to its Islamic roots and had ambiguous relationships with the Mujahideen groups on its Afghan borders.

One of the most remarkable and significant shifts away from the secular has been in India since the rise of the BJP and Hindu nationalism. Rashtriya Swayamsevak Sangh (RSS) had an aggressive paramilitary approach to Hindutva and was involved in anti-Baptist violence in Odisha in 2008. Nahendra Modi (1950–) who attended an Ashram in his youth, built his political career on a mixture of Islamophobia and commercial nous. His complicity in the anti-Muslim riots in Gujarat in 2002 enhanced his credentials as a pro-Hindu prime minister. India is the world's largest nation with its own dominant religion and Hinduism is the last surviving major example of polytheism. It also has the largest minority religious group in the world, Muslims. Naturally, an essentially anti-Muslim government has spawned Muslim opposition. Zakir Naik (1965–), the Mumbai preacher, created a huge following with his Salafi doctrine of reviving undiluted Sharia law and while he denounced general terrorism, he urged targeted violence.

Among the fault lines left behind by missionaries, one of the strangest is in Nagaland close to the Burmese border, where 88 per cent of its 2 million population are Baptist Christians who began an independence war in 1954 under the leadership of Zapu Phizo (1904–1990). India has two other majority Baptist states, Mizoram and Meghalaya.

The Sikhs too have had periods of militancy in favour of independence, religious separatism encouraged by assertions of economic neglect by the Hindu parties and educational disparity due to compulsory teaching in the Hindu language. There was continued violence 1978–92 and after Operation *Blue Star*, an Indian Army action to remove militant religious leader Jarnail Singh Bhindranwale and his followers from the Golden Temple complex in Amritsar, it was a Sikh bodyguard who murdered Indira Ghandi in 1984.

Even the world's largest officially atheist state, China, started showing signs of reverting back to Confucian ethics when Hu Jin Tao took over as Supreme Leader in 2002. He began promoting slogans like 'The Harmonious Society' and the eight virtues. President Xi regularly quoted from Confucian texts in his speeches and Confucian values are relevant to his proclaimed plan to eliminate government corruption.

In the communist dictatorship of North Korea Kim Jong Un (1984–) is the third generation of what is referred to as 'a sacred bloodline'. The embalmed bodies of both his father and grandfather are on display in the Pyonyang Palace of the Sun.

The regime remains officially anti-religious, partly as most religions are regarded as the work of imperialist invaders, but it suits the dynasty to give the state ideology some of the features of a religion; its leaders are god-like. There is some respect for what is regarded as North Korea's indigenous religion, Chondoism, founded in the nineteenth century as a mixture of Confucian ideas and native shamanism. Chondoism gained its anti-imperialist credentials by starting a large rebellion, the Donghak Peasant Revolution, in 1894, which ended in defeat and mass executions after the battle of Ugeumchi.

A different but perhaps linked trend was observable in South and Central America where adherence to the generally conservative and monopolistic Catholic regimes has deteriorated and instead there has been dramatic growth in various forms of protestant sects, particularly the Pentecostals, whose apocalyptic ideas appeal to impoverished peasants and urban workers disillusioned by corrupt governments. This has led to conflict in some regions such as Guatemala, where Rios Montt the born-again Christian dictator committed significant atrocities.

'A pseudo religious philosophy promises North Koreans a kind
of immortality through their dedication to the state.'
Antonia Blumberg, *Huffpost*

'The Chinese state organised a symposium on the contemporary
relevance of his (Confucius') teachings.'
Jonathan Watts, *Guardian Weekly*

CONCLUSION

All religious wars have non-religious features and all other wars are 'contaminated' by religion. While genuine religious wars have caused untold misery over many centuries, perhaps even more suffering has been caused by the fact that so many other wars were rendered respectable by religion.

Most wars are copy-cat wars, for it is easier to persuade people to fight for a cause if that cause has already been fought for by others. This is particularly true of religious wars; the crusades replicated themselves, as did the habit-forming sectarian rivalries like Sunni/Shiite and Catholic/Protestant.

In terms of conflict within religions, the main Protestant/Catholic rivalry 1524–1648 may have cost as many as 10 million lives, of which a large proportion died in the German Thirty Years War. Figures for Sunni/Shiite conflict are much harder to estimate, for it has lasted from 586 to the present day over a very wide area, and the figure should include the genocidal contribution of Timur.

Of Christian religious wars against non-Christians, the Middle Eastern crusades cost between one and two million lives but the Chinese Taiping up to twenty million. However, the Spanish Christian conquest of South and Central America was a catastrophe. Estimates of the demographic impact vary hugely: one states that there were 50 million indigenous people when the Spanish arrived and two hundred years later there were 2 million left. Mostly this was caused by disease. The Christian acceptance of the slave trade also caused numerous wars in Africa as chieftains fought over prisoners to sell to the European traders.

Among Muslim conquests of non-Muslims the most damaging was that of India *c.*1000–1525, which may have caused between 60 and 80 million deaths.

Of wars started in the name of Buddhism the Red Turban rebellion which brought the Ming to power must have caused at least a million deaths, though figures are unreliable. However, the Buddhist contribution, along with Shinto, to starting the Sino-Japanese and Pacific Wars cost at least thirty million. The only significant war attributable to Taoism, the Yellow Turban Rebellion against the eastern Han dynasty, cost three to seven million lives.

The level of blame attributable to religious input in all wars is extremely hard to quantify. What is certain is that almost every war received at least passive support from the relevant religions and that hardly any wars have ever been prevented by religion.

Recent wars have shown increased signs of radicalisation and suicidal fanaticism verging on paranoia. The movement of large numbers of political and economic migrants has led to isolated pockets of minority religious groups subject to real or suspected persecution. The result has been an increase in long-range recruitment, in asymmetric or terrorist warfare, and in proxy wars. Certainly, some of the early splits in Christianity were accompanied by extreme levels of violence: the Arian Wars, the Albigensian Crusade and the wars of the Reformation in Europe are examples. The levels of quasi-religious obsession evident in the Second World War, when Christianity, Shinto and Buddhism provided an eruptive legacy, were followed by a new wave of Muslim jihad following the Russian intervention in Afghanistan.

This recent radicalisation, however, creates a willingness to fight and to kill only marginally stronger than that created by the mental manipulation practised by almost all the great empires in history and in this manipulation religion played a key role.

'The attraction of religion to national identity continues apace and the usefulness to each other has been exploited time and again ... most notably in the National Socialist movement in Germany in the 1920s and 30s.'
Gary Lease, *Odd Fellows in the Politics of Religion*

APPENDICES

World Religious Affiliation Today
These figures can only be taken as very crude estimates and can make no distinction between highly committed members of a sect and those who are mere nominal adherents. For latest estimates consult Pew Research Centre website.

Christians	2.3 billion	30 per cent
Catholic	1.1 billion	16 per cent
Protestant	600 million	9 per cent
Orthodox	300 million	3.5 per cent
Muslims	1.5 billion	21 per cent
Sunni	1.35 billion	19 per cent
Shiite	150 million	2 per cent
Agnostic/atheist	1 2 billion	16 per cent
Hindus	900 million	13 per cent
Buddhist	520 million	7 per cent
Tribal/African	400 million	6 per cent
Chinese Traditional/Folk	400 million	6 per cent
Sikhs	30 million	0.5 per cent
Judaism	14 million	0.25 per cent
Jains	4 million	0.06 per cent
Shinto	4 million	0.06 per cent
Total	7.2 billion	

Chronological List of Prominent Leaders or Inspirers of Religious or Semi-religious Wars

Joshua, siege of Jericho c.15th century BC

Vishtaspa of Balk for Mazda against Turan c.15th century BC

Pharaoh Rameses II c.1250 BC

Assurbanipal of Assyria 7th century BC

Judas Maccabeus 160 BC

Datthagamini of Sri Lanka for Buddhism, 2nd century BC

Bar Kochba in Israel AD 132

Zhang Lu, for Taoism, Yellow Turbans, War of Five Pecks of Rice AD 184

Ardashir of Pars for Zoroastrianism, conquest of Persia AD 224

Emperor Constantine for Christianity, Battle of Saxa Rubra AD 312

Zana of Aksum for Christianity c.AD 350

Emperor Theodosius for Christianity AD 392

Faqing, Buddhist against Wei emperor, AD 515

Justinian I, war against Arian heretics in North Africa AD 533

Mohammed, war against Meccans 620

Waddiq, conquest of Syria for Islam 7th century

Caliph Ali, Battles against Ummayads AD 656-661

Caliph Yazid, defeat of Hussein and first Shiites AD 680

Emperor Leo, campaign against iconophiles 7th century

Charlemagne, conquest of Saxony and invasion of Muslim Spain 7th century

Otto I, conquest of Italy to found Holy Roman Empire 9th century

Alexander Nevski, defeat of Catholic Teutonic Knights by Russians

Dmitri Donskoy, defeat of Muslim tartars by Muscovites

Alfonso, Reconquista of Portugal

Pope Urban II, launch of First Crusade 11th century

St Bernard, launch of Second Crusade 12th century

Joan of Arc, holy war against the English 15th century

Charles V, battle of Mühlberg against Protestants 1546

Cortes, conquest of heathen Aztecs 16th century

Pisarro, conquest of heathen Incas 16th century

Henri III against future Henri IV, French Wars of Religion 16th century

Philip II, Eighty Years War against Dutch Protestants and the Armada 1588

Selim the Grim, attack on Shiites 1514–17

Ivan IV, capture of Kazan from Muslim Tartars 1547

Earls of Argyll and Rothes, Bishops' Wars against Anglican England 1630

Oliver Cromwell, English Civil War and attack on Irish Catholics 1644

Frederick of Palatine, Battle of White Mountain against Catholics 1619

Ferdinand II of Austria, Thirty Years War against Protestants 1619

Gustavus Adolphus, Protestant champion in Thirty Years War

Suleiman, conquests in Europe, Indian Ocean and Mediterranean 1520–66

James II, war to maintain Catholic succession 1688

John Sobieski, Holy Alliance against Ottomans, victor of the Battle of Vienna 1683

William of Orange, defeat of Catholics at the Boyne 1690

Potemkin, holy war against Crimean Muslims 1788

Hong Xiuqan, Taiping Rebellion 1850

Ito Hirobbumi, Japanese invasion of Formosa/Taiwan 1895

Hideki Tojo, holy war against Americans 1941

Saddam Hussein, attack on Shiite Iran and Ayatollah Khomeini 1980–88

Osama bin Laden, founder of al-Qaeda

Omar the Chechen, holy war against Russia

List of Major Wars in which Religion Played a Significant Role

Conquest of Canaan

Constantine's War

Arian Conflicts

Mohammed's War against Mecca

Muslim Conquests of Syria, Persia and Egypt

Muslim Conquest of Spain

Iconclast War

Carolingian Conquest of Saxony

Carolingian Conquest of Italy

Ottonian Conquest of Italy
Crusades
Teutonic Knights against East Prussia and Balkan States
The Ottoman Conquest of the Balkans
The Eighty Years War in Holland
The French Wars of Religion
The Thirty Years War
The Bishops' Wars
English Civil Wars/Wars of Three Kingdoms
American Civil War
The Asia Pacific War 1931–45

Main inter-Christian Religious or Semi-religious Wars

Arians against Catholics in Libya in 480
Justinian conquers Arian Tunisia 527 AD
Arians against Catholics War in Spain 585 AD
Iconoclast/Iconophile Wars
Teutonic Knights against Orthodox
Albigensian Crusade
Peasants' Revolt in England
Peasants' War in Germany
Eighty Years War in Netherlands
Schmalkaldic League War in Germany
French Wars of Religion
Spanish Armada Campaign
Irish Wars
Thirty Years War in Germany
Bishops' Wars in Scotland/England
English Civil War
Arguably, American Civil War

Main Sunni versus Shiite Wars

Abu Bakr defeats Musulman 631
Siffin campaign 657
Defeat of Kharijites by Ali 658
Karbala Campaign 681
Al Mukhtar revolt 686
Abbasid takeover 750
Al Mahdi/Fatimid conquest of Tunisia 909
Qarmathian Mahdi 931
Fatimids capture Aleppo 994
Almoravids conquer Morocco 1055
Almohad new Mahdi 1121
Timur attacks Muslim India 1397
Timur massacres Persian Shiites 1398
Selim the Grim campaigns against Shiites 1513 and 1517
Suleiman conquers Persian Shiites 1548–9
Sunni Mogol Aurangzeb attacks Shiites 1664
Shah Abbas supports Indian Shiites 1664
Iraq versus Iran 1980
Syrian Civil War 2012
Yemeni Civil War 2015

Main Jihads against non-Muslims

Mohammed war against Mecca 624
Conquest of Christian Syria 636
Conquest of Zoroastrian Mesopotamia and Persia 637
Conquest of North Africa 686
Invasion of India 710
Conquest of Spain 717
Failed conquest of France 720
Defeat of Chinese at Tallas 752
Muslim Conquest of half of India 977
Seljuks defeat Greeks 1071
Seljuks capture Jerusalem 1071
Jihad of Nur ad Din 1146–74

Defeat of Serbs at Kosovo 1369
Ottoman defeat of Crusaders at Nicopolis 1396
Capture of Constantinople by Ottomans 1453
Sikander of Kashmir 1473
Conquest of Hungary by Suleiman 1526
Aurangzeb campaigns against Hindus and Sikhs 1660–70
Hyder Ali invasion of Kerala 1766
Afghan Jihad against Russia 1978
Chechen rebellion 1994

Main Wars of Liberation Associated with Religion

War of Five Pecks of Rice (Tao)
Red Turbans against Yuan (Buddhist)
Reconquista of Spain (Catholic Christian)
Reconquista of Portugal
Peasants Revolt England
Removal of Tartars from Russia
Holy Alliance against Ottomans 1570
Holy Alliance against Ottomans 1693
White Lotus against Manchu 1796
Greek war of Independence 1827
Christian Taiping against Manchu 1850

Wars Caused in Part or Wholly by Buddhists or Taoists

Sri Lanka Buddhists against Hindu Tamils 2nd century BC
Taoist Red Turbans 184 AD
Faqing against Wei in China
Defeat of Sui at Hulao in 621
Harshavardamana against Chalakya 630
Revolt against Tang 719
Khmer against Cham in 1178
Kublai Khan after 1251
White Lotus/ Red Turbans revolt against Yuan in 1352
Ikko Ikki monks against Samurai 1488
White Lotus revolt against Manchus 1789

Eight Trigrams 1813
Sino-Japanese Wars 1895
Asia Japanese Russian War 1904
Pacific War 1931–45
Sri Lanka war against Tamils 1983

Estimated Casualties for Most Serious Religion-based Confrontations
Middle Eastern crusades 8 million
French Wars of religion 800,000
Ottoman attacks on Shiites 100,000
Thirty Years War 5 million
English Civil War 800,000
Taiping 20 million
Sino-Japanese War 1937–45 6 million
Pacific War 30 million

Famous Proponents of Just Religious War
Hammurabi
Moses
Samuel
Confucius
St Augustine
Mohammed
Aquinas
Urban II
St Bernard
Nichiren
St Ignatius Loyola
Guru Har Gobind
Shoin Yoshida

BIBLIOGRAPHY

Bachrach, D, S., *Religion and the Conduct of War 300–1215*, London, 2003
Barrow, R, H., *The Romans*, London, 1975
Beevor, Anthony, *The Spanish Civil War*, London, 1999
Bell, Daniel, *Confucian Political Ethics*, Princeton, 2008
Bergman,K., *Taiwan City Guide*, Taiwan, 2002
Bireley, Robert, *The Jesuits and the Thirty Years War*, Cambridge, 2003
Bonner, M., *Jihad in Islamic History*, Princeton, 2000
Bostom, Andrew, ed., *The Legacy of Jihad*, London, 2005
Bryce, James, *The Holy Roman Empire*, London, 1864
Bullock, Alan, *Hitler*, London, 1999
Burckhardt, Jakob, *The Civilization the Renaissance in Italy*, London, 1990
Campbell, Joseph, *The Power of Myth*, New York, 1988
Cantor, Norman, *The Civilisation of the Middle Ages*, London, 1994
Cavanagh, William T., *The Myth of Religious Violence*, Chicago, 2009
Choksy, Jamsheed, *Conflict and Cooperation – Justifiable Force and Holy War in Zoroastrianism*, Indiana, 1997
Cohn, Norman, *The Pursuit of the Millennium*, London, 1957
Cornwall, John, *Hitler's Pope; the Secret History of Pope Pius XII*, London, 1999
Cox, David, *The Religious Life of Robert E. Lee*, Grand Rapids, 2017
Crowley, Roger, *1453: The Holy War for Constantinople*, New York, 2005
Dale, Stephen, *Islamic World*, Ohio, 1996
Decalo, Samuel, *Coups and Army Rule in Africa*, New Haven, 1976
Ebel, Jonathan, *Faith in the Fight: Religion and the American Soldier in the Great War*, Princeton, 2010
Ebel, Jonathan, *GI Messiahs: Soldiers, War and Civil Religion*, New Haven, 2015
Ebrey, Patricia, *Illustrated History of China*, Cambridge, 1996
Elliot, John, *Imperial Spain*, London, 1964
Firestone, Reuven, *Jihad*, Oxford, 1999

Bibliography

Fisher, H. A. L., *History of Europe*, London, 1943

Fraser, Antonia, *Cromwell – Our Chief of Men*, London, 1973

Fregosi, Paul, *Jihad in the West*, London, 1998

Fukuyama, Francis, *The End of History and the Last Man*, London, 1996

Gamble, Richard, *Progressive Christians, the Great War and the Rise of the Messianic Nation*, London, 2004

Gascoyne, Bamber, *The Great Moghuls*, London, 1998

Gawthrop, Richard, *Pietism and the making of 18th Century Prussia*, Cambridge, 1993

Gibbon, Edward, *The Decline and Fall of the Roman Empire*, ed. Bury, London, 1909

Goodwin, Jason, *The Lords of the Horizons*, London, 1998

Grant, R. G., *Battle*, London. 2010

Grenke, Arthur, *God, Greed and Genocide: the Holocaust through the Centuries*, London, 2005

Guillaume, Alfred, *Islam*, London, 1969

Haldon, John, *Byzantium: a History*, Stroud, 2000

Hankins, Barry, *American Evangelicals*, New York 2009

Hardacre, Helen, *Shinto and the State 1868-1988*, Oxford, 2016

Hartnell, Nicole, *Religion, War and Ethics Source book*, London, 2014

Hashmi, Sohail, ed., *Just Wars, Holy wars and Jihads*, Oxford, 2012

Heschell. Suisannah, *The Aryan Jesus, Christian Theology and the Bible in Nazi Germany*, Princeton, 2010

Hodong, Kim, *Holy War in China*, Stanford, 2004

Hoffman,R. Joseph, *The Just War and Jihad*, New York, 2006

Holt, Mack, *The French Wars of Religion*, Cambridge, 1995

Holton, David, *Modern Japan and Shinto*, New York, 1947

Huizinga, J., *The Waning of the Middle Ages*, London, 1924

Hume, R. E., 'Hinduism and War', *American Journal of Theology* 1916

Jansen,G. H., *Militant Islam*, London, 1979

Jerryson, Michael and M. Jurgensmeyer, eds, *Buddhist Warfare*, Oxford, 2010

Johnson, James T., *The Holy War Idea in Western and Islamic Traditions*, Pennsylvania, 2002

Jones, W. R., 'English Church Propaganda against France in the Hundred Years War', *Journal of British Studies*, 1979

Juergensmeyer, Mark, *Terror in the Mind of God: the Global Rise of Violence*, California, 2003

Keay, John, *History of India*, London, 2000

Kirby, Diane, *Religion in the Cold War*, London, 2002

Kirsch, Jonathan, *God against Gods: a History of War between Monotheism and Polytheism*, New York, 2004

Kitagawa, Joseph, *Religion and Japanese History*, London, 1990

Koder, J., *Byzantine War Ideology*, Vienna, 2012

Krausz, Tibor, 'The Kaiser's Jihad', *The Jerusalem Post*, February 2011

Lawson, Tom, *The Church of England and Armed Conflict in the 20th Century*, London, 2012

Lease, Gary, *Odd Fellows in the Politics of Religion*, Berlin, 1995

Lev, Yaacov, *State and Society in Fatimid Egypt*, Leiden, 1997

Levack, Brian, *The Witch-Hunt in Early Modern Europe*, London, 2006

Longworth, Philip, *Russia's Empires: Their Rise and Fall, from Prehistory to Putin*, London, 2005

Longstaffe, Moya, *Joan of Arc and 'The Great Pity of the Land of France'*, Stroud, 2017

Maalouf, Amin, *The Crusades through Arab Eyes*, New York, 1984

Marrin, Albert, *The Last Crusade: The Church of England and the First World War*, London, 1977

Møler, Bjørn, *Religious Conflict in Africa*, Danish Institute for International Studies Report, 2006

Man, John, *Kublah Khan*, London, 2006

Marozzi, Justin. *Tamerlane – Sword of Islam* New York, 2006

Miller, R., Stout and Wilson (eds) *Religion in the American Civil War*, Oxford, 1998

Miner, Steven, *Stalin's Holy War*, North Carolina, 2003

Mote, Frederick. *Imperial China*, Cambridge, Mass, 1999

Montgomery, Bernard, *History of Warfare*, London, 1965

Moorhead, James, *Preaching the Holy War*, New Jersey, 1992

Moses, A. D., *Empire, Colonies and Genocide*, New York, 2009

Muhlenbeck, Philip, *Religion and the Cold War*, New York, 2012

North, Jonathan, *Nelson at Naples: Revolution and Retribution in 1799*, Stroud, 2018

Nye, R. B. and J. Morpurgo, *A History of the United States*, London, 1955

O'Connor, Daniel, *The Chaplains of the East India Company*, London, 2011

Oldenbourg, Zoe, *The Crusades*, London. 1998

Overy, Richard, *The Dictators, Hitler's Germany and Stalin's Russia*, London, 2004

Palmer-Fernandez, Gabriele, *Encyclopedia of Religion and War*, London, 2004

Paris, Edmund, *The Vatican against Europe*, Transl. Robson, London, 1988

Partner, Peter, *God of Battles*, Princeton, 1998

Pearse, Meic, *The Gods of War*, Downers Grove, 2007

Porter, Andrew, *Religion versus Empire: Protestant Missionaries and Overseas Expansion*, Manchester, 2004

Prescott, William H., *History of the Conquest of Mexico*, New York, 1843

Price, Neil, *The Viking Way: Religion and War in the Late Iron Age*, Uppsala, 2002

Qamar ul Huda, *Crescent and Dove*, Washington DC, 2010

Raguer, Hilari, *Gunpowder and Incense: the Catholic Church and the Spanish Civil War*, Abingdon, 2006

Rashba, Gary, *Holy Wars: 300 Years of Battles in the Holy Land*, Oxford, 2011

Reader, John, *Africa: Biography of a Continent*, London, 1998

Riley-Smith, Jonathan, *The Crusades, Christianity and Islam,* London, 2003

Richey, Stephen, *Joan of Arc,* Westport, 2007

Rummel, Walter, *Hexen und Hexenverfolgung,* Landau-Nussdorf, 2014

Runciman, Steven, *A History of the Crusades,* Cambridge, 1951

Russell, Peter, *Prince Henry the Navigator,* New Haven, 2000

Shean, J. F., *Soldiering for God: Christians in the Roman Army,* Leiden, 2010

Skia, Walter, *Japan's Holy War – the Ideology of Radical Shinto Nationalism,* New York, 2005

Snape, M. N., *God and the British Soldier,* New York, 2005

Steigmann-Gall, Richard, *The Holy Reich: Nazi Conception of Christianity,* Cambridge, 2003

Strong, Rowan, *Anglicanism and the British Empire,* Oxford, 2007

Stouraitis, Yannis, *Byzantine Approaches to Warfare,* Leiden, 2018

Thomson, Oliver, *Zealots: How a group of Scottish Conspirators Unleashed Half a Century of War in Britain,* Stroud, 2018

Tickonov, Vladimir, ed., *Buddhism in Modern Asia,* New York, 2013

Tolstoy, Leo, *Hadji Murat,* trans. London, 2006

Turnbull, Stephen, *Japanese Warrior Monks 949–1603,* Oxford, 2003

Tyerman, Christopher, *Fighting for Christendom – Holy War and Crusades,* Oxford, 2005

Ulanowski, Krzysztov, ed., *Religious Aspects of Warfare in the Ancient Near East, Greece and Rome,* Leiden, 2016

Ullman, Walter, *Political Thought in the Middle Ages,* Cambridge, 1965

Underhill, John, *Newes from America,* Boston, 1637

Valliant, G. C., *The Aztecs in Mexico,* London, 1961

Victoria, Brian, *Zen at War,* Maryland, 1997

Waley, J., *Mirrors of Morality,* London, 1981

Wang, Yuan-kang, *Harmony and War: Confucian Culture and Chinese Power Politics,* New York, 2010

Wedgewood, Veronica, *The Thirty Years War,* London, 1956

Weigel, George, *Against the Grain: Christianity and Democracy, War and Peace,* New York, 2008

Weigel, George, *Faith, Reason and the War against Jihadism,* New York, 2009

Whitton, David, *Oxford History of Medieval Europe,* Oxford, 1992

Wilkinson, Alan, *The Church of England in the First World War,* London, 2014

Wright, Robin, *Rock the Casbah: Rage and Rebellion across the Islamic World,* New York, 2012

INDEX